LAND TENURE POLICIES

LAND TENURE POLICIES
AT HOME AND ABROAD

By

HENRY WILLIAM SPIEGEL, Ph.D.
Assistant Professor of Economics, Duquesne University

Chapel Hill
The University of North Carolina Press
1941

To

GEORGE S. WEHRWEIN

PREFACE

THERE SEEMS to be no book in existence that presents in a coherent form the exposition and analysis of land tenure policies which have been developed at home and elsewhere in recent years. In the present book the attempt is made to discuss these policies from a general point of view in order to convey information and to stimulate discussion of the issues involved. The arrangement is topical and includes such subjects as objectives of land tenure policy, public control over land, the legal background, land inheritance, tenure of forest land, collective action, farm credit, and farm tenancy policy. The author has endeavored to make the discussion realistic and concrete at all points and to show the bearing of institutional factors and economic principles upon public policies. The concluding chapters contain a detailed analysis of land tenure policies in England and Germany. These countries have been selected because they exemplify land tenure policies under a democratic and a totalitarian form of government, and because the variety, range, and importance of the measures adopted in these countries call for a more elaborate discussion than the framework of the topical arrangement would permit.

There is no doubt that the attention which has been paid to farm tenancy policy in recent years is warranted. However, other important aspects of land tenure seem to be somewhat neglected, and it is to be hoped that the present book will stimulate work in land inheritance and related fields. It is here that we need an ambitious research program on a national scale to unearth the factual background and to prevent the making of generalizations based upon the few scattered field studies which are at hand at the present time.

The chapter on the legal background of land tenure is addressed to readers who have no special legal training. As it stands, many passages call for qualifications. Hence, its usefulness is limited to the reader who consults it for general purposes and not with the view of finding advice in concrete cases.

The author desires to acknowledge his indebtedness to all those who have offered encouragement, suggestions, and criticism. He is under particular obligation to his former teacher, Professor George S. Wehrwein, of the University of Wisconsin. The manuscript has been read by Professors Karl Brandt, of Stanford University; John Ise, of the University of Kansas; Norman Nybroten, of the University of Idaho; Rainer Schickele, of Iowa State College of Agriculture; and Dr. L. C. Gray, of the United States Department of Agriculture. Professor

[vii]

Max Rheinstein, of the University of Chicago Law School; Professor A. Marquand, of University College, Wales; and Mr. H. A. Hockley, of the Bureau of Agricultural Economics, Division of Land Economics, have read and criticized certain chapters. Drs. O. E. Baker and C. P. Loomis, of the Bureau of Agricultural Economics, have made helpful suggestions. Mr. M. M. Regan, of the same bureau; Mr. Leonard Kuvin, of the National Industrial Conference Board; Mrs. Katherine Wheeler, clerk of the House Committee on Agriculture; and the Honorable Marvin Jones, chairman of the same committee, have most graciously supplied information in various matters. Professor Arthur L. Rayhawk, of Duquesne University, has conducted some statistical calculations for the benefit of the book. Mr. Paul Kram, a former student of the author, and Mr. M. M. Tumin have given the manuscript more punch and clarity. To all these persons the author wishes to express his sincere thanks.

HENRY WILLIAM SPIEGEL

Pittsburgh, Pa.
August, 1940

CONTENTS

CHAPTER V

ENGLISH LAND TENURE POLICY

CHAPTER VI

LAND TENURE UNDER THE SWASTIKA

LIST OF TABLES

LIST OF TABLES

LAND TENURE POLICIES

FOUNDATIONS OF LAND TENURE POLICY

OBJECTIVES OF LAND TENURE POLICY

THE ULTIMATE motive for government interference with land tenure, farm tenancy, and, especially, the lease contract has varied according to time and place. The philosophy behind the English Agricultural Holdings Acts was an extension of the idea of protection, combined with restriction on freedom of contract. Protection in that sense meant guidance "applied to classes who, though not in any strictness 'incapable' of managing their own affairs, are, in the opinion of the legislature, unlikely to provide as well for their own interest as can the community."[1] Though the interest of the people who were directly affected by the legislation was in the foreground, implicitly the idea may have prevailed that interference on behalf of these people would further the common weal. In recent times greater stress has been laid on this aspect of government interference. This can be illustrated by Professor Pigou's attitude which supports governmental intervention on behalf of tenants in order to maximize the national dividend.[2]

In the United States, farm policies have largely been relief policies directed towards giving either agriculture or the "disadvantaged classes in American agriculture" a fair deal. This outlook is more closely related to the older idea of protection for the sake of those who need it. However, it was not seldom that the idea of protection for agriculture as a whole was associated with the claim that such protection would improve the economic condition of the whole nation. At the present time agricultural policy has passed beyond the stage of mere relief policy. It might be possible to distinguish three fundamental objectives: conservation, "adjustment" for agriculture as a whole, and help for the "disadvantaged classes."

Land Tenure Policy and Agricultural Adjustment.—What is the position of land tenure policy if it is confronted with these objectives? The term and meaning of "land tenure" is neutral and compatible with any objective; it gains life if goals are set up which the land tenure policy has to attain. If help for the disadvantaged classes is the goal, the position of the tenant is to be strengthened; he is to be enabled to become owner, or the landlord-tenant relationship is to be

[1] A. V. Dicey, *Lectures on the Relation between Law and Public Opinion in England during the Nineteenth Century* (London, Macmillan & Co., 1926), p. 262.
[2] See below, pp. 68 ff.

improved. Would such a policy be compatible with the other objective, "adjustment" for agriculture as a whole? In many instances
the answer cannot be affirmative. Improving the conditions of the
tenants would make many of them more productive[3] and might prevent, in many cases, their transfer to occupations where they could
produce goods which satisfy a more expansive demand. Moreover, a
more diversified cultivation in the South would compete with or curtail purchases of products of the Middle West. On the occasion of the
discussion of the farm tenancy program before Congress, Secretary
Wallace admitted that the bill in question would be a "very slight"
encouragement of the back-to-the-land movement.[4] The fears of those
who regarded the program as a stimulus to production could not be
allayed by Undersecretary Wilson's statement that the land required
for the tenant program would be land which is already under cultivation at the present time.[5]

However, these considerations have little significance under present
economic conditions. A higher or lower occupational mobility of the
farmers is important only so far as the economic system permits their
diversion to occupations where they can produce utilities which meet
a more expansive demand. There is no doubt that there are plenty of
goods and services of that kind. But as long as unemployed people
and resources cannot be brought together, there is no reason for op-
posing a policy, the alternative of which might result in increasing the
number of unemployed industrial workers. Since the employment
opportunities which farming offers have become all-important, there
is not much sense in refraining from improving the lot of the tenant
for fear he might remain in farming or increase his productivity. A
similar kind of reasoning applies to the agricultural development program of such enterprises as the TVA and the Grand Coulee irrigation
project, which are censored by some because "when the agricultural
development . . . has been provided for, there will be more subsidies
to keep part of it out of cultivation."[6]

Land Tenure Policy and Conservation.—A conservation policy, in
general, is compatible with a land tenure policy, the latter being understood as aiming at the improvement of the conditions of the disadvantaged classes. If the tenure system secures for the farmer the products
of his improvements and enables him to look forward to many years
of farming on the same farm, he will be more of a conservationist in
his management than a tenant who shifts every one or two years and

---

[3] However, if they produce more cash crops, their purchasing power as consumers might also increase, to the benefit of other farmers.

[4] Farm Tenancy, *Hearing* before the Committee on Agriculture, House of Representatives, 75th Cong., 1st Sess., on H. R. 8, Serial A, p. 255 (1937).

[5] *Ibid.*, pp. 32, 52.

[6] L. Robbins, *The Great Depression* (New York, Macmillan Co., 1936), p. 136.

receives no compensation for his improvements. Hence, conservation policies and tenure policies are not only compatible but complementary to each other. However, it is doubtful if the land tenure policies which have been propounded so far in the United States will ever result in that degree of conservation which the European peasant applies to his land. It has been asked why the government should pay the American farmer for conservationist practices since European peasants practice conservation[7] without receiving specific payments for such management. However, the European peasantry is preserved by tariff fences and receives prices for its products which are 100 and more per cent above the prices which the farmer receives in the United States. If the government conserves the peasant, it does not have to conserve the land. Subsidies for conservation practices which are raised by progressive taxes are superior to high prices for farm products which hit the poor consumer harder than they do the rich.

While tariff fences and high prices of agricultural products explain why the European peasant is financially able to practice conservation, they do not explain why he makes use of this ability. It is here that land tenure and tenure policies come into play. Restrictions on the alienation of land, on its divisibility, inheritance, and utilization tend to confirm the peasant in his conservationist practices. There are, however, definite limits to the success of a land tenure policy which aims at conservation. Unless there is stringent compulsion, such a policy will be most successful in confirming the farmer in his conservationist practices, but it cannot bring about a management of the conservationist type overnight. Conservation is not rooted in laws or in the tenure system, but in the outlook and spirit of the agriculturist. Tenure laws and customs may strengthen him in this spirit, but they cannot create it. On the other hand, it must be stressed that suitable tenure institutions, though they do not create the conservative spirit, are necessary prerequisites to the rise of that spirit. Indeed, one can go so far as to grant that there is a positive correlation between a suitable tenure setup and the strength of the conservationist spirit of the farm population. Applied to the American farmer, this means that he will be willing to practice conservation if he can reap the fruits of his conservation. Adjustments in the tenure system which secure him these fruits will bring about a certain amount of conservation. However, it is highly questionable whether such measures as the introduction of primogeniture, combined with restrictions on the alienation of farms, would induce the American farmer to change his outlook to one which approaches that of the European peasant who is used to thinking in generations. Measures of this type find response only if they are an expression of the prevailing attitude, spirit, and outlook of

[7] The technical question concerning differences in need is beyond the scope of this book.

the agriculturist. The formation of this spirit and outlook is the result of a century-old tradition. Changes in the law cannot substitute for this tradition.

It is again another question whether, in the United States, conservation to the degree applied by some European peasants is desirable if it can only be brought about by a similar spirit and similar institutions. A study of land tenure in Germany will show that the social disutility of such institutions is too great to justify experiments in that direction. As Professor G. S. Wehrwein has formulated it:

In our anxiety to control erosion, prevent the destruction of forests or to curb speculation we seem to accept uncritically the policies of Europe without recognizing fundamental differences. It is one thing to formulate land-use policies for a nation with abundant resources and approaching a stationary population and quite another for a nation with limited resources but which insists on stimulating population increase for reasons which cannot be separated from the social philosophy, ideology and nationalistic ambitions of that nation. . . . There is something admirable about American land tenure, a free system which has permitted landless laborers and penniless immigrants to climb the agricultural ladder. . . .[8]

LAND TENURE AND PUBLIC CONTROL OVER LAND

William Penn wrote in 1701: "I hope reason of state shall never be one to violate property."[9] One hundred and fifty years later, Toqueville wondered about the high esteem in which property was held in the United States, and he ascribed this attitude to the institutions of equalitarian democracy where men "dread revolutions." As he said, "In no country in the world is the love of property more active and more anxious than in the United States; nowhere does the majority display less inclination for those principles which threaten to alter, in whatever manner, the laws of property."[10] In the meantime, inequality in the distribution of wealth has gradually increased, and the stratification of society, though it has not yet become as fixed as in Europe, has rapidly progressed. Yet public opinion is still attached to the institutions of the equalitarian period and inclined to attribute to property in fee simple the character of a natural law which does not stand alterations and adjustments to changing social conditions. So far, only a few seem willing to endorse the view that "the system of private land tenure which happens to prevail at one moment in some country is not the only possible system of land tenure. The only pos-

[8] "Public Control of Land Use in the United States," *Journal of Farm Economics,* XXI (1939), 75-76.
[9] Quoted in Charles A. Beard, *The Idea of National Interest* (New York, Macmillan Co., 1934), p. 24.
[10] Alexis de Toqueville, *Democracy in America,* tr., H. Reeves (New York, Barnes, 1855), Pt. 2, Bk. 3, Chap. 21.

sible alternative is not the nationalization of the land. The alternative may be any one of the innumerable other systems of private land tenure."[11]

While there was a tendency throughout the nineteenth century to remove restrictions on property owners, a complete coalescence of the law of land and the law of movables was nowhere attained. To be sure, Blackstone had maintained the sacredness of property before the law: "So great, moreover, is the regard of the law for private property, that it will not authorize the least violation; no, not even for the general good of the whole community."[12] However, the sovereignty of the English Parliament could supersede the right of the property owner like any other right. American constitutional law, while sanctioning Blackstone's view by embodying it in the Constitution, created such devices as the right of eminent domain and the police power which supersede the property right when it seems necessary to do so for the sake of the public interest. There are still other restrictions on the right of the property owner. The common law recognizes various "natural rights" of the neighbor against the owners of abutting land. They are not permitted to interfere with the "enjoyment" of neighboring owners by their mode of utilization, for example. Regarding conservation, it was said in 1909 that "it is, in fact, doubtful, whether the ownership of land, or even the right to carry on business, was at any time in our legal history absolute and unrestricted."[13]

On the Continent, especially in Germany, the relics of the old order were much more numerous; their continuance throughout the nineteenth century help to explain the arrival of a new feudalism at the present time. The emancipation of the peasants, while in itself a product of liberalism and laissez faire, was intermingled with so large an amount of government interference that complete freedom was far from being materialized. Add to this the interplay of political forces which determined the outlook and spirit of the local peasant population and dominated agricultural credit, and it becomes obvious that no traditional aversion against public control over land could come into existence. Furthermore, the utilization of certain types of land resources such as forest, water, and mines was always the subject of a more or less stringent government control.

The present tendency to restrict the right of the landowner has led to the revival of the ancient distinction between real property and movables. This distinction had faded away when land was regarded

[11] Walter Lippmann, *An Inquiry into the Principles of the Good Society* (Boston, Little, Brown and Co., 1937), p. 270.

[12] *Commentaries on the Laws of England* (4 vols. Oxford, 1765-69), I, 139.

[13] A. A. Bruce, "The Conservation of Our Natural Resources and of Our National Strength and Virility," *University of Pennsylvania Law Review*, LVIII (1909), 161.

as a marketable commodity like movable goods which the owner could alienate, bequeath, mortgage, and utilize at his own discretion. While the present tendency is to uphold the absolute right of the owner of movables, increasing restrictions on the right of the landowner have made the differences between land and other forms of wealth more conspicuous.

The romantic philosophy behind the view that there is a fundamental difference between real property and movable goods is well illustrated in the following words of Coleridge:

When shall we return to a sound conception of the rights to property —namely, as being official, implying and demanding the performance of commensurate duties! Nothing but the most horrible perversion of humanity and moral justice under the specious name of political economy, could have blinded men to this truth as to the possession of land—the law of God having connected indissolubly the cultivation of every rood of earth with the maintenance and watchful labor of man. But money, stock, riches by credit, transferable and convertible at will, are under no such obligation; and, unhappily, it is from the selfish, autocratic possession of *such* property that our landowners have learnt their present theory of trading with that which was never meant to be an object of commerce.[14]

The return of a similar philosophy of property has expressed itself in many other formulations. They all stress the restrictions, some by taking them into the definition of property, and others, in their most extreme form, by changing property into "a restricted functional right of usufruct which can be held by the farmer only if he fulfills the duties imposed upon him by the nation."[15] Where this concept of property is used, it will be accompanied by the tendency to draw the logical conclusion from the separate treatment of land and movable goods and to establish a special legal order not only for the farmers' land but for the farmers themselves. Under corporativism the unity of the common law is given up, and we find the substitution of a diversified legal order for the various occupational groups in place of the equalitarian order of the common law.

The tendencies toward restriction on property rights are strongest where the government has acquired land which is redistributed. "It is certainly not the view of liberals that the state, having once regained the fee simple, should part with it again."[16] In earlier times this view was based upon the intention to prevent the accruing of the "unearned

[14] *On the Constitution of the Church and State* (2nd ed. London, 1830), pp. 46-47, quoted in R. J. White (ed.), *The Political Thought of S. T. Coleridge* (London, Cape, 1938), pp. 163-64.

[15] K. Brandt, "Public Control of Land Use in Europe," *Journal of Farm Economics*, XXI (1939), 64.

[16] L. T. Hobhouse, *Liberalism* (New York, Holt & Co., n.d.), pp. 175-76.

increment" to a farmer who has been granted his land by the government. At the present time restrictions on this type of property are advocated for other reasons, in the main for the sake of the new holder who is regarded as needing protection against the dangers arising out of the liberty to alienate, utilize, mortgage, subdivide, or bequeath his land at his discretion. While there is strong opposition against curtailment of the fee simple in the United States, some restrictions are imposed upon the mortgagor under the Bankhead-Jones Farm Tenant Act and under the mortgage terms of many leading agencies. Likewise the management of those holders who borrow under the rehabilitation program is supervised to a certain degree. Clients who are tenants are required to have written rental contracts which assure equitable tenure arrangements and reasonable security of occupancy.[17]

In view of the strong aversion to restrictions on fee simple, other arrangements are used which bring about similar results as restrictions on property rights. Some of the programs of the Farm Security Administration provide for a temporary substitution of lease arrangements in place of the transfer of property rights. Under the rural homesteads program the farmer rents the farm for several crop years before entering contract for purchase. If the farmer proves satisfactory at the end of the trial lease, he may purchase the farm.[18]

There is one by-product of recent agricultural policies which may turn out to have important effects upon real property. At some places some of the "bases" which have been established for the marketing of a number of agricultural products can be alienated from the land which produces the commodity without alienating the land at the same time. Professor H. C. Taylor has drawn a number of interesting conclusions from this observation and has pointed out that a part of the value of the real estate has been transferred to the base, which is intangible property.[19] This part will be greater, the less use can be made of the land without the base. If the importance of such bases increases, and if they become separately marketable to a greater extent than they are now, "then, maybe, we will come one day where somebody, instead of inheriting a farm will inherit an allotment."[20]

[17] *Report* of the Administrator of the Farm Security Administration, 1938, pp. 4-5.   [18] *Ibid.*, p. 16.
[19] "Land Tenure and the Social Control of the Use of Land," *Proceedings* of the Fifth International Conference of Agricultural Economists, 1938, special reprint, pp. 4-5.
[20] *Farm Tenancy*, Hearing before the Committee on Agriculture, House of Representatives, 75th Cong., 1st Sess., on H. R. 8, Serial A (1937), p. 312.

II

THE LEGAL BACKGROUND OF LAND TENURE IN THE UNITED STATES

DEVELOPMENT OF AMERICAN LAND LAW

SINCE ALL LAND tenure policies aim at the maintenance of or changes in the legal relationship between man and the land, an understanding of the means and ends of land tenure policy requires a certain amount of knowledge of the legal framework within which the land tenure policy operates. To be sure, the goals of the land tenure policy are not legalistic, but are set by politics and economics. However, the means to attain these goals consist largely of changes in the existing system of real property, notwithstanding the fact that there is a wide domain of administrative action based upon discretion, and that education offers many possibilities of guiding individual action without changing the law. With reference to these alternative methods of land tenure policy, the general statement holds true that "the regulation of social affairs by adjudicating and adjusting private rights" is more compatible with the objectives of liberalism than is the further extension of administrative action. "The one is the method of a common law; the other the method of the prerogatives of superior persons. The one is the system of democratic liberalism, the other of authoritarian collectivism."[1]

American land law is part of the English common law. In England the Norman Conquest has led to a specific organization of rights in land which is different from any other type of landholding. In the eleventh century the King assumed the supreme right over all land. He, the lord paramount, divided the land among his tenants-in-chief, or mesne lords, who had no original rights in the land but only those which they could derive from the King's grant. The mesne lords, in their turn, transferred the land to their vassals, the tenants-in-demesne, or tenants paravail. One link of the chain was closely connected with the other, and all land belonged, in the last analysis, to the King. The occupier and mesne lord held the land upon the condition of the performance of certain services. All land had become "feudal" land as contrasted with "allodial" land which the owner possesses in his own right. "Tenure" was the relationship between the grantor and grantee of the right in land, and all landholders were tenants or subtenants

[1] Lippmann, *An Inquiry into the Principles of the Good Society*, p. 273.

of the King. For all practical purposes the kind and quantity of the services to be rendered by the tenants was of the greatest importance. While there was no absolute ownership aside from that of the King, the gradual abolition and monetization of the services changed some types of landholders into virtual owners as early as the seventeenth century.

Tenure, hence, in its narrowest meaning, denotes this feudal relationship between lord and overlord. It is a controversial question among contemporary jurists whether tenure, in this institutionalized sense, ever existed in the United States. Some courts have held that there were no limits to the extent to which the common law was adopted in the colonies, while others maintained that only that portion was adopted which was applicable to colonial conditions. Jefferson denied the existence of tenure in the strongest terms. The Saxons, he said, had held the land in absolute dominion. Feudalism was introduced by William. "America was not conquered by William the Norman. . . . Possessions there are, undoubtedly, of the allodial nature."[2] Other writers held the opposite view. Whatever validity can be attributed to either one of these doctrines, the fact remains that, in colonial times, oaths of fealty to the lord were taken, and services, often nominal rents, rendered. The situation after the revolution is much more doubtful. Some authorities argue that the feudal position of the paramount lord which was previously occupied by the King passed to the state with other sovereign rights. The statutes or judicial decisions have declared tenure nonexistent in some states—Connecticut, New York, Maryland, Virginia, Ohio, Wisconsin, West Virginia, Minnesota, California, and, possibly, Kentucky.[3] These statutes and decisions can be interpreted either as declaratory acts which merely elucidated the existing legal situation, or as constitutive acts which changed the law.

The opinion which regards the acts as declaratory fits well the other theory which propounds a general abolition of "tenure" in the United States. Some advocates of that theory have made especial reference to the Ordinance of 1787.

This noble statute struck the key-note of our liberal system of land law not only in the states formed out of the public domain, but also in the older states. The doctrine of tenure is entirely exploded; it has no existence. Though the word may be used for the sake of convenience, the last vestige of feudal import has been torn from it. The individual title derived from the government involves the entire transfer of the ownership of the soil. It is purely allodial, with all the

[2] *The Writings of Thomas Jefferson,* ed., H. A. Washington (9 vols. New York, Derby, 1861), I, 138-39.

[3] H. T. Tiffany, *The Law of Real Property,* Vol. I, §19. Hereafter cited as *Real Property.*

incidents pertaining to that title as substantial as in the infancy of Teutonic civilisation.[4]

At first glance, the question whether there ever was such tenure in the United States seems to be of a highly academic nature. However, it has to be taken into account that public control over land is more easily accepted by public opinion and by the legal profession if the legal tradition links the owner or occupier of land with the general public and does not vest absolute ownership in him. In England, where the doctrine of tenure was never given up, various schemes of land reform and even the proposal of land nationalization found a wide response because the people were accustomed to regard the right of the owner or occupier as limited.

OWNERSHIP AND TENANCY

The distinction between ownership and tenancy is, of course, based upon differences in the legal position of owner and tenant. However, in the technical language of the law, ownership often embraces what is called tenancy in common parlance. Tiffany, an authority on real property law, proposed to use the concept of ownership "without reference to the greater or less duration of the rights involved." He defines ownership as "the idea of rights in some particular person or persons (the owner or owners) to use the land according to his or their pleasure, and to demand that others refrain from such use" and distinguishes it from the rights to dispose of lands not based on ownership, for example.[5] According to this definition a tenant farmer would have to be called an owner, a conclusion which Tiffany justifies by referring to the observation that a tenant farmer talks of "my farm." For the sake of expediency, and in order to avoid misunderstanding, such a use of the term ownership is, in general, avoided in the following pages.

Estates.—In the language of the law, rights in land are called estates. The main points of a classificatory scheme of estates are as follows:[6]

I. Freehold estates.—The period of duration of these estates is not positively ascertained.
   A. Estates of inheritance.—These estates pass to the owner's heirs.
      1. Estates in fee simple.—They pass to collateral as well as to lineal heirs.
      2. Estates tail, or fee tail, pass only to lineal heirs.

[4] *Land Office Report*, 1870, pp. 28-29, quoted in Shosuke Sato, *History of the Land Question in the United States*, pp. 100-101.
[5] *Op. cit.*, Vol. I, §2.   [6] *Ibid.*, §25.

B. Estates not of inheritance, life estates.
   1. Life estates created by voluntary act.
   2. Life estates created by law.

II. Estates less than freehold, or leasehold estates.
   A. Tenancy for years.
   B. Tenancy at will.
   C. Tenancy from year to year.
   D. Tenancy by sufferance.

As can easily be seen, the main principle of division rests on the time during which the estate is in existence. Freehold estates last for a period whose end is not definitely ascertained. On the other hand, leasehold estates are in existence only during a certain length of time. Freehold estates may either pass to the holder's heir, or may exist only during his lifetime.

Property.—For all practical purposes the fee simple is the most important freehold estate of inheritance. The fee simple denotes what is commonly called property or ownership. Modern legal theory conceives of property as a bundle of rights which together form the most comprehensive type of domination which the law confers upon the citizen. None of these rights is absolutely essential to the concept of property, which is characterized by its being paramount and permanent. An owner in fee simple may dispose of his land at his will, may alienate it and pass it to his heirs, and make any use of it he pleases. He may go so far as to injure and destroy it, provided his action does not amount to a "nuisance."

Corporate Ownership of Land.—The acquisition of land by corporations is limited in most of the states to an amount which is necessary for or reasonably incidental to carrying out the purposes of their creation. Within these limits the corporations are likewise entitled to transfer their property. Not infrequently there is an exception to the prohibition of the acquisition of lands by corporations. This permits the acquisition of land for the collection of debts due the corporation, apparently the method by which the insurance companies and a great many other investment corporations have been acquiring farm lands. The admitted asset value of the farm real estate owned by the twenty-six largest legal-reserve life insurance companies domiciled in the United States has increased from $82,000,000 in 1929 to $529,000,000 in 1938. These figures refer only to farm real estate acquired in satisfaction of debt; farm real estate under contract of sale has increased from $9,000,000 to $82,000,000 during the same period.[7]

[7] *Investigation of Concentration of Economic Power,* Hearings, February 12, 1940, before the Temporary National Economic Committee, 76th Cong., 3rd Sess., Part 10-A, pp. 180-81 (1940).—According to testimony of Mr. Glenn Rogers, manager

In addition there are a few states which permit the acquisition of land for the collection of debts due the corporation, but require that the corporation divest itself of the land within a specified period. One of these states is Oklahoma, which enacted a statute in 1937 according to which the corporation has to dispose of the land within a period of seven years.[8]

In a few states there are more rigid restrictions on the activity of religious corporations,[9] and a Kansas statute of recent date provides that no corporation shall be granted a charter, and no foreign corporation shall be given permission to do business if it is engaged in agriculture or horticulture, except cattle ranching.[10] The statute has been upheld by the courts.[11] Similar bills are pending in other states.

The agricultural census of 1940 will supply information about corporate ownership of land by making available the number of landlords who are corporations. At the present time the number of corporations engaged in agriculture and the amount of their business cannot positively be ascertained, and it is not possible to investigate the effects of the described restrictions upon the formation of corporations engaged in farming. The following table shows the number of corporations which are engaged in agriculture and related industries and file federal income tax returns. These figures have to be used with great caution, since the industrial classification is not strictly comparable from year to year. The classification is based on the predominant industry of each concern, but, because of the diversified activities of many corporations, the industry group may not contain corporations engaged exclusively in the industries in which they are classified. Moreover, the comparability of the industrial classification for 1934 and subsequent years with that for years prior to 1934 may be materially affected by the discontinuance of the privilege of filing consolidated returns, except by railroads. The predominant industry on which the consolidated return was classified may not coincide with the predominant industry of the various affiliated concerns. On the whole, the classification used by the Treasury Department probably exaggerates the importance of the corporation in agriculture. It includes in agriculture "a wide variety of enterprises, such as the United Fruit Company, whose range of operations far transcends what 'farming' ordinarily embraces."[12]

---

of the farm-loan division of the Metropolitan Life Insurance Company, before the Temporary National Economic Committee, this company is the "largest farmer" in the United States, owning approximately 1,430,000 acres of farm land, which represents an investment of $79,800,000. This land is in 7,531 farms.

[8] Chap. XLVI.

[9] Tiffany, *op. cit.*, Vol. V, §1376.   [10] *Laws of 1931,* Chap. CLIII, §1.

[11] State *v.* Sledd Farm Corporation, 137 K. 697 (1933).

[12] Leverett S. Lyon, *et al., Government and Economic Life* (2 vols. Washington, The Brookings Institution, 1939), I, 493, 496.

TABLE 1

CORPORATION INCOME AND EXCESS-PROFITS TAX RETURNS 1916-37; AGRICULTURE AND
RELATED INDUSTRIES*

Year	Number of corporations	Year	Number of corporations
1916	7,274	1927	9,905
1917	9,660	1928	10,265
1918	7,887	1929	10,615
1919	8,298	1930	10,961
1920	9,186	1931	11,014
1921	8,724	1932	10,977
1922	9,092	1933	10,490
1923	9,360	1934	10,526
1924	9,758	1935	10,084
1925	9,904	1936	9,860
1926	10,688	1937	8,169

*Treasury Department, *Statistics of Income.*

Homestead Exemptions.—Land is liable for the debts of its owner.
However, there are statutory or constitutional provisions in most of the
states which exempt the homestead or residence of the owner from
forced sale, in order to protect the family home. In general, the homestead must be occupied by the owner. Occupation by a tenant is not
sufficient. The extent of the exemptions differs in the various jurisdictions. There are exceptions from the exemption for certain classes of
debts, and in some states the owner can waive the right of exemption.
Occasionally there are also restrictions on mortgages on homesteads.
According to constitutional provisions, a homestead in Texas can be
mortgaged only in order to secure the purchase money or the cost of
improvements. The voluntary alienation of the homestead requires,
in general, the consent of the wife of the owner. Other restrictions on
the alienation of homesteads in Arkansas and California, have been
repealed.[13]

Entails.—Estates in fee tail, the other class of freehold estates of
inheritance, are of no great importance any longer. Such estates pass
only to lineal heirs, and, if there are no such heirs, the land reverts to
the grantor. This rule was stated in the statute *De Donis conditio-
nalibus* of 1285. The statute was finally abolished by the English real
property reform legislation of 1925. In the United States it was never
recognized in South Carolina, Mississippi, Iowa, and Oregon. In other
jurisdictions—New Hampshire and Maryland—it was held repealed by
state laws. Some states—Alabama, Georgia, Indiana, Kentucky, Maryland, North Carolina, and New York—have expressly changed fee tails
into estates in fee simple. In other states—Connecticut, Ohio, and
Rhode Island—fee tails can still be created, but after the death of the

[13] Tiffany, *op. cit.,* Vol. V, §§1332 ff.

donee the estate becomes one in fee simple in his issue.[14] Where estates
in fee tail are still in force, the holder of such an estate cannot bar the
entail by his will, or devise the land. Moreover, there are restrictions
on the liability of the land for debts of the holder.

For the purposes of this book a discussion of the freehold estates
not of inheritance, or life estates, is superfluous. Such estates may be
created by voluntary act for the life of the donee or for the life of
another person than the donee, or by law as in the case of a surviving
spouse who acquires an interest in the freehold of the deceased spouse.

Leasehold Estates.—This other principal class of estates embraces
what is commonly called tenancy. The essential element is that the
time for which the lease is granted has to be less than the duration
of the right which the lessor has in the land. Leases are distinguished
according to the period of time for which they are made. There are
tenancies for years, from year to year, tenancies at will, and tenancies
by sufferance. The tenancy for years is made for a certain length of
time, not necessarily for years. Tenancies from year to year are
periodic tenancies. They are made for a certain period and will continue for subsequent successive periods of the same length, unless they
are terminated by due notice. A tenancy at will can be determined at
any time by either the landlord or the tenant. Tenancies by sufferance
occur when a tenant holds over after termination of the lease, and, in
some states, squatters are viewed in this category.

At common law there are no restrictions upon long-term leases.
However, there are statutory and constitutional provisions in some
states, which provide for term limits. These provisions are relics of a
time when the remembrance of the ancient feudal bonds was more
intense than it is at present. The term limits were regarded as necessary obstacles to prevent the rise of new obligations of a perpetual
nature.

Form of the Lease.—The Statute of Frauds of 1677 provided that
leases which are not put in writing and signed by the parties are regarded as leases at will only, with the exception that leases which do
not exceed three years can be made without any writing if "the rent
reserved to the landlord, during such term, shall amount to two thirds
parts at the least of the full improved value of the thing demised."
The statutes of the various states have modified this rule to a considerable extent.[15] In some states the period for which an oral lease
may be made has been reduced to one year. Other statutes do not
contain any exception at all.

In some states an oral lease within the prohibition of the statute
creates a tenancy at will, while in others the periodic payment of rent
is regarded as a sufficient reason for bringing about a periodic tenancy.

[14] For a full discussion see Tiffany, *op. cit.*, Vol. I, §§34 ff.
[15] *Ibid.*, §§80 ff.

However, it has been held that the creation of a term without writing is directly contrary to the statute. Though this interpretation might protect the public, it neglects the fact that the requirement of a written lease grants protection to the lessee rather than to the lessor, so that there is no sense in punishing the lessee for nonfulfillment of that requirement. The establishment of a tenancy at will which is terminable at the landlord's pleasure puts the tenant in a very unfavorable position. However, in some jurisdictions an oral lease has been regarded as valid if followed by improvements of the lessee.

Rights and Duties of the Tenant.—While an owner-occupier, whose farm is not mortgaged, is entitled to make any use whatsoever of his land, a tenant has to abstain from waste; that is, he has to utilize the holding without unreasonable injuries to the land. It is interesting to note that "the general tendency of the American courts has been to restrict the application of the English law of waste, in order to adapt it to the conditions of a new and growing country, and to stimulate the development of the land by the tenant in possession."[16] Conditions have changed sufficiently to justify a reversion of this tendency. In England a conversion of meadow into arable land, or of arable land into wood, or conversely, has been generally regarded as waste since it amounts to an alteration in the character of the rented land. While this rule has not been applied in the United States, a complete change in the utilization may amount to waste according to American law.[17] In England the cutting of timber trees was only permitted upon land where that type of utilization was customary and part of the regular profits. It was said in 1939 that in the United States "in view of the quantity of land which is here available for use only by a clearing away the timber thereon, it is usually held that a tenant is not guilty of waste if he cuts timber to a reasonable extent in order that he may cultivate the soil, and the fact that he sells the timber so cut is immaterial."[18]

At common law the rent is regarded as part of the profits and, therefore, is due after the period for which it is paid. However, advance payment is often provided by custom or express provision. The amount of the rent must be certain or capable of reduction to certainty. It can be made dependent upon the fluctuations of variables, as the price of grain, or the income of the tenant.[19] In some states the landlord's right to distress for rent is still recognized.[20]

The tenant's right to remove fixtures which he has annexed is not generally recognized.[21] If the lease is terminated at a time which the tenant, without his fault, could not foresee, he has a right to take the annual crops which he has sown before the lease was terminated. How-

[16] *Ibid.*, Vol. II, §630.
[18] *Ibid.*, §634.
[20] *Ibid.*, §§918 ff.
[17] *Ibid.*, §632.
[19] *Ibid.*, Vol. III, §889.
[21] *Ibid.*, Vol. II, §§606 ff.

ever, the tenant from year to year does not have this right in many jurisdictions.[22]

Tenancy as a form of land tenure creates a more elaborate system of legal relationships than does ownership. The division of functions, rights, and duties creates potential sources of conflict for which the law must provide. The more complex this network of relationship becomes, and the more the factors of production are split and divided among the parties, the more detailed the legislation has to become. However, legal provisions are often insignificant if they can be ruled out by contractual agreements which serve the ends of the more powerful party. On the other hand, rigid compulsory provisions of the law may not serve their ends. Statutes which intend to influence such items as the amount of rent or the termination of the lease have to delegate a certain amount of discretionary power to administrative or judicial bodies.

Licensees and Croppers.—A licensee is not a tenant, since he has no possession. He has merely the permission to use the land for a specified purpose and has no interest in the land which could be asserted against a third person. The license can be in writing or oral and is, in general, freely revocable. However, if the licensor is bound by contract not to revoke the license, he may become liable for damage if he violates the contract.[23]

A cropper is regarded as a tenant if he has exclusive possession. The courts are inclined to deny that he has possession if the landowner retains the right to control and supervise the management. Other decisions have regarded the delivery of the landowner's share by the cultivator as the criterion of a rent and a lease contract. A cropper who is not a tenant is an employee hired to do work for a share of the crop. Landowner and cropper are not regarded as partners since the gross returns and not the profits are shared.[24]

THE ALIENATION OF LAND

The freedom of alienation which the owner enjoys is regarded as a substantial characteristic of his right. Consequently, the law does not recognize restrictions on the right of the owner to alienate his property, although the law itself could be modified by legislative action. Land cannot be transferred under the condition that the one who acquires it does not transfer it to a third person. A provision which imposes a penalty in the case of such a transfer is void. In general, it is not possible to restrain the right of the owner in some specific way or for some specific purpose: the owner cannot be prohibited from mortgaging his property, from transferring it to some particular person, or in some particular manner.

[22] *Ibid.*, §601.
[23] *Ibid.*, Vol. I, §79; Vol. III, §832.   [24] *Ibid.*, Vol. I, §78; Vol. II, §604.

There are two qualifications of this general rule. In a few states restrictions for a "reasonable time" are held valid. Some courts have recognized the validity of a provision which prohibits the alienation to any except particular named individuals, or except to a certain class of individuals, or a provision that the property shall not be sold without having first been offered to a person named. Other courts have held such provisions invalid.

The general rule is based on the reason that restrictions on the right of alienation would be "repugnant to the nature of the estate." Yet, as Tiffany asserts,

it is so repugnant merely because the courts have so regarded it. . . . The real basis of the rule . . . is to be found in considerations of public policy adverse to the withdrawal of property from commerce, and the check upon its improvement and development which must result therefrom . . . there is no interest remaining in the grantor to be benefited by such a restriction, and consequently no reason why these considerations of public policy should be denied their full effect.[25]

The importance of this rule as a check on land policies is obvious. If the federal government or another public agency wants to dispose of land and transfer it, it cannot prevent the purchaser from selling the land for speculative purposes, from mortgaging it, from renting it, or from distributing it among his heirs, unless the agency is authorized to do so by statutory provisions. The rule was stated at a time when one could not conceive of a person or agency who would be benefited by restrictions of the described type. The situation has changed now. When the proposals for a tenant purchase program were before Congress, it was suggested that the tenant, who would be enabled by government aid to purchase a farm, should not be given a complete title at once after having paid for the land. His right to alienate the land should be restricted, or he should at least be only entitled to sell the land back to the government. Otherwise cash offers would hold out a large temptation. The proposal was opposed by the Farm Bureau Federation on the ground that education is better than government restriction which would be contrary to sound American jurisprudence. A member of the House took the stand that the proposal would amount to "taking tenants and making them wards of the government." Chairman Jones of the House Committee on Agriculture likewise was of the opinion that the purchaser must be given fee simple after the farm has been paid for. Otherwise, he stated, "I do not think you can get the more ambitious type of man."[26] Correspondingly the Bankhead-Jones

[25] *Ibid.*, Vol. V, §1343.
[26] *Farm Tenancy*, Hearing before the Committee on Agriculture, House of Representatives, 75th Cong., 1st Sess., on H. R. 8, Serial A (1937), pp. 146, 157, 226, 240, 315.

Farm Tenant Act grants full title to a purchaser who has been given a loan under the provisions of the act. However, if the borrower transfers the farm before full payment is made, the Secretary of Agriculture is authorized to declare the balance immediately due. Less than five years after the making of the loan, no final payment shall be accepted, or release of the interest be made, without the consent of the Secretary.

Deed Restrictions.—While most restrictions on the alienation itself are thus prevented, restrictions on the utilization of land (deed restrictions) affect a subsequent transfer under certain circumstances, especially if the second purchaser knows about the restrictions at the time he acquires the land. Such restrictions do not have to be agreed upon in connection with the transfer of the land, but can be enacted independently. However, "the courts do not favor restrictions upon the utilization of land, and that a particular mode of utilization is excluded by agreement must clearly appear."[27] The restriction can be enforced not only by the person with whom the agreement was made, but also by other persons who have an interest in the observation of the provisions of the agreement. It is obvious that there are wide possibilities in the use of deed restrictions as a means to secure conservationist farm management practices, for example.

Methods of Land Transfer.—Land is transferred by means of a conveyance which requires a deed. If the attempt is made to transfer land by means of an oral agreement, a grantee who has made improvements on the land is entitled to a valid document in writing.[28] In order to ascertain the title of the grantor, the grantee has to depend on the record of previous conveyances. The Torrens system which requires the registration of titles in order to ascertain the ownership of all parcels of land has not generally been introduced in the United States. It has been adopted by a few states in a modified form, usually on an optional basis. The transfer transaction itself requires a greater amount of formalities and inexpediencies under the Torrens system which vests the power to issue conclusive title certificates in the government. However, this system has certain definite advantages over that which is generally applied in the United States. The title certificate is absolutely reliable, and there is no need to examine the previous titles when a transfer takes place.[29]

Besides this common method of transferring land *inter vivos,* there are many other methods of disposing of land. Federal or state land is usually transferred through the grant of a patent which is signed in the name of the president or by the governor. Moreover, an owner may dedicate his land to a public use by means of an implicit or express declaration. The ownership of land which is held in adverse possession may change. New land which has been formed by accretion

[27] Tiffany, *op. cit.,* Vol. III, §858.

[28] *Ibid.,* Vol. IV, §§966, 1236.   [29] *Ibid.,* Vol. V, §§1314 ff.

or alluvion may be acquired by the owner of the borderland. The states may acquire land whose owner dies intestate without heirs. The ownership of land may change by force of a judicial process or decree, because of tax delinquency, or because the state has appropriated it for public use under the power of eminent domain. Finally, death is an important cause of changes in the ownership of land. It passes to the heirs according to the rules of intestate succession or according to the provisions of the will.

The relative importance or the various ways of changing the ownership of farms is shown in the following table. From 1927 to 1939, 6 to 9 per cent of all farms have changed ownership per year. Up to 1931 the largest number of changes in ownership were brought about by voluntary sales and trades. During the depression the increase in foreclosures of mortgages and in bankruptcies resulted in making that type of change in ownership larger than any other. Changes in ownership on account of tax delinquency increased more rapidly than any other type during that period. There was also an increase in changes on account of inheritance transfers or gifts. Taking all farms as a whole, the mobility was much greater during the depression than before or afterward; it reached its peak in 1933 with 9.36 per cent of all farms changing ownership.

TABLE 2

NUMBER OF FARMS CHANGING OWNERSHIP BY VARIOUS METHODS, PER 1,000 OF ALL FARMS, 12 MONTHS ENDED MAR. 15, 1927-39*

Year	Voluntary sales and trades (a)	Delinquent tax	Foreclosure (b) of mortgages, bankruptcies, etc.	Inheritance and gift	Administrators' and executors' sales (c)	Miscellaneous and unclassified	Total
1927	28.3	5.1	18.2	8.8	7.0	1.1	68.5
1928	26.3	5.2	17.6	8.9	6.7	1.3	66.0
1929	23.5	4.7	14.8	8.5	5.4	1.1	58.0
1930	23.7	5.1	15.7	9.3	6.1	1.6	61.5
1931	19.0	7.4	18.7	9.4	5.7	1.7	61.9
1932	16.2	13.3	28.4	10.4	6.2	2.1	76.6
1933	16.8	15.3	38.8	13.1	7.0	2.6	93.6
1934	17.8	11.1	28.0	12.6	6.7	2.4	78.6
1935	19.4	7.3	21.0	12.2	7.1	2.1	69.1
1936	24.8	5.9	20.3	12.3	7.4	2.2	72.9
1937	31.5	4.3	18.1	9.9	8.4	1.8	74.0
1938	29.9	3.1	14.3	7.7	8.2	1.6	64.8
1939 (d)	28.2	3.4	13.4	7.6	8.0	1.5	62.1

*B. R. Stauber and M. M. Regan, *The Farm Real Estate Situation*, Circulars, U. S. Department of Agriculture.
(a) Including contracts to purchase (but not options).
(b) Includes loss of title by default of contract, sales to avoid foreclosure, and surrender of title or other transfers to avoid foreclosure.
(c) Includes all other sales in settlement of estates.
(d) Preliminary.

Land Inheritance.—In previous times the inheritance of land and movables followed different rules. Land passed to the blood relatives and was free from liability for the debts of the deceased, while the movables were used for the payment of his debts. Today land and movables are generally treated alike. However, there are still some relics of the old distinction, as, for example, the provision that land shall not be applied to the payment of debts until the movables have been used. In some states movables and land pass to different heirs.

If an owner dies without having devised his land by will the land passes to his blood relatives according to the rules of descent. These rules grant priority to the children of the deceased; if there are no children, the parents or collateral relatives inherit the land. At common law priority was given to the eldest son who alone inherited. When there were sons, the daughters were excluded from the inheritance. When there were no sons, the daughters received equal shares. In England these rules were abolished by the real property reform legislation of 1925 which applies the same principles to the inheritance of land and movables. Since then, all children share equally in the land of the deceased. In the United States the same principle has applied in all jurisdictions for a long time. The surviving spouse receives certain interests, the amount being dependent upon the number of children and other circumstances.

If the owner has devised his land by will, the land is distributed in accordance with the provisions of the will. There is freedom to bequeath in the United States; however, children who are omitted from the will are granted in many jurisdictions the share which they would receive if there were no will.

III

FACTS AND FACTORS IN EUROPEAN AND AMERICAN LAND TENURE

THE INHERITANCE OF FARM LAND

INHERITANCE laws, according to Toqueville, ought to be placed at the head of all political institutions.[1] In European countries land inheritance is regarded as the heart of the tenure system. According to Georges Sorel, "the inheritance of land is so closely connected with the juridical sentiments of a people that it is possible to use different inheritance laws as characterizations of different societies. It is there that the local laws fight their last battle against the unifying tendencies of centralized governments, and sometimes, win them."[2] In the United States the importance of land inheritance has not yet reached its acme. It is growing at a rate in proportion to the increase of the time distance between the first and the present generation of settlers. In most sections of the country this period exceeds another generation's lifetime.

Inheritance and the Distribution of Wealth.—It is no exaggeration to say that the inheritance customs which prevail in a region determine the social structure of that region to a large extent. Inherited wealth, said Hobhouse, is "the main determining factor in the social and economic structure of our time."[3] Inheritance in all its forms is one of the most powerful factors accounting for the unequal distribution of wealth. As H. D. Dickinson has shown, this cause of the unequal distribution of wealth operates with a much higher intensity than the others and is cumulative in a way the others are not.

Incomes derived from work are increased with progressive difficulty, whereas those derived from property are increased with regressive difficulty. . . . While one who relies on personal exertions for his livelihood finds, after a certain point, increasing difficulty in increasing his output of efficiency-units, one whose income is due to legal claims is able, owing to the diminishing marginal utility of income, to increase the number of those claims the more easily the more he already has.[4]

These considerations hold true in whatever manner property may be inherited. They are valid even where the property of the deceased is equally distributed among his children. However, the tendency to-

---

[1] *Democracy in America*, I, 49.
[2] *Introduction à l'économie moderne* (2e éd. Paris, Rivière, 1922), p. 74.
[3] *Liberalism*, p. 197.
[4] *Institutional Revenue* (London, Williams & Norgate, 1932), pp. 173-74.

wards increasing inequality is much more pronounced when the property passes to one heir. There is enough statistical evidence at hand to illustrate this conclusion. In France property, especially land, is equally divided among the children of the deceased. In England it is customary to prefer a single heir. Consequently wealth is much less unequally distributed in France than in England. The inequality of the distribution of property in England was even more pronounced before the World War when 9 per cent of all Englishmen owned 63.7 per cent of all the wealth. There is no doubt that the discontinuance of the traditional inheritance customs which call for preference of the eldest son is among the factors which have brought about this change. Figures indicating the distribution of wealth in England and France are presented in the following tables.

TABLE 3

CUMULATIVE PER CENT DISTRIBUTION OF CAPITAL ACCORDING TO AMOUNT OWNED AND NUMBER OF OWNERS, ENGLAND AND WALES, 1911-13 AND 1924-30*

Amount of capital £	1911-1913		1924-1930	
	Per cent of total capital owned	Per cent of all persons owning capital	Per cent of total capital owned	Per cent of all persons owning capital
Less than 100....	11.1	88.3	6.4	78.6
" " 1,000....	21.0	97.0	16.8	94.1
" " 5,000....	36.3	99.1	33.8	98.3
" " 10,000....	45.8	99.5	43.8	99.1
" " 25,000....	59.7	99.8	58.2	99.6
" " 100,000....	78.2	99.9	76.8	99.8
Total..............	100.0	100.0	100.0	100.0

*G. W. Daniels and H. Campion, *The Distribution of National Capital* (Manchester University Press, 1936), pp. 30, 51.

TABLE 4

CUMULATIVE PER CENT DISTRIBUTION OF WEALTH, ACCORDING TO VALUE OF ESTATES PROBATED IN FRANCE IN 1935*

Value of estates, francs	Per cent of value of all estates probated	Per cent of all estates probated
Less than 50,000..............	25.3	86.9
" " 100,000..............	37.4	93.8
" " 500,000..............	64.4	99.1
" " 1,000,000..............	74.0	99.6
" " 2,000,000..............	83.1	99.8
" " 5,000,000..............	91.7	99.9
Total.....................	100.0	100.0

*Annuaire statistique, 1936 (Paris, Imprimerie Nationale, 1937), pp. 228-29.

Primogeniture.—Unequal distribution of inherited property among the heirs may have its origin in the law itself or in a testament. If the law provides for an unequal distribution, its provisions may either call for application to all cases, or only to those where the deceased has not provided in his will for a different distribution.

When the eldest or youngest son is predetermined to inherit the farm, a stationary tenure system tends to become established. The stability is attained at the cost of the disinherited children. In earlier times urbanization has facilitated the absorption of the disinherited children into other occupations, and they have been credited with part of the advance of English commerce and industry. They also have formed a link between the landed gentry and the urban classes in England. However, all this was true under conditions of a rapidly expanding economy. Under present conditions the cities do not offer many opportunities for job-seeking farmers' sons. If they have to leave the home farm, they will either increase the number of unemployed people in the cities, or, if there are restrictions on their freedom to choose their residence, they will become agricultural laborers. In an expanding economy, primogeniture may mobilize the forces of progress. In a stationary or contracting economy, it tends to perpetuate the existing stratification of society.

Primogeniture is often accompanied by absentee ownership unless there are restrictions on the separation of ownership and cultivation of land. Restrictions of this type prevent the development of a tenant class and the advancement of the agricultural laborer. If they are combined with restrictions on the alienation of land, tenancy becomes the highest rung on the agricultural ladder. Restrictions on the alienation of land, especially on its divisibility, have to be appraised in the light of the rule that divisibility of resources which facilitates their transference maximizes the national dividend.[5] Restrictions of this type tend to perpetuate the existing distribution of land property and the size of the farms. They discourage such improvements in the proportion of the productive factors as the renting of additional plots of land. They are just as obnoxious when they apply only to farms of a certain size which is regarded as favorable. Every farm has its own optimum size, and the establishment of a general standard is incompatible with such elemental facts as the unequal distribution of labor and capital among the holdings, the qualitative difference of the factors of production, and the necessity of their permanent readjustment in view of technological progress.

Primogeniture and alternative systems of land inheritance will be more fully discussed in connection with the entailed farms legislation in Germany. Free divisibility of inherited land is usually associated

[5] See A. C. Pigou, *Economics of Welfare*, pp. 142, 158 f.

with part-ownership and a high mobility of land property so as to secure farms of an economical size.

Land Inheritance in Europe.—Generalizations concerning the influence of the system of land inheritance upon the tenure of agricultural land are often misleading. It is necessary to survey the whole complex of concrete factors which, in addition to the inheritance system, determine the tenure setup in a given country. France, Belgium, Holland, and England have high percentages of tenancy, though the prevailing inheritance customs are quite different. There is freedom to bequeath property at will in both England and France. However, the English tradition favors a single heir, while an equitable distribution of the estate among all children of the deceased is preferred in France. The rigidity of both these systems has been mitigated in recent years by legislative acts. It was possible in England until 1939 to "cut off a child without a penny." Such absolute freedom does not exist any longer. Now the courts are authorized to grant reasonable provisions to children who have been omitted from the will.[6] In France the formal freedom of testamentary disposition has for long been outweighed by a system of large "compulsory portions" which can be claimed by the relatives. It is the characteristic feature of the French inheritance system that these portions are usually not commuted in cash payments. Instead of mortgaging the farm, the heirs divide it. Under this system, parceling has become excessive. However, it was not until 1938 that certain provisions of the Civil Code in regard to successions of rural property were modified. It is still the rule that all children can claim equal portions of the estate. But certain provisions of the law of February 7, 1938, result in benefits for the heir who takes over an undivided estate. A decree of June 17, 1938, goes still further. This decree provides that an estate containing an agricultural holding of less than 200,000 francs (about $4,000) in value may remain undivided in spite of the opposition of a co-heir if it is requested by the surviving spouse having an equity in the farm and living thereon, or by any heir, if the deceased has children under age. The estate, then, is declared indivisible for a period not exceeding five years. The declaration may be renewed until the decease of the surviving spouse or the coming of age of the youngest child. The decree further provides for exemptions from taxation in favor of heirs who avoid the division of agricultural estates.

These changes seem moderate when compared with the large-scale establishment of entailed farms under the Nazi regime in Germany. However, an appraisal of the French reforms has to take into account the deeply-rooted custom and legal tradition, both of which favor equal treatment of all children. In England a different course was adopted

[6] Inheritance (Family Provision) Act, 1938, 1 & 2 Geo. 6, c. 45.

as early as 1285, when the statute *De Donis* gave support to a system of primogeniture. Though this system has become less rigid during the later centuries, a complete legal change did not occur until the Real Property Reform Laws of 1925. Even before that time the owner could bequeath his estate by his will to some person other than his heir-at-law. The latter had preference only if the owner died intestate. Under the new rule, on the owner's death intestate the estate no longer passes to the heir-at-law, but the land is treated as if it were personalty. The inheritance of real and personal estate follows the same rules. However, the importance of the measure should not be overestimated. As a custom primogeniture still prevails to a large extent among the owners of large estates in England even though it now is necessary to bequeath the property by will. However, the decline of the custom is illustrated by the breaking-up of many estates and the resulting increase in owner-occupancy in recent years.

Land Inheritance in the United States.—In colonial America descent to the eldest son prevailed in accordance with the rules of English law. However, there had been opposition to primogeniture since the beginning of the eighteenth century. The attacks culminated in Jefferson's successful fight against primogeniture in Virginia. The Ordinance of 1787 provided in Section 2 that "the estates both of resident and non-resident proprietors in the . . . territory, dying intestate, shall descend to, and be distributed among their children and the descendants of a deceased child in equal parts."

In Louisiana, South Carolina, Ohio and Mississippi primogeniture was never recognized. During the period from 1777 to 1798 it was abolished in Georgia, North Carolina, Virginia, Maryland, New York, South Carolina, and Rhode Island. Primogeniture was not the only alternative to a system of equal division of the estate among the children. In Pennsylvania and other states the pious colonists had taken refuge with the Mosaic prescription, and in accordance with Deuteronomy 21:17 and I Chronicles 5:1, they granted the eldest son the double portion of the other children. Jefferson had opposed this principle: "If the eldest son could eat twice as much, or do double work, it might be a natural evidence of his right to a double portion; but being on a par in his powers and wants, with his brothers and sisters, he should be on a par also in the partition of the patrimony."[7]

For over a century land has been equally distributed among the children of the deceased. However, the abolition of entails and primo-geniture was not effective enough to result in a complete disappearance of these institutions. In Maine, Massachusetts, Delaware, and Rhode Island entails are still admitted, though the holder is entitled to convey the property in fee simple. Other states do not have any provisions

[7] *The Writings of Thomas Jefferson*, I, 43.

relating to the subject. However, there is not much doubt that the courts of these states would decline to recognize entails, though the statute *De Donis* of 1285, whose last relics were abolished in England in 1925, seems to be still in force there. Today these rules are curiosities and of historical interest only, though the continued existence of some large estates in New England until the middle of the nineteenth century has been attributed to them.

To what extent the division of inherited land takes place at the present time is an open question. Professor Max Sering reported fifty years ago that in some of the oldest regions of the East the undivided transfer of the farm was customary.[8] As long as the disinherited children could find plenty of free land in the West or employment opportunities in the cities, this custom did not result in an increase in tenancy. In the twenties Professor Wehrwein described the conditions in a Wisconsin county where many families had held the farm for generations. The custom was based upon primogeniture, the "Bohemian Contract," and similar institutions.[9] No evidence is available concerning how widespread such local customs are.

Division of inherited land is often checked by the lack of villages which facilitate the interchange of small plots of land. However, the studies of Kolb and Brunner show that the number of villages and the village population are increasing at the present time. In 1935 the amount of part-ownership was the highest ever recorded, and some part of the additionally-rented land seems to result from inheritance divisions. Moreover, one inherited farm, divided and used for additional leases, increases the potential mobility of the surrounding farms which can be divided in the same manner; the next division further intensifies this development; and so on. The problem of how far this process has already gone deserves an investigation, as does the whole question of land inheritance, which should be dealt with in a comprehensive study covering a field as broad as possible.

Most of the investigations into the inheritance of agricultural land in the United States show the amount of land in a certain region which is acquired by inheritance. In most cases the percentage of land or farms acquired by inheritance ranged between 5 and 25 per cent. Obviously the percentage is highest in the older parts of the country.

Present Tendencies.—It is impossible to formulate any objectives of land tenure policy with reference to land inheritance until a study of the described type is at hand. Nevertheless, it is interesting to compile a record of the few statements referring to such a policy. Professor Richard B. Morris has pointed out that "the philosophers of the Cotton Kingdom, convinced that conservativism was the best weapon

[8] *Die landwirtschaftliche Konkurrenz Nordamerikas* (Leipsic, 1887), pp. 169 ff.

[9] "The Problem of Inheritance in Land Tenure," *Journal of Farm Economics*, IX (1927), 163 ff.

for self-preservation, advocated, prior to the Civil War, the creation of entails, and the re-introduction of primogeniture."[10] Morris himself raises the question whether "agrarian readjustments," such as the trend towards tenancy, the displacement of the smaller freehold in the New South by the large plantation and the tenant farmer, and the advantages of the large plantation organization will necessitate a change in our rules of succession.[11] L. C. Gray holds the view that

the successive subdivision of farms for the purpose of equal inheritance has in some areas produced farm units too small for successful operation. In the development of a family holdings program, we shall have to face the probability of a large portion of the farm population remaining on the land. We may need to take steps to insure that the farms established by this program are not rendered submarginal for agriculture by undue subdivision through inheritance.

O. E. Baker suggests

as a compromise the incorporation of the farm, a division of the shares of stock among the children, but with the heir who operates the farm paid a manager's salary, which should take precedence over dividends.

J. S. Davis recommends research and education, but also state legislation in order to alleviate the debt burden on the heir who takes over the farm and mortgages it in favor of the other heirs.[12]

Extreme caution is necessary in view of these proposals, inasmuch as they point towards the substitution of new inheritance laws in place of the present system of equal treatment of all children. The terrible predictions of alarmist writers respecting the consequences of the division of landed property are based upon a few local studies, and there is very little evidence for the belief that they hold good for the whole country. Even then the social costs of primogeniture would still be higher than those of the present system which facilitates a certain amount of social mobility. The supporters of the present order are probably incomparably more numerous than the advocates of primogeniture. However, they are seldom heard, and the few statements of the subject which can be found do not all contain an a priori dismissal of primogeniture. Restrictions on equalitarian inheritance would destroy what is left of the agricultural ladder and would amount to a regress to the ideas of the statute *De Donis* of 1285.

[10] *Studies in the History of American Law*, p. 124. The philosopher of the Cotton Kingdom is George Fitzhugh, *Sociology for the South* (Richmond, Va., A. Morris, 1854), pp. 189-93.   [11] *Ibid.*, p. 125.
    [12] Gray, "Land Policies and National Progress," in *Proceedings* of the Association of Land Grant Colleges and Universities, Fiftieth Annual Convention, 1936, pp. 44-45; O. E. Baker, Ralph Borsodi, and M. L. Wilson, *Agriculture and Modern Life*, p. 170; Davis, "Observations on Agricultural Policy," *Journal of Farm Economics*, XIX (1937), 876.

THE TENURE OF FOREST LAND

The Case for Intervention.—The leading principles of land tenure policy as applied to forest land have been ably formulated by Antonio de Viti de Marco, who says "As for the forests, . . . the State . . . is not so bad a producer in this field as it has shown itself to be in other forms of landed and industrial property, when compared with private producers."[13] Among the reasons for this superior or, to say the least, equal position of the government are certain characteristic specific features of forestry. The planting of forests requires a large initial capital. The economy is increased when wide areas are taken into cultivation. There is no need for that special oversight and care which characterizes the more intensive types of cultivation. Ultimately the waiting power of a corporate legal entity like the state is incomparably greater than that of an individual owner, since its life is virtually perpetual.

Moreover, there are two more reasons which call for special consideration of governmental interference in the field of forestry. Our economic system is based upon the principle that the product of investments accrues to the person who is responsible for the investment. If a part of the product accrues to other persons or to the general public, "self-interest will not," as Professor A. C. Pigou has stated it, "tend to make the national dividend a maximum; and consequently, certain specific acts of interference with normal economic processes may be expected not to diminish, but to increase the dividend."[14]

We omit here a repetition of the elaborate analysis upon which Professor Pigou's conclusion rests. Applied to forestry the argument confronts us with the fact that there is a divergence between the whole product of an investment in forestry and that part of the product which accrues to the investor. For, as Antonio de Viti de Marco puts it, two utilities are derived from the forests: the private profits to be made from the sale of timber, and the general benefits which forests confer upon the community.[15]

[13] *First Principles of Public Finance*, tr., Edith Pavlo Marget (New York, Harcourt, Brace & Co., 1936), p. 71.   [14] *Op. cit.*, p. 172.

[15] The character of these benefits has undergone considerable change in the course of time. In the past century the beneficial effect of forests on the climate was emphasized, while the search for employment opportunities, conservation consciousness, and the emergence of a semi-permanent war economy, mixed with the strife for national self-sufficiency, have now placed other benefits in the foreground. The changes in the character of the beneficial effects have led to forest policies in countries which indulged in laissez faire before. Henry Sidgwick, writing of the beneficial effect on the climate in 1887, said, "In England . . . this consideration can scarcely have practical importance."—*Principles of Political Economy* (2nd ed. London, Macmillan & Co., 1887), p. 477. Eighty years before, Lord Sinclair had called a forest "our great domestic foe."—Élie Halévy, *A History of the English People in 1815*, tr., E. I. Watkin and D. A. Barker (New York, Harcourt, Brace & Co., 1924), p. 202. Today it is said that nothing "calls more definitely for

The cost of maintaining the forest is borne exclusively by the proprietor, who sets against this cost only the private utility to be derived from the timber and the pasturage, and does not take account of the public utility of the forest as such. For this reason, the moment that it is to his interest to cut down the forest, and it is to the interest of society to preserve the forest, society must assume that part of the cost to which the public utility corresponds. Only then is the economic calculation complete.[16]

This is virtually the same conclusion at which Professor Pigou arrives. However, Pigou, in the main, proposes to compensate for the divergence between social and private cost by means of a system of bounties and taxes and of "extraordinary encouragements" of investments in the specific field of industrial activity where the full product does not accrue to the investor.[17] When the government assumes the utilization of forests, the conflict between private and public interests does not arise. Then all cost is borne by the community, and all benefits are conferred upon it. However, when the government imposes restrictions upon the private utilization of forests, it should grant compensation. "The compensation is merely that part of the cost which the State assumes in order to preserve the public utility of the private forest."[18]

The case for government interference with forestry is supported by another reason which arises from people's attitude towards the future. Professor Pigou says:

If we set out a series of exactly equal satisfactions—*satisfactions*, not objects that yield satisfactions—all of them absolutely certain to occur over a series of years beginning now, the desires which a man will entertain for these several satisfactions will not be equal, but will be represented by a scale of magnitudes continually diminishing as the years to which the satisfactions are allocated become more remote. This reveals a far-reaching economic disharmony. For it implies that people distribute their resources between the present, the near future and the remote future on the basis of a wholly irrational preference. When they have a choice between two satisfactions, they will not necessarily choose the larger of the two, but will often devote themselves to producing or obtaining a smaller one now in preference to a much larger one some years hence. The inevitable result is that efforts directed towards the remote future are starved relatively to those directed to the near future, while these in turn are starved relatively to efforts directed towards the present.[19]

---

sustained national effort than afforestation."—Lord Addison, *A Policy for British Agriculture*, p. 273. [16] *Op. cit.*, p. 73.

[17] *Socialism versus Capitalism* (London, Macmillan & Co., 1937), pp. 42-43; and his *Economics of Welfare*, p. 192. [18] A. de Viti de Marco, *op. cit.*, p. 73.

[19] *A Study in Public Finance* (2nd ed. London, Macmillan & Co., 1929), pp. 117-18.

As he adds, this maladjustment between desire and satisfaction which is the result of the defectiveness of our telescopic faculty makes us see future pleasures on a still more diminished scale when the future satisfaction will not be our own.

In extending the summation of pleasure . . . over all time and all sentience, it is to be considered that, just as egoism is never so perfect but that distance in time renders pleasure less attractive, so utilitarianism is never so perfect but that persons whose interests are widely separate will not each "count for one" to the other. . . . The average citizen cannot be expected to care much for the interests . . . of fellow-citizens outside his own class, nor at all for remote posterity.[20]

Edgeworth attributed so much importance to this conclusion that he asked for its consideration if utilitarianism is to be adopted as the rule of political action. An application of these principles to forest policy calls for a correction of the tendency to turn forest resources "more than they ought to be—maximum aggregate satisfaction being taken as our goal—to the use of immediate consumption, and less than they ought to be to the use of distant consumption."[21] Pigou again proposes a system of bounties. However, he has no illusions about the difficulties of calculating the proper amount of the bounties and of the administrative cost involved. Hence, for the sake of expediency, one could be inclined to prefer government ownership of forest resources to a system of bounties supplemented by restrictions on private utilization.

There is no use attributing much value to the rate of interest as the guiding principle of forest utilization. Contrariwise, the principles derived from the preceding discussion imply that "normal" economic behavior as guided by the rate of interest cannot bring about such utilization of forest resources as would maximize the national dividend. Suppose there is an alternative between a perpetual, fixed yield and an increase in the yield by 25 per cent during a certain length of time. Suppose further that the resource is fully exploited and used up at the end of that time. If the choice is made dependent upon the greater profitableness of either one, an equilibrium can be calculated at which the advantages of both procedures are balanced. The equilibrium would be attained after

32.986 years, if the rate of interest is	5	per cent
27.617 " " " " " " "	6	" "
23.791 " " " " " " "	7	" "
20.915 " " " " " " "	8	" "
18.674 " " " " " " "	9	" "
16.887 " " " " " " "	10	" "

[20] F. Y. Edgeworth, *Papers Relating to Political Economy* (3 vols. London, Macmillan & Co., 1925), II, 101.

[21] Pigou, *A Study of Public Finance*, p. 119.

That means that under the assumption of a rate of interest of 5 per cent the perpetual utilization would be less profitable than the wasteful exploitation, if the latter can be continued for thirty-three years.[22]

The Case against Intervention.—In view of this example it is hardly understandable that the opponents of government interference with forestry have argued that there are no special problems involved in forest production which would justify state action.[23] It is maintained that the great length of the production period does not call for special consideration, and that the security of the investment, the expected increments in the value of timber and the social advantages of forest ownership compensate for the low interest on the investment. As is often the case, the rate of interest is credited with bringing about automatic adjustment; if the rate is lowered, logging operations are curtailed and the production period is lengthened. The resulting decline of the timber supply leads to an increase in its price, attributed to the interest reduction for still another reason. The general statement is made that the lowering of the interest rate brings about an expansion of the productive activities of those industries which use timber. Hence, the increased demand results in higher prices.[24]

Experience has shown that such an automatic effect of changes in the rate of interest, assuming that it exists, does not prevent wasteful exploitation of forest resources by private owners. The opponents of government interference with forestry may be right when they argue that the social advantages of forest ownership compensate for the low interest on the investment and induce the owner to disregard economic advantages; then the utilization of forest resources may be in accordance with the welfare requirements of the community. However, the community still has to pay for the social cost which is involved in such a utilization. The only difference is that the payment does not consist of bounties to the forest owners secured from the general public in the form of taxes, but of social advantages which have to be conferred upon the owners of forest resources. The question of what kind of payment seems preferable does not directly concern the economist. In a democracy the statesmen will endeavor to prevent the rise of a class of large landowners whose functions are fulfilled only when social privileges are bestowed upon them.

However, it cannot be denied that government ownership of forests gives rise to serious economic problems. Without the guiding principle of the interest rate and outside of the framework of the price system,

[22] The example is adopted from Sven Helander, *Rationale Grundlagen der Wirtschaftspolitik* (Nürnberg, Krische, 1933), p. 63.

[23] For a summary of these arguments see Martha Stephanie Braun, *Theorie der staatlichen Wirtschaftspolitik* (Leipsic and Vienna, Deuticke, 1929), pp. 85 ff.

[24] *Ibid.*, pp. 87-88.

the government, perhaps, will not have such information as the amount of forest resources to be employed, or when to utilize them.[25] Yet in a country where many resources and much man power are unemployed, this problem is of secondary importance, and an application of the crude engineering standpoint would, perhaps, be a lesser evil than the wasteful exploitation by private owners.

Types of Government Action.—The government can interfere with the private utilization of forest resources in three different ways.[26] State interference may, first of all, take the shape of mere assistance and encouragement. "Subsidies for planting or other work, loans on favourable terms, premiums and rewards for good management, gifts of land, reduction of or exemption from taxation, grants for education and research, free advice and assistance, propaganda, distribution of seeds and plants, and cooperation in protection from fire" are among the encouraging devices which forestry enjoys in most countries. In a few countries where the economic importance of forestry is only slight, government intervention is confined to these measures.

In the United States public control over private forest utilization has been largely directed at the prevention of devastation, through cooperation and other measures aiming at the control of disease, insects, and fires. At present efforts are made to go beyond these preventive measures and turn to a more positive policy. Moreover, the federal government has been aiding in the establishment of farm woodlands—the Clarke-McNary Act of 1924—and the management of woodland, and several states have encouraged forestry by means of special tax legislation. The lumber code of the NRA called for a policy of conservation, the continuance of which was agreed upon by the leaders of the lumber industry when the NRA collapsed.[27] Publicly supported forest research is conducted on a wide scale. The policies directed toward greater government activity in the field of forestry may possibly be supported by the traditional responsiveness of public opinion to the special requirements of forest resources. This tradition found expression in the Timber-Culture Act of 1873[28] and has been revived by the current trend in favor of conservation.

The second step which the government may take in its forest policy consists of legal compulsion and restrictions. "Apart from the question of protection of the forests, control is generally strictest in countries where home-grown supplies are a matter of vital importance, as in central Europe, or where timber production is one of the main indus-

[25] See *Collectivist Economic Planning*, ed., F. A. von Hayek (London, Routledge, 1936), pp. 3-8.

[26] Cf. H. S. Troup, *Forestry and State Control*, pp. 17 ff., upon which the following summary is based.

[27] Henry T. Buechel, "Labor Relations in the West Coast Lumber Industry, 1935," p. 56. Master's thesis, State College of Washington, 1936.

[28] Cf. B. H. Hibbard, *A History of the Public Land Policies*, pp. 411 ff.

tries, as in the Baltic countries."[29] Professor Troup, the holder of the chair of forestry in the University of Oxford, has conveniently arranged these measures under the following headings: compulsory preservation of existing forests, prevention of speculation in woodlands, compulsory afforestation or regeneration of felled areas, prevention of forest devastation, compulsory working on the principle of the sustained yield, restriction as to rotation of size of trees to be felled, limitation of area or quantity of material to be felled, requirements as to silvicultural practice and other operations, and measures to secure proper forest management.[30] Measures of this type reduce the proprietary rights by restricting the alienation, indebtedness, and inheritance of land, by prohibiting changes in its use, and by prescribing certain practices and prohibiting others. Such measures have been pushed forward to the utmost degree in Germany and Italy. In Germany forestry had developed well under the protection of feudal relics. Its social costs were borne by the people, who had to make compensation for the lack of profitableness of the forest enterprise by conferring social privileges upon the *Junkers*. Now the government has assumed the role of the feudal lords.[31] In Italy the *Battaglia del rimboscimento* ("Battle of Reforestation") has led to the establishment of a special *Milizia forestale* ("Forest Militia") which supervises the reforestation and pacifies the secret or open opposition.

Direct state management, the third form of government interference with forestry, can be found in a few countries.[32] State management may either be applied as a punitive measure, if the private owner does not live up to the forest laws, as in Norway and India, or it may be based upon a contractual agreement between the owner and the government, as in France, Great Britain, and India. Another type of state management can be found in Switzerland where the government is authorized to consolidate private forest lands which are required for the public welfare.

Public ownership of forest land is the alternative and the supplement of public control over private utilization of forests. The extent of public ownership in various European countries is indicated in the following table. In those countries where there is only a small area of forests, the percentage of forest land which is under private ownership tends to be large. It is small in those countries where the importance of forest resources is slight. Where there are exceptions to this rule, utilization of the private forest land is usually regulated and controlled by the government, as in Norway, Germany, Sweden, and Finland.

[29] Troup, *op. cit.*, pp. 18-19.   [30] *Ibid.*, pp. 19-22.
[31] Franz Heske, *German Forestry* (New Haven, Yale University Press, 1938), pp. 276 ff. Readers of this book do well to consult the review by Professor Zon in the *New Republic*, August, 1938, pp. 55-56.
[32] Troup, *op. cit.*, pp. 22-24.

TABLE 5

RELATIVE IMPORTANCE OF FOREST LAND, AND AMOUNT OF LAND UNDER PRIVATE OWNERSHIP
SELECTED COUNTRIES*

Country	Forest land, per cent of total area	Forest land under private ownership, per cent of all forest land
Ireland	1.4	78.7
Great Britain	5.4	88.3
Holland	7.8	81.0
Denmark	8.1	72.3
Hungary	12.6	72.8
Belgium	17.8	51.8
Greece	18.5	20.4
Italy	18.7	63.0
Lithuania	18.8	15.3
France	19.2	62.5
Estonia	20.2	19.3
Poland	21.5	63.9
Rumania	24.2	51.2
Switzerland	24.3	27.7
Norway	24.7	80.6
Latvia	25.2	14.6
Portugal	26.2	94.0
Germany	27.5	50.2
Bulgaria	28.8	18.2
Yugoslavia	30.6	33.6
Albania	36.0	6.3
Sweden	56.5	76.1
Finland	73.5	58.5

*Werner Junghans, "Forstwirtschaftliche Aufgaben und Probleme der europäischen Länder," *Weltwirtschaftliches Archiv*, XLVIII (1938), 560 ff.

Public ownership of forests is increasing at the present time. The British Forestry Commission, established in 1919, has become the largest single landowner in the country and has acquired 1,000,000 acres of land. The commission has great difficulty in obtaining new land.[33] In the United States federal agencies acquired 21,000,000 acres from July 1, 1933, to December 31, 1937. Almost half of the newly acquired land consists of forest land—about 48 per cent. The total acreage of land in federal ownership as of June 30, 1936, was 387,000,-000 acres. Of that area, 148,000,000 acres were under the custody of the Forest Service. The national forests are operating on a sustained-yield basis.

The distribution of the forest area by type of ownership is shown in the following table.

[33] Lord Addison, *op. cit.*, p. 267.

TABLE 6

FOREST AREA OF THE CONTINENTAL UNITED STATES*

Type of ownership	Forest land	Commercial forest land
Public:	Thousands of acres	
Federal......................	152,720	88,815
State and County.............	17,480	10,635
Total Public............	170,200	99,450
Private:		
Farm.......................	185,475	152,580
Other.......................	258,885	242,870
Total Private...........	444,360	395,450
Total Public and Private..	614,560	494,900

*Hearing before the Subcommittee of the Committee on Appropriations, House, 75th Cong., 3rd Sess., on the Agricultural Department Appropriation Bill for 1939, p. 378.

It has been recommended that the amount of forest land under public ownership be doubled. This recommendation is based upon a detailed investigation which has shown that there is no need for a complete abandonment of private ownership of forest resources. Under appropriate government control, there is still a place for private forests in areas where it is possible to make a profit out of them.[34] In recent times much attention has been paid to the employment capacity of forestry, and the "provision of useful employment for rural people is bound to receive more and more attention in planning programs of forest development."[35] If this aspect of the forest problem is put in the foreground, a new evaluation of the public ownership of forests may have to be made.

TAXATION AND LAND TENURE

Taxation of farm land influences the tenure system in various ways. In the United States there is ample evidence that small properties are burdened with the property tax to a higher degree than large and higher-priced properties which tend to be underassessed.[36] While this example points to an unintentional effect of taxation, which may facilitate concentration of land, absentee ownership, and tenancy, there are various instances of intentional effects of tax policies upon

[34] National Resources Board, Part VIII of the Report on Land Planning: *Forest Land Resources, Requirements, Problems, and Policy* (Washington, 1935), pp. 56 ff.

[35] W. N. Sparhawk, *Forests and Employment in Germany*, United States Department of Agriculture, Circular No. 471 (1938), p. 2; Lord Addison, *op. cit.*, pp. 270 ff.

[36] Roy G. Blakey, *Report on Taxation in West Virginia*, 1930, p. 11. See also various Experiment Station bulletins: Minnesota, No. 277 (1931), pp. 10-14; Texas, No. 458 (1932), pp. 17-18; Louisiana, No. 231 (1933), Pt. 2, p. 17; Ohio, No. 459 (1930), p. 35.

land tenure. The progressive land tax of New Zealand, in force from 1891 to 1931, provided for differentiation according to size of estate, character of tenure, and residence of owner. It is generally recognized that taxes of this type contributed to the breakup of many large estates and to the decrease in absentee ownership in New Zealand and Australia.

The decline in population growth and urbanization has greatly reduced the strength of the argument of the single taxers. Since "unearned increments" have not only ceased to accrue[37] but have been wiped out in many cases, the proposals of Henry George have lost their appeal. The most that present attempts aim at is prevention of government subsidies from accruing solely to the landlords.

In the United States the depression has led to a growing sentiment in favor of the exemption of owner-occupied homes, at least partially, from taxation. Homestead exemptions of that type, which tend to destroy the local tax base, have been enacted in a few states. These proposals were often supported by references to the tendency of homestead exemptions to promote farm ownership and prevent land speculation and farm tenancy, since the exemption would inflate the value of owner-operated land. However, if this is to be the goal, the exemption has to amount to a considerable sum. Even then capitalization will take place only if a certain permanence of the exemption is expected.

The homestead exemption grants privileges to owner-occupiers. Other proposals are directed toward discrimination against tenure types which are regarded as socially undesirable. However, the advocates of special taxation of landowning corporations often forget that corporate ownership, at the present time, is involuntary in more cases than it is voluntary. Discriminate taxes which grant the corporations a certain amount of time for selling their holdings could take this factor into account. Taxes of this type, if capitalized, might lower land values.

High-tenancy regions often are high-tax regions, and it is probable that high taxes influence the owner to become a tenant, especially when he has a small equity. Farm taxes in the United States continued to rise until 1929, whereas land values and rents declined after 1920. Undoubtedly this may have operated as an economic inducement to some farmers to become tenants. In general, high farm real-estate taxes tend to increase tenancy, and it has been said that a tax system which contributes to bankruptcy is responsible for the substitution of tenants in place of owners.[38] The amount of tax sales is indicated in Table 2

[37] William Allen White has based a fascinating "economic theory" upon this observation.—*The Changing West* (New York, Macmillan Co., 1939).

[38] B. H. Hibbard, "Taxation in Relation to Land Utilization," in *Conference on Economic Policy for American Agriculture at the University of Chicago*, p. 49.

above. However, cause and effect may be reversed when we find a high tax rate in an area of high tenancy. One reason may be that the tenant votes it against the landlord.

For the United States as a whole for the year 1930, it has been estimated that 21.9 per cent of the gross rent received by owners of cash-rented farms was required for taxes on these farms.

Among the individual states the highest proportion of gross cash rent required for taxes is shown for Michigan, where the percentage was 56.6, followed next by Pennsylvania, with a percentage of 46.9, and the lowest percentage of 11.1 is shown for Alabama, followed closely with 12.4 per cent for Arkansas. In 16 states the percentage was under 20; in 19 states between 20.0 and 29.9; in 9 states between 30.0 and 39.9; in 3 states, between 40.0 and 49.9.[39]

The value of these calculations should not be overestimated because differences of the lease contracts are not taken into account therein. In one case the term of the lease may be long, or the tenant may receive compensation for improvements, while in others it may be different.

Regarding the relationship between income and taxes of owner-operated and of rented farms, the different types of income do not result in a great difference of the percentage relationship of taxes to net rent or net return of land respectively. Where taxes on owner-operated property are high or low, those on rented property move, in general, in the same direction.[40]

Inheritance Taxes.—Inheritance taxes in various forms are used as means to attain widely different objectives of land tenure policies. Progressive death duties have contributed to the breakup of large estates in England. The opposite policy is followed in France, where the system of succession has resulted in excessive parceling. A decree of June 17, 1938, provides for remedial action by modifying certain provisions of the civil code, and by granting certain exemptions from taxation to co-heirs in cases where the division of an agricultural holding has been avoided.

In England a quarter of all farmers bought their farms during the period from 1914 to 1927. Many of them did so not because they wanted to become owners but in order to prevent possible disturbances through the sale of the land by their landlords who needed cash for the payment of inheritance taxes. The English inheritance tax yields 10 per cent of the national tax revenue. The amount of tax paid for agricultural land is not recorded separately. It has been estimated to amount to £1,700,000 in 1931-32 and £1,991,000 in 1932-33.[41] French

[39] W. B. Jenkins, *Taxes on Farm Property in the United States,* Department of Commerce, Fifteenth Census of the United States, 1930 (Washington, 1933), p. 78.

[40] W. Coombs, *Taxation of Farm Property,* United States Department of Agriculture, Technical Bulletin No. 172 (Washington, 1930), pp. 34-44.

[41] *Hansard,* Fifth Series, Vol. 280 (1934), Col. 467.

inheritance taxes yield 5 per cent, and German inheritance taxes less than 1 per cent of the national tax revenue. In the United States the federal tax has become more important in recent years because of the reduction of the initial exemption from $100,000 to $40,000, and because of the considerable increase in rates. The federal estate tax yields about 5 per cent of the total federal tax revenue, and the inheritance taxes of the states amount to 4 per cent of their total tax revenue.[42]

The English death duties were enacted comparatively late. The reforms of 1907, 1909, 1919, and 1925 increased the rate of progression. Under present conditions the tax on an estate containing 30,000 acres of land amounts to £200,000. The valuation of the estates is said to be on the average one third above the effective value of the land and its buildings to the owner in possession.[43] Death duties are held to have led to a reduction of the fixed capital to be sunk in inherited land which is kept by the landlord. They have caused other landlords to sell part of their estates in order to pay the tax. These duties are adversely criticized by the English conservatives,[44] while others point to the fact that it would take a hundred and fifty years to reduce an estate from £2,500,000 to below £300,000. If the rates are applied to an estate of £25,000, it will take fourteen generations before it falls below £10,000.[45] In 1909 the Treasury was authorized to accept land in payment of death duties. So far this power has never been assumed, and land offerings were invariably rejected by the Treasury. Some reformers are inclined to advocate a reversal in this policy of the Treasury. Such proposals are made either because of the difficulties of the landowners in making payments in cash, or in order to facilitate public ownership of land.

According to the traditional analysis of the incidence of taxation, the inheritance tax cannot be shifted. The heir cannot place the burden of the tax upon the tenant, because its levy is the result of particular circumstances, not of conditions which generally prevail among the landlords. If he attempts to shift the tax, the tenant will move to other land. If the landlord has a monopoly, he will still not shift the tax, because he already charges a monopoly rent. These theoretical considerations may call for modification in view of the fact that full mobility of the tenants, to say the least, is as rare a phenomenon as full mobility of any other productive agent.

[42] W J. Schultz, in *Encyclopaedia of the Social Sciences* (New York, Macmillan Co., 1932), VIII, 43 ff.; *Facing the Tax Problem* (New York, Twentieth Century Fund, Inc., 1937), p. 22.

[43] Lord Lothian, in the London *Times*, July 10, 1936.

[44] *Hansard*, Fifth Series, Vol. 291 (1934), Cols. 117-36.

[45] G. F. Shirras, *Science of Public Finance* (3rd ed. London, Macmillan & Co., 1936), pp. 529-30.

LAND TENURE AND COLLECTIVE ACTION

Land tenure in the Western world[46] has remained comparatively unaffected by the trend toward collectivism. Instances of coöperative farming are rare. Collectivist cultivation of the soil is mostly the off-spring of a specific spiritual or religious outlook of the coöperators. Hence, it can be found among the Dukhobors in Canada as well as among the Jewish settlers in Palestine. The leading men on the Delta Cooperative Farm in Hillhouse, Mississippi, are ministers. The few coöperative farms which existed in Czechoslovakia originated from the spirit of the back-to-the-land movement and of the postwar settlement legislation, which had broken up the large estates. It has been said that the coöperative management of farms cannot compete with that of private enterprises

because it lacks (1) the necessary pressure toward the strict and continuous fulfilment of the members' duties, (2) the necessary mobility of management and its adaptation to new conditions, and (3) particularly, the possibility of utilizing the egotistic motives of the individual coöperator as an inducement for improving the efficiency of his work, motives which are inherent to private business with its wage-stimulus. If each member has to work only for the big pot, he is interested, first of all, in leisure at the cost of the others.[47]

Yet this realistic approach is confined in its application to progressive conditions of farming. If these do not prevail and if the general standard of farming is low, the establishment of coöperatives may mean progress. This is particularly true if conditions are so bad that any change means improvement.

Some of the European examples of tenant coöperatives deserve further investigation in order to examine their adaptability to conditions in the South. Here and in Europe such coöperatives could be established only with government help, or under conditions improved by private benefactors. The Delta Cooperative Farm, founded by Sam Franklin and Sherwood Eddy,[43] was supplied with credit which carried interest of only 2.5 per cent. Besides that, the coöperative enjoys the leadership of the excellent men who founded it, and its membership consists of an elite of farmers who proved their biological and mental fitness and who probably are above the average. In the first year the twenty-four white and colored sharecropper families from Arkansas earned an average cash income of $327.53 per family from their 2,000-acre cotton farm. They grow not only cotton, but cultivate gardens, tend a poultry farm and a hog farm, and manage a store as a consumers'

[46] For the development in Russia see L. E. Hubbard, *The Economies of Soviet Agriculture* (London, Macmillan & Co., 1939).

[47] Friedrich Aereboe, *Agrarpolitik*, pp. 188 f.

[48] Cf. N. Read, in the *Carolina Magazine*, March, 1937, pp. 3 ff.

coöperative. Profits are divided in proportion to the amount and quality of the work done. Advance dividends replace the old "furnish" system. The coöperative sells at current prices for cash only. Ownership passes into the hands of the members in proportion to the repayment of the capital investment. Large-scale production on the most scientific lines and economy in financing are mentioned as reasons for the cheaper production of cotton by coöperatives than by individual small holders. If the reported facts can stand a critical investigation and the test of more experience, the experiment deserves encouragement and imitation. However, there are critical statements regarding the financial success of the Delta coöperative as compared with other cotton farms:

It would take an expert farm accountant to draw anything like a controlled comparison between the groups, but on the face of the figures it would seem that such comparison would probably indicate that the Delta cooperators, given an extremely favorable interest rate and management furnished by philanthropy, succeeded in making slightly if any more than their neighbors under the existing system.[49]

The Farm Security Administration has set up some farming coöperatives under its rehabilitation program. The land is leased from the FSA, and the rent is 3 per cent of the appraised investment in land and buildings, plus insurance, taxes, and maintenance. The settlers are supplied with the usual rehabilitation loans of the FSA. The coöperatives are chartered by the state as corporations. No man has any particular plot as his own, but the members are assigned to jobs wherever their efforts are needed. The corporation pays each man fifteen cents an hour as an advance against the annual dividends. Policies are decided by the members; but the manager, who is an appointee of the FSA, has authority to modify decisions.[50] During the first year, average monthly work hours were 250, or a wage income of $37.50 a month. Since the corporations were just starting, no dividends were declared for the first year.[51]

Tenant coöperatives play a considerable role as agencies of improving land tenure in two countries of Southern Europe, the conditions of which are comparable to those of the American South. While we know very little of their effect on production, more information is available on their organization and management. They are organized in two forms: either the lease is collective while the work is done individually, or the work is also done collectively. The first type is to be found in Rumania; both types are organized in Italy. In both coun-

[49] T. J. Woofter, in the *New Republic*, October 20, 1937, pp. 303-04.

[50] For a full description see "Thirty-Three Families Join in Two Cooperative Farms," in the *Weekly Kansas City Star*, April 6, 1938. The article has been reprinted by the Farm Security Administration.

[51] New York *Times*, February 12, 1939.

tries the coöperatives served as the means of replacing the usurious sublessors. The prewar distribution of Rumanian land—.64 per cent of the population owned more than 99.36 per cent—was immobile on account of lack of capital and adequate agencies for credit. The Rumanian Mortgage Bank aided only the holders of the large estates, while farmers and tenants were forced to take refuge with usurers. Because of the lack of capital, purchasing and even renting of farms became more and more difficult. The institution which developed from these conditions was that of the sublessor who made the burden of the tenants still heavier. In order to remedy these evils, tenant coöperatives were favored by two laws in 1903 and 1909. As a result of the farmers' revolution of 1907, the law of 1909 provided that the state and corporate land should be rented only to tenant coöperatives which thus replaced the sublessors. The coöperatives worked well. They were controlled by a central office which sent a well-trained agricultural expert to each coöperative. The coöperatives divided the land into lots and assigned them to the members; they supplied the latter with seed, machinery, and teams, supervised the cultivation, and organized the sale of products. Coöperatives developed rapidly until the war. The holding of each member averaged around ten to twelve acres and tended to become larger with the increase of coöperative tenancy. The size of such holdings was a little larger than the average farm in Rumania. After the war, the agrarian reform opened the way for land-buying coöperatives which replaced the tenant coöperatives. No demand for this form of land tenure existed after land had become available through the expropriation of the estates. The progress and decline of the tenant coöperatives is as follows:

TABLE 7

TENANT COÖPERATIVES IN RUMANIA, 1903-32*

Year	Number of coöperatives	Number of members	Cultivated area, acres
1903	3	......	12,202
1905	87	......	75,545
1907	103	11,118	92,376
1909	273	36,371	470,587
1911	378	62,009	699,971
1913	465	76,678	925,981
1923	162	17,942	212,338
1926	117	13,829	106,610
1932	42	3,286	14,091

*M. V. Pienesco, "Agricultural Cooperation in Rumania," *International Review of Agriculture, Monthly Bulletin of Agricultural Economics and Sociology*, XXV (1934), 533 ff.

Both the described types of tenant coöperatives can be found in Italy. The coöperatives acquire land by means of a cash or share lease, sometimes also by purchase. In those coöperatives where the whole productive process is organized along coöperative lines, all the work is done collectively and is unified and centrally organized. The members are not much different from wage workers who are supervised by a manager. Where the work is done individually, the coöperatives act as sublessors. They assign distinct plots to the individual members who cultivate the land without coöperating in every stage of production. This type of organization has been more successful than the former because the individual responsibility of the member and the dependency upon his own efforts stimulated his efficiency. The tenant coöperative also fulfills functions other than renting, as common purchasing, financing, and insuring. In 1920 a special branch of the Coöperative Credit Bank was established to improve the supply of credit for the purposes of tenant coöperatives. The Italian tenant coöperatives enjoy other preferences based upon special legislation, and such favors as the administration bestows upon them. Both types have been supported by the various political parties in earlier times. Under the Fascist regime they have been united in a centralized organization in 1930, which is subdivided into regional units which supply the member coöperatives with technical and economic advice. In 1928 there were 314 such coöperatives with 46,724 members. They cultivated 441,977 acres of rented land. By the end of 1937 this figure had dropped to only 200,000 acres.[52]

In more recent times we find similar tenant coöperatives in Hungary. The small holders who were not supplied with land by the so-called agrarian reform of 1920 established tenant coöperatives, which have access to the general credit coöperatives. They rent land, finance the lease, and sublet it to their members. There were 56 tenant coöperatives in 1929 which rented more than 70,000 acres with about 4,000 families living on these farms. The results are praised by Hungarian writers.

No coöperatives, but associations of small gardeners which rent land and let it in small plots to their members for noncompetitive horticultural purposes, can be found all over Europe. The organization of coöperatives did not prove successful here.

With reference to the effect of land tenure upon other forms of coöperation, it is generally recognized that tenants do not lend themselves easily to coöperation. Tenants are more mobile than owners, and their marketing and buying is often under control of the landlord. Jesse Collins spoke of his

firm conviction that cooperation is the natural offspring of ownership and can flourish only in countries where ownership is the predominant principle. This, I think, is abundantly proved by its history and present position in other countries. It had no existence in Denmark

[52] W. Ebenstein, "The Fate of Coöperation Under Fascism," *Journal of Politics*, I (1939), 401.

(where it is now seen at its best) when the land tenure in that country was more or less similar to our own. It was only when—in the last century—the old tenure was changed by the legislation into one of ownership that the system took root and flourished. In a country like ours (or rather Great Britain, for Ireland has escaped) where the great mass of the cultivators are tenants holding from year to year, many of them here today and gone tomorrow, cooperation must be an exotic.[53]

Organizations of tenants which do not take part in the letting operations have recently developed in the United States. The Southern Tenant Farmers Union was organized as an independent union in Arkansas in the late summer of 1934. In October, 1936, the union claimed a membership of about 30,000, thus being the largest bona fide agricultural workers union in the South. In 1937 it affiliated on an autonomous basis with the United Cannery, Agricultural, Packing, and Allied Workers of America, a CIO affiliate which was organized in the same year. The Southern Tenant Farmers Union withdrew from affiliation with the UCAPAWA in March, 1939.

There are also a few collectivist ventures on the part of the landlords. Organizations of landlords existed in prewar Rumania. There "trusts" of sublessors were established which exploited the tenants. The monstrous land distribution—5,385 landlords owned half of the farm land—and the lack of capital and of credit agencies aggravated the plight of the tenants. Monopolies with similar tendencies developed in Sweden on account of the land purchases of the big lumber corporations.

In recent years other forms of collective action have developed. Collective lease contracts were set up by landlord and tenant organizations in Italy and are now generally adopted by the contracting parties.[54] Coöperative renting was provided for in the Farm Tenancy Law of March 23, 1935, of the Spanish Republic.[55] In Germany model lease contracts were drafted by public bodies; these contracts have to be used for all renting arrangements in agriculture.[56]

Collective action on the part of landlords and tenants was encouraged in an Oklahoma statute of 1937 which conferred upon a government agency the duty to improve the tenancy situation by assisting landlords and tenants in taking advantage of existing farm organizations, associations and coöperatives, and by organizing them whenever needed for their mutual benefit. The statute was repealed in 1939.[57]

[53] Letter to W. J. Ashley, 1908, reprinted in Anne Ashley, *W. J. Ashley. A Life* (London, King, 1932), p. 136.
[54] The best account of these activities is given in C. T. Schmidt, *The Plough and the Sword*, Chap. VII.
[55] *Annuaire Internationale de législation agricole*, XXV (1935), 756 ff. (Chap. VII, arts. 32-42). [56] See below, pp. 128 ff.
[57] *Oklahoma Laws*, 1937, S. B. 272; 1939, S. B. 82. See below, p. 76.

Tenancy and Farm Credit.—Farm tenancy and farm credit fulfill similar functions by supplying the farmer with outside capital. To a certain degree[58] they can be substituted for each other. Hence, it is not surprising to find that there are relatively fewer mortgages on tenant-operated farms than on owner-operated farms. In 1935, 25.1 per cent of all tenant-operated farms had mortgages, as compared with 41.5 per cent of all owner-operated farms. Moreover, owner-operated farms, although representing but 57.2 per cent of all farms, bore 64 per cent of the total debt; 68.9 per cent of all mortgaged farms were operated by owners. This divergency between owner- and tenant-operated farms was already in existence in earlier years, but has been intensified during the depression, when the mortgage debt on tenant-operated farms declined more rapidly than the mortgage debt on owner-operated farms. This has been explained in part "by the large volume of distress transfers of mortgaged owner-operated farms to non-operating owners with a complete liquidation of debt."[59]

Influence of Credit upon Tenancy—Denmark.—Abundance of farm credit will, generally speaking, make tenancy decrease. An illustrative application of this rule can be found in Denmark. It has been said that "the Danish farmer does not have to deal with a landlord; he has substituted for him a lendlord."[60] In that small country, where co-operatives participate in the agricultural life to a high degree, tenancy is almost nonexistent, while farm credit is utilized more than elsewhere. The total mortgage debt in 1926 amounted to 50 per cent of the value of the properties mortgaged. During the following years the debt ratio has increased as a result of the decline in land values. In 1933 the total mortgage debt on rural property was 70 per cent of the aggregate value of the farms.[61] In 1919 the percentage of farms operated by tenants was only 4.5, and 92.4 per cent of all farms were operated by owners. Correspondingly, only 5.6 per cent of all farm land is cultivated by tenants. The purchaser of a Danish farm can acquire mortgage credit up to 70-75 per cent of the farm value. There are also facilities for credit for working capital at reasonable conditions. Owing to its dependency upon exports, Danish agriculture was badly stricken by the agricultural depression. Great indebtedness, the

[58] "Under existing institutional facilities a farmer is allowed to rent a larger volume of capital (in the form of farm land and buildings) than he is permitted to borrow."—T. W. Schultz, "Capital Rationing, Uncertainty, and Farm Tenancy Reform," *Journal of Political Economy,* XLVIII (1940), 314.

[59] *Farm Mortgage Indebtedness in the United States,* detailed summary, United States Departments of Commerce and Agriculture (Washington, 1937), p. 1.

[60] T. W. Schultz, in *The National Farm Institute Symposium on Land Tenure,* Iowa Agricultural Experiment Station, Bulletin No. 357 (1937), p. 305.

[61] G. Costanzo, *Agricultural Indebtedness* (Rome, International Institute of Agriculture, 1937), p. 55.

pacemaker of high land values, resulted in a severe crisis, which proved the weakness of the Danish land tenure system midst decreasing prices of agricultural products. In recent times the plight of the Danish farmers resulted in producers' strikes. "The land has been burdened with debt to the extent that interest charges and amortization are out of all proportion of its productive power." If one keeps this in mind, the "Danish way" of reforming tenancy loses much of its attraction. Moreover, "in spite of all the legislation to encourage the rural population to remain in the country, the movement to the urban districts has continued."[62]

Influence of Credit Upon Tenancy—United States.—On the other hand, lack of farm credit may result in a high amount of tenancy. It seems that the slow development of organized agencies for farm credit in the United States has been an important factor accounting for the expansion of farm tenancy. Even today the degree of farm indebtedness is not high if compared with that of many European countries. According to special inquiry as of January 1, 1932,

25 per cent of the mortgaged farms reporting were indebted for 25 per cent or less of their value

38 per cent of the mortgaged farms reporting were indebted for between 25 and 50 per cent of their value

21 per cent of the mortgaged farms reporting were indebted for between 50 and 75 per cent of their value

11 per cent of the mortgaged farms reporting were indebted for between 75 and 100 per cent of their value

5 per cent of the mortgaged farms reporting were indebted for more than 100 per cent of their value.

In relation to the value of agricultural real estate, including both mortgaged and unmortgaged farms, mortgage-secured credit has been estimated to be 19.3 per cent in 1930. Owing to the decline in land values, this ratio increased to 28 per cent in 1933. When land values recovered and the farm debt decreased, the trend reverted. The ratio declined to 23.8 per cent in 1935 and was again 19.8 per cent in 1937.[63] The ratio of mortgage debt to the value of mortgaged farms operated by full owners was 39.6 per cent in 1930 and 50.2 per cent in 1935.[64] The rise is due to the loss in the value of farm real estate.

[62] J. W. Gannaway, Jr., and E. Gjessing, "Danish Land Legislation—An Appraisal of Recent Trends," *Foreign Agriculture*, February, 1937, p. 65.

[63] Donald C. Horton, *Long-Term Debts in the United States* (United States Department of Commerce, Bureau of Foreign and Domestic Commerce, Washington, 1937), p. 109; J. Wesley Sternberg, "Trend of Long-Term Debts in the United States, 1934-1937," *Survey of Current Business*, XIX (1939), 13.

[64] *Farm Mortgage Indebtedness in the United States,* detailed summary. Cooperative survey, United States Departments of Commerce and Agriculture (Washington, 1937), p. 12.

The proportion of owner-operated farms mortgaged increased from 27.8 per cent in 1890 to 42 per cent in 1930. In only five states more than half of the farms are mortgaged. The total volume of farm-mortgage indebtedness is shown in the following table.

TABLE 8

CHANGES IN THE VOLUME OF FARM MORTGAGE INDEBTEDNESS, UNITED STATES, 1910-38*

Year	Volume of debt (millions of dollars)	Relatives	
1910................	3,320	100	35
1920................	7,858	237	83
1925................	9,361	282	99
1928................	9,461	285	100
1930................	9,241	278	98
1933................	8,500	256	90
1935................	7,770	234	82
1936................	7,500	226	79
1937................	7,255	219	77
1938................	7,082	213	75

*1910-1935: Horton, *Long-Term Debts in the United States*, p. 107; 1936-1938: Sternberg, "Trend of Long-Term Debts in the United States, 1934-1937," *Survey of Current Business*, XIX (1939), 11.

The average amount of mortgage debt of an owner-operated farm is lower than that of a tenant-operated farm. This difference has been explained by the difference in the average size of owner and tenant-operated farms.[65]

The aggregate amount of farm mortgage debt in the United States is only four times higher than in Germany, seven times higher than in Switzerland, and ten times higher than in Denmark.[66] In view of the fact that the aggregate value of farms and the agricultural output of these countries amounts to a much smaller fraction of value and output of American agriculture, the farm-mortgage indebtedness in the United States appears comparatively small, so that a considerable amount of tenancy can be expected offhand. This observation fits well Professor W. G. Murray's view that "up to this time, experience has shown that credit extended by governmental agencies, state and federal, has not been successful in keeping tenancy down."[67] There was not enough credit, and the credit which was obtainable was too expensive. Consequently the view has been expressed that "a notable increase in family-owned and operated farms might be brought about through a further extension of sound long-term credit facilities for those best fitted by character and training to use them successfully."[68]

[65] David L. Wickens, *Farm Mortgage Credit*, United States Department of Agriculture, Technical Bulletin No. 288 (Washington, 1932), pp. 17-18.

[66] The comparison is based upon figures reported in Costanzo, *op. cit.*

[67] "Governmental Farm Credit and Tenancy," *Law and Contemporary Problems*, IV (1937), 507.

[68] National Industrial Conference Board, *American Agricultural Conditions and Remedies*, Preliminary General Review (New York, 1936), p. 14.

During the depression the per-cent decline of the aggregate amount of debts on tenant-operated farms was greater than that on owner-operated farms.[69] There is evidence that the various lending agencies adopted different lending policies with respect to owner-operated and tenant-operated farms. The aggregate mortgage debt secured by farms operated by tenants and managers amounts to 56 per cent of the aggregate mortgage debt secured by farms operated by owners. Offhand one might expect that the proportion of mortgages on tenant- and on owner-operated farms in the portfolios of the several lender groups is in the vicinity of this ratio. However, the federal land banks, land bank commissioners, and individual lenders "discriminate" against tenant-operated farms, while the commercial and savings banks, joint-stock land banks, mortgage companies, life-insurance companies, and other lenders "discriminate" against owner-operated farms. This attitude is illustrated in the following tables.

It is obvious that such a wide difference in the distribution of mortgages by tenure is the result of intentional differences in the lending policies of the credit agencies. The regulations of the federal agencies called for a preferential treatment of owner-operators. The private credit agencies prefer investments of large amounts in a single transaction. Since tenant-operated farms, in general, represent larger

TABLE 9

PERCENTAGE OF FARM MORTGAGE DEBT SECURED BY FARMS OPERATED BY OWNERS AND BY TENANTS AND MANAGERS, 1935*

Lender	Per cent of mortgage debt secured by farms operated by owners	Per cent of mortgage debt secured by farms operated by tenants and managers	
		Actual figures	Hypothetically expected figures (based on average)
All lenders.................	64.1	35.9	....
Individuals................	70.8	29.2	39.6
Federal land banks and land bank commissioners.......	68.3	31.7	38.2
Commercial and savings banks....................	57.2	42.8	32.0
Joint-stock land banks.......	56.7	43.3	31.8
Mortgage companies........	54.6	45.4	30.6
Life insurance companies....	54.5	45.5	30.5
Others....................	61.1	38.9	34.2

*Horton, *Regional Variations*, pp. 9 ff.

[69] For figures, see D. C. Horton, *Regional Variations in the Sources and in the Tenure Distribution of Farm Mortgage Credit, Outstanding January 1, 1935* (United States Department of Agriculture, Bureau of Agricultural Economics, February, 1938), pp. 9 ff.

TABLE 10

PERCENTAGE OF TOTAL MORTGAGE DEBT ON OWNER-OPERATED AND ON TENANT- AND
MANAGER-OPERATED FARMS HELD BY THE PRINCIPAL LENDING GROUPS, 1935*

Per cent of total mortgage debt	Federal land banks and land bank commissioners	Life insurance companies	Commercial and savings banks	Individuals	Others	All lenders
On farms of owner-operators.	34.9	14.0	8.1	27.1	15.9	100
On farms operated by tenants.	28.9	20.8	10.7	19.9	19.7	100

*Horton, *Regional Variations*, p. 15.

properties, these institutions will grant relatively more mortgages on tenant-operated farms than on those operated by owners.[70]

Influence of Credit Upon Tenancy—France.—Tenancy can be due to the lack of agencies of farm credit as well as to the disinclination of the farm population to burden the holdings with debts. Mortgage indebtedness is still regarded as a disgrace by the French peasants. Few people would buy or sell a farm without full payment in cash. The division of land between the heirs prevents the farm from being mortgaged for the benefit of the dispossessed heirs. The indebtedness of the French farm land as a whole is estimated as amounting to 12 per cent of its value. Other reasons for this situation have been stated by Professor H. Sée. The favorable conditions are

brought about by the decline of the desire to acquire more land, by the difficulty to enter into new debts because of the decrease in land values, and by the lack of well organized farm credit. Contrary to its model, the Prussian *Landschaften*, the *Crédit Foncier* worked almost exclusively for the benefit of the cities. Almost all creditors of farm mortgages are private individuals. This source becomes less productive as investments in stocks and bonds increase among the land population. Hence, the interest rate of mortgages, including all expenses, is as high as 8-9 percent. Credit for improvement has also been limited as much as possible.[71]

The demand for working capital has increased constantly since the intensive cultivation requires more money.

The limited indebtedness had the favourable effect that the small burden of interest helped the farmers to overcome the decrease in prices. On the other hand, the lack of working capital was an obstacle to intensive culture. That is proved by the insufficient use of industrial fertilizer.[72]

[70] See Wickens, *op. cit.*, pp. 37-40; Horton, *Regional Variations*, pp. 16-17.
[71] *Französische Wirtschaftsgeschichte* (2 vols., Jena, 1936), II, 398-99.
[72] *Ibid.*, p. 401.

As the Danish example illustrates, easy access to and wide use of credit, together with absence of tenancy, does not work for the benefit of the farmers during periods of depression. Although low farm indebtedness often corresponds to tenancy, generalizations are likely to mislead. Farm credit at reasonable terms is accessible in Holland, yet a great deal of tenancy remains, perhaps facilitated by the fact that credit for tenants, too, is readily procurable. In other countries the tenant credit problem led to great difficulties.

Working Credit for Tenants.—The laws of many countries provide that the creation of mortgages on movable goods requires the transfer of possession of these goods. This requirement makes it hard for the tenant to obtain working credit when he is unable to provide other than personal security. In Germany the Tenant Credit Law of 1926 improved the situation by enabling the tenant to mortgage his stock without transfer of possession. The law requires recording of the mortgage in a public register. Only a licensed tenant-credit corporation may grant such loans. The mortgage has the same rank as the landlord's lien. In the case of a foreclosure, the credit agency and the landlord both can claim half of the proceeds of the tenant's stock. These measures were intended to be only temporary but have become permanent. Similar credit agencies exist in Switzerland, Italy, and Poland. The Scandinavian countries permit the conveyance of the tenant's property to a creditor while the possession remains with the tenant. He regains full ownership after satisfying the creditor's claim. In the United States the system of local production-credit associations established by the Farm Credit Administration enlarged the tenant's agencies of credit. However, in order to provide for the necessary security, he must obtain a waiver from the landlord.

In France statutes of 1894 and 1899 created a system of regional credit associations. Their management, which was reorganized in 1920 and 1926, is based upon local agencies which supply their members with credit secured by bills of exchange which are discounted by the regional agencies. The regional agencies can also grant advances. They are controlled by a central office which makes the state credit accessible to them. The tenant's credit is short-termed and secured by *warrants agricoles,* which are mortgage certificates of nonperishable products held by the tenant in trust. In order to protect the creditor's interest, the management of the farm is subject to supervision. The warrants are nonnegotiable instruments. As mentioned before, the French farmers do not too often avail themselves of this means of credit, the winegrowers being the most frequent users. Long-term credit is given only to holders of small parcels of land. Its security is noteworthy; the credit is given after the farmer has taken out a life insurance policy.

Influence of Farm Prices.—By keeping marginal costs low, abundant and cheap working credit induces the farmer to cultivate extensively. It then becomes profitable to utilize the earning capacity of the farm in excess of its optimum productivity. Yet credit agencies, adjustments in rent, or improvements of the terms of the lease can seldom outweigh the effects of an insufficient level of farm prices. "If the price question is taken care of reasonably well the land ownership problem will be solved automatically. . . . The one or two hundred dollars per acre at which modern farms are bought or held must be forthcoming out of their income derived from their operation, or a class of people distinct from operators must own them."[73] A Swiss farmers' organization has made an illuminating study of the effects of an increase in the prices of agricultural products as compared with the reduction of farm debts or interest. The comparison, which is reproduced in the following table, illustrates that a relatively small increase in the prices of agricultural products increases gross returns to a much greater extent than a considerable reduction of farm debts or interest. Only where the debt is relatively high, an interest reduction by 25 per cent has a greater effect upon gross returns than an increase in prices by 5 per cent. Taking all farms together, a price increase of 10 per cent would, on the average, bring about the same result as a reduction of debt or interest by 58 per cent.[74]

TABLE 11

EFFECT OF INCREASE IN AGRICULTURAL PRICES COMPARED WITH EFFECT OF DECREASE IN FARM DEBT OR INTEREST, BY AMOUNT OF FARM DEBT. SAMPLE STUDY OF SWISS FARMS, 1932*

Amount of debt	Number of farms	Gross return per hectare	Interest per hectare	Increase In Gross Return Per Hectare as Result of:			
				Increase in agricultural prices		Reduction of debt or interest	
				by 5 per cent	by 10 per cent	by 25 per cent	by 50 per cent
francs		francs	francs	francs	francs	francs	francs
Under 1,000......	74	707	14.37	35.30	70.70	3.59	7.19
1,000 – 2,000......	60	786	61.87	39.30	78.60	15.46	30.93
2,000 – 3,000......	63	848	101.94	42.40	84.80	25.58	50.96
3,000 – 4,000......	85	861	156.82	43.00	86.10	39.20	78.40
4,000 – 5,000......	86	906	187.76	45.30	90.60	46.94	93.88
5,000 – 6,000......	62	1,032	221,67	51.60	103.20	55.42	110.84
6,000 – 7,000......	41	1,143	256.24	57.10	114.30	66.31	132.62
Over 7,000......	93	1,375	370.80	68.70	137.40	92.70	185.40

*Die Ueberschuldung und Entschuldung der schweizerischen Landwirtschaft, Mitteilungen des Schweizerischen Bauernsekretariates, No. 109 (Brugg, 1934), p. 44.

[73] B. H. Hibbard, in *The National Farm Institute Symposium on Land Tenure,* Iowa Agricultural Experiment Station, Bulletin No. 357 (Ames, 1937), p. 320.

[74] *Die Ueberschuldung und Entschuldung der schweizerischen Landwirtschaft,* Mitteilungen des Schweizerischen Bauernsekretariates, No. 109 (Brugg, 1934), p. 45.

LAND VALUES AND THE RATE OF INTEREST

Students of finance have made the observation that the cost of farm credit is still relatively high, compared with the cost of credit to urban business enterprises. This is true in spite of the fact that the field of agricultural credit has been permeated by governmental interference, which has considerably reduced the rate of interest. The fear has been expressed that low interest rates, created by political pressure, might permit land values to advance above the level that can be maintained by subsequent purchasers. "The result may be well to increase the number of farm tenants more rapidly than the newly enacted Farm Tenancy Bill can place present tenants in the farm-owner class."[75] When the Bankhead-Jones Farm Tenant Act was under discussion, similar fears were expressed. It was said that the low interest rates which were proposed in order to enable tenants to buy farms would inflate land values. Chairman Jones, of the House Committee on Agriculture, and Secretary Wallace elaborated on devices to prevent real-estate booms as a result of low interest rates. Mr. Jones expressed the opinion that the limitation of the advantages to small owner-operators would be of help.[76]

However, it seems rather doubtful whether these fears have much validity. A complete discussion of this problem would require the formulation of a theory of land valuation and is beyond the scope of this book. The general statement that a fall or rise in the rate of interest will cause a rise or fall respectively in the value of land neglects to take into account the fact that there are two variables in the picture, both of which determine the capitalized value. The observation has been made that the ordinary businessman is inclined to pay more attention to the series of expected yields than to the capitalization factor. There is no reason for expecting a different attitude on the part of a farmer, especially if he looks forward to paying back his mortgage within a definite period of time as he does under the conditions of the tenant-purchase program. To say the least, an anticipated change in the price of his products or in his operating costs will be given just as much attention as the interest rate,[77] and "no interest rate can be low enough to permit a positive capital value to be derived from negative or zero profits."[78]

---

[75] A. A. Dowell, "Land Booms and the Mortgage Rate of Interest," *Journal of Farm Economics*, XX (1938), 231-32.

[76] *Farm Tenancy.* Hearing before the Committee on Agriculture, House of Representatives, 75th Congress, 1st Sess., on H. R. 8, Serial A (1937), pp. 255-57.

[77] Cf. D. H. Robertson, "Mr. Keynes' Theory of Money," *Economic Journal*, XLI (1931), 403.

[78] F. Machlup, "The Rate of Interest as Cost Factor and as Capitalization Factor," *American Economic Review*, XXV (1935), 465.

TABLE 12

LAND VALUES, INTEREST RATES OF FARM MORTGAGES, AND GROSS FARM INCOME,
UNITED STATES, 1900-34*

Year	Value of Land, Buildings, Livestock & Machinery		Interest rate of farm mortgages, per cent (b)	Gross Farm Income	
	Total, in million dollars	Per acre, dollars (a)		Total, in million dollars	Per acre, dollars (a)
1900	20,440	24.37	7.18	3,655	4.36
1901	22,532	26.74	7.08	3,755	4.46
1902	24,624	29.09	6.97	3,924	4.64
1903	26,717	31.40	6.84	4,261	5.01
1904	28,809	33.71	6.71	4,392	5.14
1905	30,901	35.99	6.60	4,523	5.27
1906	32,993	38.24	6.48	4,928	5.71
1907	35,086	40.48	6.36	5,352	6.17
1908	37,178	42.70	6.25	5,633	6.47
1909	39,270	44.89	6.13	6,238	7.13
1910	40,991	46.65	6.33	6,643	7.56
1911	42,217	47.62	6.37	6,327	7.14
1912	44,311	49.55	6.16	6,784	7.59
1913	46,134	51.15	6.04	6,975	7.73
1914	46,507	51.13	6.23	7,028	7.73
1915	49,199	53.63	6.13	7,395	8.06
1916	53,803	58.16	6.02	8,914	9.64
1917	60,437	64.79	6.03	12,832	13.76
1918	66,083	70.27	6.36	15,101	16.06
1919	65,930	69.53	7.38	16,935	17.86
1920	77,924	81.52	6.94	13,566	14.19
1921	70,733	74.49	6.81	8,927	9.40
1922	61,706	65.42	7.14	9,944	10.54
1923	60,090	64.13	6.68	11,041	11.78
1924	58,028	62.35	6.42	11,337	12.18
1925	57,018	61.69	6.07	11,968	12.95
1926	57,032	60.88	6.01	11,480	12.25
1927	55,876	58.86	6.08	11,616	12.24
1928	56,244	58.48	5.95	11,741	12.21
1929	57,230	58.74	5.89	11,941	12.26
1930	57,248	58.02	5.80	9,454	9.58
1931	51,382	51.37	5.85	6,968	6.97
1932	42,952	42.36	5.92	5,337	5.26
1933	35,458	34.51	5.82	6,406	6.24
1934	36,646	35.20	5.15	7,265	6.98

*Leonard Kuvin, *Private Long-Term Debt and Interest in the United States* (New York, National Industrial Conference Board, 1936), p. 72.
(a) Acreage of land in farms for inter-census years estimated by the Bureau of Agricultural Economics.
(b) Interest charges on farm mortgage debt (interest "payable," Kuvin, p. 133) as percentages of farm mortgage debt.

The development of the postwar land boom is an apt illustration
of the negligible role of the interest rate. The year 1920 when land
values were at their peak followed upon the year 1919 when the interest rate of farm mortgages was substantially higher than in any
other year between 1900 and 1934. In 1934 land values were lower
than in any other year since 1907, with the exception of 1933; how-

ever, the interest rate was the lowest recorded during the first thirty-four years of the current century. As the preceding table illustrates, the correlation between gross farm income and land values seems to be definitely more significant than that between interest rates and land values. Hence, the necessity of low interest rates for farm mortgages should not be regarded as a serious obstacle to a tenant-purchasing program, especially since land values are certainly not too high at the present time. It is a strange attitude to complain about the alleged effects of a low interest rate and, at the same time, propagate better prices for agricultural products, which admittedly have the same effect. Those who regard low land values as a necessary prerequisite of a farm tenant program should pay at least the same attention to this variable as to the rate of interest.[79]

Control by "Lendlords."—During the last decade the relative importance of the various lending agencies holding farm mortgages has undergone important changes. The federal land banks and land bank commissioners now hold 40 per cent of the aggregate farm mortgage debt. The tripling of their share occurred at the expense of the life-insurance companies and individual lenders. The development is as follows:

TABLE 13

FARM MORTGAGE DEBT HELD BY PRINCIPAL LENDING AGENCIES, UNITED STATES, 1929, AND 1934-37*

Lending agencies	PER CENT OF FARM MORTGAGE DEBT				
	1929	1934	1935	1936	1937
Federal land bank and land bank commissioner.....................	12.9	32.7	38.1	39.8	40.0
Joint-stock land banks...............	6.8	3.3	2.3	1.8	1.5
Life insurance companies........... ..	22.8	16.5	14.1	12.9	12.6
State and national banks........... ..	10.3(a)	6.5	6.5	6.7	7.1
State credit agencies (b)........... ..	1.0	1.0	.6	.5	.4
Individuals, endowments, educational institutions and others......... ..	46.2	40.0	38.4	38.3	38.4
Total farm mortgage debt.....	100.0	100.0	100.0	100.0	100.0

*Sternberg, "Trend of Long-Term Debts in the United States, 1934-1937," *Survey of Current Business*, XIX (1939), 14 (adapted from reports on farm mortgage debt by Donald C. Horton and E. G. Enquist, Jr., in the May, 1938, and the November, 1938, issues of the *Agricultural Finance Review*).
(a) Figures are for 1930.
(b) Rural Credit Board of South Dakota, Bank of North Dakota, and Department of Rural Credit of Minnesota.

[79] William Allen White goes as far as to say: "By way of a solution of the southern farm problem, the federal government is doing two self-destructing things: trying to subsidize the tenant farmer so that he can buy land and break up the plantation system, and at the same time the federal government is trying to subsidize the price of cotton, making it so high that the planters can afford not to sell the land at a price the tenants can pay." *Op. cit.*, p. 60.

A discussion of the causes of these changes would be beyond the limits of our topic. However, the change will undoubtedly affect land utilization and farm management to a considerable degree. Public agencies as creditors of mortgages will be inclined to follow policies which differ from those of private lenders. They will be inclined to lay stress on the public interest in proper farm management practices and conservation.[80] Moreover, insurance companies are reported to have eliminated from their lending program territories of small loan activity, farms of low value, farms in arid regions, very large farm mortgages, specialized farms, and so on.[81] Some of the specific reasons for this discrimination will not be present in the case of public lending agencies.

Control of lending agencies over agriculture may be preventive or restrictive. Preventive control is involved in the decision of the lending agencies to grant or decline loans.

The influence of credit extension in an area may be either a positive or a negative one from the standpoint of encouraging a desired land use. As an example, if the detailed study of an area indicates that wise public policy should exclude further settlement considerable pressure to prevent unwarranted occupation could be exerted through definite announcement that credit by governmental agencies or those supervised by the government would not be made available to persons who settled in that locality.[82]

On the other hand,

There are several methods of encouraging particular types of land use through the extension of credit. They may take the form of making special requirements as to the use and manner of the use of the loan funds, of publicity as to credit facilities available for certain purposes, differential interest rates, and favourable methods of payment. . . . As an example, suppose an area study indicates the need of larger farm units in a particular locality or region. Liberal credit policies could be adopted which would encourage present operators to borrow for the purpose of acquiring additional land. Lower interest rates on such loans could be defended on the basis of benefits which would accrue to society because of the more desirable use of land obtained.[83]

The above types of control are applied in selecting the debtor and in granting credit. A different type of control may be exerted over indebted farmers. This control may be stipulated in the credit instru-

[80] See E. C. Johnson, "Farm Credit Policy as a Factor in Soil Conservation," *Journal of Land and Public Utility Economics*, XV (1939), 377-82.
[81] M. Woodruff, Jr., *Farm Mortgage Loans of Life Insurance Companies* (New Haven, Yale University Press, 1937), pp. 37 ff.
[82] Donald R. Rush, "Credit as a Factor in Land Policy," *Land Policy Circular* (United States Department of Agriculture, Bureau of Agricultural Economics), March, 1938, pp. 11-12.   [83] *Ibid.*, pp. 12-13.

ment, or it may be covenanted if the farmer is in default. The mere fact that the farm is mortgaged implies already a certain amount of control over its utilization. The occupier is obliged not to commit waste; that is, he has to utilize the holding without unreasonable injuries to the land.[84] Moreover, the mortgage agreement often contains specific provisions which secure conservationist farm management practices, for instance. Mortgages which are granted under the provisions of the Bankhead-Jones Farm Tenant Act contain such covenants as the Secretary of Agriculture shall prescribe to assure that the farm will be maintained in repair, and waste and exhaustion of the farm prevented, and that such proper farming practices as the Secretary shall prescribe will be carried out.

However, there are some legal limits to that type of control. The mortgagor's obligation cannot be extended beyond the time when the mortgage is paid. A mortgage agreement is void, which, in effect, may prevent the mortgagor from enjoying the land as freely after payment of the debt as before the creation of the mortgage. The courts have regarded such stipulations as extorted from the emergency of the borrower. Likewise an agreement was held void which grants the mortgagee an option to purchase the mortgaged property.[85]

The creditor's control over a farmer in default is usually combined with a more or less elaborate debt adjustment scheme. There may be statutory bases for such schemes, or they may entirely rest upon private agreement and upon the willingness of the lender to abstain from foreclosure. Such willingness has been shown by public lending agencies and by nonpublic banks as well. Moreover, it has been stated that often banks are less willing to foreclose than private creditors. This attitude of the banks is not surprising, for the banks are less inclined to press land values down than a private creditor would be; they shy at the odium which is attached to bank foreclosures, and they do not have as much at stake as a private investor.[86]

Experience in Australia.—During the Great Depression the member states of the Australasian Commonwealth established debt adjustment schemes for farmers. These schemes are of great interest because of the combination of rehabilitation and supervision under laws which adhere to the democratic tradition of these states. In New South Wales the Farmers' Relief Act, 1932-1935, provides for a stay order which protects the farmer's assets from proceedings by all of his creditors. The farmer may receive advances from the Farmers' Relief Board for the management of the farm and maintenance of the family. His liabilities are conditioned to the present value of his assets; no indi-

[84] Tiffany, *Real Property*, Vol. V, §1428.
[85] *Ibid.*, §1382.
[86] W. R. Maclaurin, *Economic Planning in Australia, 1929-1936* (London, King, 1937), pp. 219-220.

vidual creditor can take unfair advantage, and each will receive his share when distributions are available.[87] The board which administers the act consists of three members, two of whom are representatives of the farmers and of the farm creditors. The director of the board issues a stay order if he is of the opinion that the farmer needs assistance under the act, that he has prospects of ultimate financial rehabilitation, and that his past conduct and dealings are such that he deserves assistance. Applications for stay orders can be made by the farmer, and, under certain restrictions, by a creditor. Generally the stay order is in force for three years.

If the director decides to issue a stay order, he will appoint "some fit and proper person (which may be a corporate body) to act as supervisor of the estate of the farmer in respect of whom the stay order has been granted." The supervisor usually is situated as conveniently as possible to the farmer's property. He is required to furnish at least one bond of £2,000. The farmer is entitled to state his preference for the appointment of a particular supervisor.

The supervisor method has been adopted in order to avoid the centralization of the control of farmers' affairs in a large government department such as would be necessary for that purpose. It is the opinion of the Government that by dealing direct with his particular supervisor probably in an adjoining country town, there will be avoided the delay and congestion that may arise from concentration in one office of the affairs of a large number of farmers. It is further hoped that the farmer will become personally acquainted with his supervisor and that a better understanding of his circumstances will exist than if the farmer were compelled to deal by correspondence with a Government Department. In order to encourage the greatest freedom and confidence between farmer and supervisor the latter will be called upon to observe absolute secrecy in regard to the farmer's affairs.[88]

Upon his appointment the supervisor becomes the statutory agent of the farmer. He does not interfere with the management of the farm or the marketing of the products, but may do this if the board so directs him. He receives all money payable to the farmer and pays out of the receipts certain disbursements outlined in the act. Moreover, the supervisor has certain powers of sale which can be exercised with the consent of the board in cases where the farmer has assets which are not required for the working of the farm and is unable to meet the current expenses of the farm. The farmer cannot sell or mortgage his property without the consent of the board.

It is anticipated that the Board will use the existing supervisors for the purposes of conducting negotiations with creditors and assisting

[87] New South Wales Farmers' Relief Board, *An Explanation of the Provisions and Benefits of the Farmers' Relief Act, 1932-1935* (Sidney, Kent, 1935), pp. 5-6.

[88] *Ibid.*, p. 11.

farmers to compound their schemes. In addition the Board may appoint a certain number of practical men to report on the prospects of the farmer and his ability to satisfactorily carry on his operations on the basis of his readjusted debt position.[89]

The cost of the supervisor is not to exceed 3 per cent of the gross proceeds. "The supervisor does not need to be a farmer, but must be a man with some financial and business training with a good knowledge of rural interests. One supervisor may administer the affairs of a number of farmers."[90]

As the Farmers' Relief Board states, "The pivotal point in the administration is the supervisor."[91] There were fifty-six supervisors on June 30, 1937. They administered 1,557 cases. While one supervisor was in charge of no less than 205 cases, another handled just one. Virtually all supervisors are accountants.[92] In order to coördinate policies throughout the estate and to secure a uniform interpretation of the act, the board appointed inspectors who visit the supervisors at certain intervals.[93] However, the advantages of the decentralized administration were generally appreciated.[94]

It can provide prompt and efficient service of the utmost value in dealing with emergencies peculiar to rural industry, and makes possible that personal contact which can do so much to prevent misunderstanding, avoid delay, and check any influence that might otherwise operate adversely against the ultimate rehabilitation of the individual farmer.[95]

The board mentions the fact that in certain instances there have been difficulties in bringing the supervisors to

an appreciation of the fact that they are not merely receivers, and that the administration calls for a thorough analysis of the farmers' troubles at the outset, and the continued application, under competent practical guidance, of a constructive policy of management designed to overcome those troubles.[96]

On the other hand,

experience to date has shown a ready response on the part of most creditors to a reasonable offer to compromise, realising that such offer

[89] *Ibid.*, p. 24. [90] *Ibid.*, p. 11.

[91] *Report* on Operations of the Farmers' Relief Board during Year Ended 30th June, 1934 (1935), p. 2.

[92] Legislative Assembly, 2nd Session, New South Wales, 1938, *Report* on Operations of the Farmers' Relief Board during Year Ended 30th June, 1937 (1938), p. 6.

[93] *Ibid.*

[94] *Report* on Operations of the Farmers' Relief Board for Year Ended 30th June, 1935 (1935-1936), p. 3.

[95] *Report* on Operations of the Farmers' Relief Board for Year Ended 30th June, 1936 (1937), p. 2.

[96] *Report* on Operations of the Farmers' Relief Board for Year Ended 30th June, 1937 (1938), p. 2.

is made only after a full investigation of the farmer's position, and is based on the value of the farmer's assets and the productive capacity of the settler's business.[97]

Opposition against the act has centered against the control of the farmer's income,

many farmers not appreciating the fact that before they are entitled to a writing-off of portions of their debts they must, in fairness to all concerned, be prepared to submit their affairs to a close investigation by an impartial authority. This investigation would be valueless unless it carried with it the complete supervision of the income and expenditure during the period in which it was undertaken. In addition, a number of farmers do not realize that their working assets have depleted to such an extent that it is essential for them to go through a period of reconstruction covering one or two years before they could hope to be able to meet their commitments even on adjusted basis.[98]

[97] *Report* on Operation of the Farmers' Relief Board for Year Ended 30th June, 1936 (1937), p. 4. 　　　　　　[98] *Ibid.*

IV

FARM TENANCY POLICY

IN SPITE OF the well-known differences between American farmers and European peasants, and between American and European land tenure, manner of living, and thinking, an investigation into the state of farm tenancy in some European countries might be of value for a better appreciation of the main issues in the present discussion of a farm tenancy reform in the United States. It is safe to say that tenancy decreased considerably during the last decades, particularly in England and in the Balkans. This development has led to new farm indebtedness. The agrarian reform in the Balkans occasioned a strong demand for credit, for the owners of the divided estates had to assume debts for compensation payments to the former owners and for implements, equipment, and buildings which the change rendered necessary. Hence, many tenants became owners, but indebted ones. With the exception of conditions in England, this is the most significant recent instance of the working of the agricultural ladder in Europe. Besides the large-scale changes in East and South Europe which were brought about by political measures and not by the working of the tenure system itself, tenancy in Europe is seldom a step toward ownership. It is the permanent status of the overwhelming majority of tenants. Moreover, in many European countries with a large and stable farm laboring class, tenancy itself is the peak of an agricultural career often aspired for and rarely attained.

A comparative study of tenancy as a form of land tenure in various countries involves delicate problems. Such a comparison has to deal with all the facts and tendencies which are related to the system of land tenure. It is indeed not the single institution which has to be compared but the whole system of land tenure, even the agricultural situation as a whole. The importance and meaning of tenancy in different countries cannot be appraised by means of quantifications and statistical measurements, because such measurements are significant only in so far as the facts covered by them have a common denominator. Under this reservation we present the percentages of tenant farmers and of land under lease.

Difference in Appreciation of Tenancy.—A striking difference exists in the social esteem in which tenancy is held in the United States and in Europe. In this country where the institution of home and farm

TABLE 14

PERCENTAGE OF TENANT FARMERS AND OF LAND UNDER LEASE, SELECTED COUNTRIES *

Tenant farmers, per cent of all farmers		Land under lease, per cent of all farm land	
United States.......(1935)	42.1 (a)	United States......(1934)	45.0
Denmark...........(1919)	5.6	Ireland............(1929)	2.5
Estonia............(1929)	5.6 (b)	Estonia............(1929)	4.4 (e)
Germany...........(1933)	6.2 (c)	Denmark...........(1919)	5.6
Switzerland.........(1921)	7.0 (d)	Lithuania..........(1930)	9.2
Lithuania..........(1930)	8.3	Germany...........(1933)	10.7
Latvia.............(1929)	8.9	Canada............(1931)	12.6
Canada............(1931)	10.2	Latvia............(1929)	14.6
Finland............(1929)	11.1	Switzerland........(1929)	15.0 (f)
Greece.............(1929)	11.4	Sweden...........(1932)	26.7
Norway............(1929)	14.3	France............(1929)	40.1
Sweden............(1932)	19.6	Holland...........(1930)	49.0
Italy..............(1931)	32.0	Belgium...........(1929)	59.1
France.............(1929)	34.1	England & Wales. .(1927)	64.0
Holland............(1930)	46.7	Scotland..........(1934)	67.0
Belgium...........(1929)	51.8		
England & Wales....(1927)	63.0		
Scotland...........(1934)	76.0		

*International Institute of Agriculture, *The First World Agricultural Census*, Bulletins 1-42 (Rome, 1930 ff.).
(a) An additional 10.1 per cent are part-owners.
(b) An additional 15.1 per cent are tenants on state lands.
(c) An additional 41 per cent are part-owners.
(d) An additional 2 per cent are part-owners.
(e) An additional 14.1 per cent are under state lease.
(f) An additional 6 per cent are operated by part-owners.

ownership plays such an important role, tenancy is regarded by many as a social disease. This attitude is deeply rooted in the American tradition. As early as 1787 Tench Coxe spoke of the ideal American economy where "in the foreground we should find the mass of our citizens—the cultivators, (and what is happily for us in most instances the same thing) the independent proprietors of the soil."[1] Later on Senator T. H. Benton expressed the following view:

Tenantry is unfavourable to freedom. It lays the foundation for separate orders in society, annihilates the love of country, and weakens the spirit of independence. The farming tenant has, in fact, no country, no hearth, no domestic altar, no household god. The freeholder, on the contrary, is the natural supporter of a free government; and it should be the policy of republics to multiply their freeholders, as it is the policy of monarchies to multiply tenants. We are a republic, and we wish to continue so: then multiply the class of freeholders.[2]

According to Toqueville, who made his keen observations at about the same time as did Senator Benton, the absence of tenancy in the

[1] See H. Hutcheson, *Tench Coxe, A Study in American Economic Development* (Baltimore, Johns Hopkins University Press, 1938), p. 80.
[2] *Thirty Years' View* (2 vols., New York, Appleton Co., 1854-56), I, 103-4.

United States was "much less attributable to the [democratic] institutions of the country than to the country itself. In America land is cheap, and anyone may easily become a landowner; its returns are small, and its produce cannot well be divided between a landowner and a farmer."[3] Toqueville also showed that, in the absence of these conditions, democratic institutions rather tend to raise rents and shorten the lease terms. The subsequent development has shown the validity of his analysis to a striking degree. The democratic institutions could not prevent the rise of tenancy when land became more expensive, keen competition for it arose, and the growing of cash crops facilitated the division of the produce among landlord and tenant.

An important reason for the disrepute in which farm tenancy is still held seems to be that the conditions in the South are generalized by many observers. If one speaks of the tenant's plight, it is too often the sharecropper in the Cotton Kingdom who is thought of. This misconception is supported by some misleading arrangements of the census. However, there seems to be hope that these arrangements will be corrected in the future, and croppers will be enumerated as farm laborers.[4] The Census of Agriculture of 1940 has made an important contribution by making possible a statistical treatment of an entire plantation as a unit.

Moreover, many students of American farm tenancy have neglected some facts which J. D. Black has emphasized in a recent publication. The true extent of farm tenancy is not as great as it may appear at first glance. The working of the agricultural ladder is still effective to some degree, and the alternative is not farm tenancy or farm ownership but tenancy or a larger quota of hired men and of indebted owners.[5] However, there is much doubt whether a moderate reform of the lease contract could bring about a change in the social appreciation of farm tenancy. The traditional outlook is definitely in favor of farm ownership, which is regarded as an important element in civic education, and the ownership of farm land is conceived not as a mere economic institution but as "a patent of nobility." It has been stated by conservative observers that the amount of tenancy "should be no greater than that needed to facilitate a regular movement of young men into the status of farm operators and from tenancy to ownership with a minimum of permanent accumulation of land either in the ownership or in the tenancy status."[6] The amount of tenancy necessary to facil-

[3] *Democracy in America*, Pt. 2, Bk. 3, Chap. 6.

[4] K. Brandt, "Fallacious Census Terminology and Its Consequences in Agriculture," *Social Research*, V (1938), 19 ff.

[5] J. D. Black and R. H. Allen, "The Growth of Farm Tenancy in the United States," *Quarterly Journal of Economics*, LI (1937), 393 ff.

[6] Chamber of Commerce of the United States, *Farm Tenancy in the United States* (Washington, 1937), p. 40.

itate such a movement has been estimated as 30 per cent.[7] However, since the agricultural ladder at the present time is no longer an axiom but has become a postulate, it is the permanent tenant whose situation is the essence of the tenant problem in the United States.[8]

In many European countries, farm tenancy has been the pacemaker of agricultural progress and is regarded as a sound and necessary component of the tenure system. It has been recognized that in times of depression the position of the tenant is often superior to that of an owner-operator. Especially in England the function of the landlord as a shock absorber is generally acknowledged. In other countries the most striking instances of poor tenancy conditions were improved by the various agricultural reforms after the World War. At the present time there are no farm economists in Europe who would generally and unconditionally condemn farm tenancy. The change which occurred during the past century is illustrated by statements like that of Arthur Young that "the magic of ownership turns sand into gold and rocky grounds into scenes of fertility," or by the aphorism of A. Thaer, the father of scientific farm management, that the farm is the beloved wife of the owner, but the tenant's mistress whom he intends to leave. Only a few contemporaries of these men regarded tenancy as equivalent or supplemental to ownership. F. List, who belonged to that small group, spoke of the 'absurd argument that the cultivator ought to be the owner" and stressed the fact that the agricultural ladder requires a sufficient number of tenant farms.[9]

The observation that tenancy is not in disrepute in Europe is illustrated by the fact that it has been used as a means of land resettlement in various countries—Yugoslavia, Estonia, Holland, England, and Italy. However, when expropriated land is rented to tenants, the settlers do not feel completely secure. If their relation to the land is not stronger than a lease, another political change may cause its loss.

The restrictions on the rights of settlers on new holdings established with government support have brought forth tenure types which are similar to tenancy even if the holder has a proprietary right in the land. In some of the settlement legislations tenancy was preferred in order to prevent the accruing of the "unearned increment" to the settlers. "While conservative policy is to establish a peasant proprietary which would reinforce the voting strength of property, the liberal

[7] See H. C. Taylor, "What Should Be Done About Farm Tenancy," *Journal of Farm Economics*, XX (1938), 145.

[8] G. S. Wehrwein, "Place of Tenancy in a System of Farm Land Tenure," *Journal of Land and Public Utility Economics*, I (1925), 83.

[9] "Die Ackerverfassung, die Zwergwirtschaft und die Auswanderung (1842)," in *Werke* (Berlin, Hobbing, 1928), V, 439-441. List used the concept of an agricultural ladder ("Stufenreihe," p. 441). So did W. Roscher, *Nationalökonomik des Ackerbaues* (10th ed. Stuttgart, 1882), p. 181 ("unabgebrochene Stufenleiter").

policy is to establish a state tenantry from whose prosperity the whole community would profit."[10]

The Inadequacy of Tenant Law.—The question arises why it is in our time that the legal framework of farm tenancy is regarded as inadequate. Both under the common and Roman law systems, the legal foundations of tenancy were laid many centuries ago. They have proved satisfactory to both landlord and tenant during a long time. Is the higher sense of social consciousness and the tendency toward greater security responsible for the reformatory attitude toward farm tenancy, or is this attitude the result of economic or agricultural changes? It seems that the situation in which farm tenancy finds itself today is to be ascribed to all these factors. In the course of centuries tenancy had developed into one of the bonds which formed the network of feudal servitude in Europe. Whenever the political inferiority of the peasants was abolished or mitigated, the economic dependency continued. The legal basis of farm tenancy in the United States originated from the feudal system, and tenancy performed the function of a feudal institution during the prerevolutionary era. After the revolution, farm tenancy as a form of land tenure with no vestiges of feudalism seems to have been rare. It was not until the reconstruction period that farm tenancy emerged as an institution of greater significance. It fulfilled the function of the abolished slavery system in the South where the political emancipation did not imply economic freedom.

During the frontier period, farm tenancy was a means of facilitating migrations. Its disadvantages became more evident when a steadier and more intensive cultivation developed which was accompanied by the increasing use of farm machinery, fertilizer, irrigation, and other measures which multiply the tenant's capital and labor expenditures. This factor leads to another cause of the dissatisfaction with the traditional form of farm tenancy. Broadly speaking, both the Roman and common law systems do not recognize an essential difference between the renting of a book, costume, lodging, or farm. The Roman law concept of lease originates from the *locatio conductio,* which comprised not only leases of land and movable goods, but also the contracts for work and labor which were regarded as the employer's lease of the workman's capacity to work. The modern statutes of Roman origin still contain relics of this idea.

The common law distinguishes between the "hire" of movable goods and the "lease" of real property, but not between the leasing of lodgings and farms. In conformity with this concept tenants are regarded as consumers and usufructuaries of another's property. This idea implies that the land is considered as the only factor of produc-

---

[10] Hobhouse, *Liberalism,* pp. 175-76.

tion, while the productive power of the tenant is more or less incidental. The law regards him as a consumer of the productive power of
the land, not as a producer. This concept was possibly adequate in
times when the tenant's labor and capital outlay were small, when
cultivation was extensive, and when the regenerative power of constant
and proper cultivation was not recognized in all its implications.
Under present conditions farm tenancy is a division of functions, and
the importance of the tenant's functions has gradually increased. That
is why the philosophy behind the tenancy law has become inadequate.
If the law does not secure for the tenant the value of fixtures he leaves
behind, or if it does not settle the period of the lease according to the
ripening time of some improvements, it is not surprising that the
tenant's farm equipment is poorer than that of the owner, and that
he leaves the farm after having wastefully exploited the land. A different conduct would amount to an unexpected gift to the landlord.
The changes in agriculture have brought about the necessity of compensation for improvements and of adjustments in the duration
of leases. Contractual agreements have not helped to eliminate the
inadequacies of the law. Certain characteristics of the lease market
account for that. Its specific structure influences the amount of rent
as well as the other obligations of the parties.

THE FORMATION OF RENTS AND THE LEASE MARKET

The rent is a contractual obligation and not a residuum like the
economic rent. Unless there is perfect competition, there will be a
divergency of contract and economic rent. The bargaining parties
stipulate a contract rent, which is in a more or less close relation to
the economic rent. During the subsequent lease term this relationship
between contract and economic rent may change. The change is less
violent in the case of a share rent, which follows closely the fluctuations
of economic rent brought about by price changes. Not so, cash rents.
The prices of agricultural products might fall, while cash rents remain
stable for quite a while. This tendency proves burdensome for the
tenant, especially in case of a long-term lease. It has been often
observed that tenants' losses are "not met soon enough or generously
enough by abatements of rents."[11] If a reduction is finally granted, it
is preceded by losses of the tenant and attempts to pay the old rate.
Thereby a part of the tenant's capital goes to waste. If the lease term
is short, the tenant often abstains from asking for a reduction in rent,
since the landlord might give him notice.

It has also been observed that a rise in prices does not at once
lead to a rise in cash rents, and, more generally, that changes in cash
rents lag several years behind changes in prices. As it has been said

[11] See J. H. Clapham, *An Economic History of Modern Britain* (3 vols., New
York, Macmillan Co., 1938), III, 77.

with reference to a concrete case, "Landlords were broken in to remission and abatement. There were still arrears of reduction due in some places. Old tenants who survived had their lost capital to replace; new ones would take no risks."[12]

The rate of interest is another of the factors which are of influence upon the determination of rents. It may be stated as a general rule that those farmers who stand nearest to the money market press strongest for the highest return on their capital, while others are more willing to accept lower returns. Moreover, an operator who uses only his own assets is freer in neglecting higher returns than the operator who uses outside capital or assets belonging to someone else. This is so, provided that he does not have to pay a low rate of interest for special reasons, as in the case of credit given by relatives, friends, co-operatives, or the government, or when land is rented from a relative. In addition to the return on the goods supplied by the landlord, many tenants have to secure a return to the landlord for his supervisory services. In most cases the return on the goods and services supplied by the tenant is of the nature of a residue which remains after the contractual claims of the landlord have been satisfied. The tendency of rented farms to yield returns which are sometimes higher than those on owner-operated farms has brought forth misleading statements as to the higher efficiency of tenant farming and the like. Such conclusions are correct when high returns of rented farms are not the result of a predatory exploitation of the land, of reckless waste of materials, or of a curtailment of the reward for the labor and capital supply of the tenant.

Sometimes the landlord will content himself with a rent which is considerably lower than the rate of interest would call for. Such cases occur when the landlord is unable to assume the management of the farm, when he holds the land with the intention to wait for an increase in its value in the future, when he holds it for building purposes, and when there is a prestige, sentimental, or amenity value attached to the ownership of land. The occurrence of such cases is demonstrated by the relatively low percentage relation of the rental to the selling value of some farms and by lower gross returns on the capital investment of some landlords than a first farm mortgage would yield.[13]

When both the landlord and the tenant are very remote from the money market, the relationship between interest rates and rents disappears. This may happen in districts where banking and farm credit

[12] *Ibid.*, p. 38; Viscount Astor and B. Seebohm Rowntree, *British Agriculture*, p. 387.

[13] In 1930 it was estimated for the United States that gross rents represented 5.1 per cent of the farm value of rented farms. These gross returns on capital investments ranged from 3.1 per cent in Maryland to 10.6 per cent in Mississippi.—W. B. Jenkins, *Taxes on Farm Property in the United States*, Fifteenth Census of the United States, 1930 (Washington, 1933), p. 78.

is not widely used, or where the distribution of land property is too immobile to be influenced by the money market.

The Lease Market.—Another phenomenon which affects the amount of rents is produced by differences between real-estate market and lease market, particularly evident when the supply of capital is scarce. Since there is less capital required for renting a farm than for purchasing one, there are relatively more persons in the market who are able to rent a farm than there are prospective purchasers of farms. This factor tends to bring about different trends of rent and land prices and creates a keener competition for leases than for purchases. The smallness of the required capital has its bearing also upon the mind of the prospective tenant. He is more likely than a buyer to assume liabilities which he cannot meet. In addition thereto, the absence of that degree of fixity of investment which is characteristic of investments in real estate strengthens the inclination of the tenant to overburden himself and to be careless in assuming obligations. This tendency may be intensified by the fact that a tenant's failure in business does not involve a loss so great as that of an owner-operator.

It has often been observed that the rent of poor land is comparatively higher than the rent of good land. The same is true with respect to small and large holdings. The reasons therefor are similar to those which have brought forth the phenomenon that the slums of the cities yield higher rents than the better districts. However, while the slums supply only housing facilities, the small farm-holding supplies housing as well as opportunity for work. The tenants of the slums have a stronger withholding power than the tenants of small farm-holdings.

Some of the factors which raise the demand for leases also increase their supply. Since the capital required by the tenant is smaller than that of an owner-operator, business failures and losses in production result more easily in an abandonment of the farm. Consequently, farms are put again on the lease market and increase the supply. However, the significance of this process should not be overemphasized. It is necessary to bear in mind that the increase in the supply is in no way based on an increase in the actual amount of land available for leases. The increase in the supply corresponds to that multiplication of tenants' demand which results from the frequent change in the possession of rented farms. It is insufficient to satisfy a demand which has increased for other reasons.

Although the rent is a price, its formation does not follow all the rules regarding the determination of prices in modern economic life. The formation of rents is dependent to a very high degree upon the personal characteristics of the bargaining parties, and particularly upon those of the tenant. Often the rent is not determined by capitalistic calculations but by the tenant's vital desire to use his working power. Then, the amount of the rent is related rather to the intensity of his personal needs than to objective conditions, and the tenant's personal circumstances will force him into engagements which he cannot meet. There are no statistics available which show how many cases of shifting are due to nonfulfillment of contractual obligations of the tenant, but there is no doubt that many of the 34.2 per cent of tenants who seem to be on the move at least once a year would keep their farms longer if they were able to meet the terms of the lease.

The tenant's plight becomes worse if the bargaining power of the landlord is strengthened by a tendency toward monopoly. In this connection two monopolistic tendencies are to be distinguished. If farming is the only occupation in a certain area, the landlords are enabled to grant or refuse access to opportunities for work. On the other hand, if there are more tenants seeking farms than are available, and land is held by a few large owners, the land monopoly of the lessors becomes effective. Both tendencies are often mixed, but it is necessary to distinguish them since both call for different remedies. The relative insignificance of industries in parts of the South has brought forth an illustration of the landlords' control over the access to opportunities for work. When tenants were dispossessed involuntarily on account of the acreage reduction of the AAA, acts of violence occurred, since the croppers had lost their only opportunity for making a living. In other regions the scarcity of available land and the keen competition among tenants has brought about serious dislocations.

Keen competition among tenants has introduced a serious form of instability [in Iowa]. Particularly in the northwestern and southern parts of the state, more tenants are looking for farms than there are farms to go around. These tenants, desperately searching for a farm, bid the rent up, sometimes knowing they cannot live up to their promises. The bidding among tenants has resulted in unduly high cash rentals for grassland under crop share leases in the northwestern and southern part of the state, thus further discouraging conservation.[14]

Hence, it may happen that the strength of their bargaining power enables landlords to increase the rent so high "as to leave the tenants but bare subsistence, and so prevent them from having the capital—or in bad times even the physical vigor—requisite to render their labor adequately efficient." The result

is quite a possible one, even on the supposition that all parties are actuated by enlightened self-interest; since even when an increase in the incomes of tenants . . . would lead to a more than equivalent increase in the value of their labor, it is obviously not the interest of the landlord to furnish the increment of income unless he is to profit by the increased efficiency. Now in the case we are considering, the in-

[14] R. Schickele and C. A. Norman, *Farm Tenure in Iowa, No. I,* Iowa Agricultural Experiment Station, Bulletin No. 354 (Ames, 1937), p. 171.

creased produce would in the first instance be appropriated by the tenant; and even where the loss to the landlord would ultimately be compensated by a rise in rent or perhaps by greater regularity in payment, the prospect of this compensation may easily be too remote and dubious to induce a prudent landlord to make an immediate and certain sacrifice of income in order to obtain it.[15]

Reports on the amounts of net rents are not numerous. Investigations into gross rents are often of little significance, because the significance of the rent as expressed in units of money depends upon several other terms of the lease contract which do not have a common denominator and cannot be quantified so easily. The same amount of money rent is of different weight if the tenant, for instance, pays taxes or receives compensation for improvements, or if he does not. These defects in the comparison of rents could be avoided by calculating constructed rents based upon money payments and other terms of the contract.

Rents and Mortgages.—The peak which the trend of rents reaches at a certain time seems to be important for the further development of farm mortgage debts. The increased rent tends to become capitalized in the form of higher mortgages. If the rents decrease later, the volume of mortgages remains steady for many years. Hence, it is safe to say that the peak of rents determines the amount of indebtedness for a long period. The development of land values, rents, and farm mortgage holdings in the United States since 1914 illustrates this conclusion. Farm real-estate values and rents reached a peak in 1920 and 1921, while the long upward trend in the volume of farm mortgage debt was not checked before 1928.[16] The increase in debt after 1920 was only to a small degree the result of an increase in the number of mortgaged farms, and the conclusion seems justified that the increase in debt was largely due to additional mortgaging facilitated by the high farm values and rents of 1920 and the preceding years. However, it must be taken into account that credit was easily obtainable in these years. The indebtedness was far below its limits in 1920, when the ratio of mortgage debt to the value of the mortgaged farm averaged around 30 per cent.[17]

THE ECONOMIC FOUNDATION OF FARM TENANCY POLICY

Professor Pigou, of the University of Cambridge, is virtually the only economic theorist of repute who has ever attempted to vindicate farm tenancy policies on the basis of strictly economic reasoning.

[15] Sidgwick, *Principles of Political Economy*, pp. 479-80.

[16] Stauber and Regan, *The Farm Real Estate Situation, 1935-36*, United States Department of Agriculture, Circular No. 417 (Washington, 1936), p. 20; *The Farm Debt Problem* (Washington, 1933), 73rd Cong., 1st Sess., H. D. 9, pp. 8, 10.

[17] *The Farm Debt Problem*, p. 15.

Pigou's analysis is based upon his distinction between the marginal social net product and the marginal private net product.

The marginal social net product is the total net product of physical things or objective services due to the marginal increment of resources in any given use or place, no matter to whom any part of this product may accrue. It might happen, for example . . . that costs are thrown upon people not directly concerned, through, say, uncompensated damage done to surrounding woods by sparks from railway engines. All such effects must be included—some of them will be positive, others negative elements—in reckoning up the social net product of the marginal increment of any volume of resources turned into any use or place. . . . The marginal private net product is that part of the total net product of physical things or objective services due to the marginal increment of resources in any given use or place which accrues in the first instance—i.e. prior to sale—to the person responsible for investing resources there.[18]

Since the economic subjects are, in the main, only concerned with the private net product of their actions, they will attempt to equalize the values of the marginal private net products of resources which they invest in various lines of entrepreneurial activity. There will be no tendency toward equalization of the values of the marginal social net products unless the marginal private net product and the marginal social net product are identical. "When there is a divergence between these two sorts of marginal net products, self-interest will not, therefore tend to make the national dividend a maximum; and, consequently, certain specific acts of interference with normal economic processes may be expected, not to diminish, but to increase the dividend."[19]

This argument also gives support to government interference with forestry and to conservation policies. In the case of forestry the interest of society may call for preserving a forest at a time when it is to the interest of the owner to cut it down. If the owner preserves it, he has to be compensated for the divergence between that part of his product which accrues to society and that part which accrues to him. A similar case can be found when the owners of durable production goods, of which the investor is a tenant, leave the work of maintaining and improving them to the temporary occupiers. The main difference between this case and that of forestry rests upon the fact that the forest owner who preserves the forest in the interest of society renders services to the general public and thus cannot receive compensation by means of contractual agreements. On the other hand, the tenant who makes improvements which benefit the landlord renders services to a party to his lease contract, and the divergence between the private and the social net product can be alleviated by a modification of that con-

[18] *Economics of Welfare*, pp. 134-35. [19] *Ibid.*, p. 172.

tract.[20] The extent of the divergence varies in accordance with the arrangements of the contract between landlord and tenant, and the terms of the contract are based upon varying requirements of technical convenience, tradition, custom, and comparative wealth of landlords and tenants.[21] In this connection Pigou refers to the Irish landlords, who are poorer than the English, and thus leave more of the expenditure on land to their tenants than do the English landlords. An analysis of the various types of lease contracts discloses that the "primitive type of contract between landlord and tenant, in which nothing is said about the condition of the land at the end of the lease," tends to maximize the difference between the private and the social net product. The private net product is much shorter under this system "which merely provides for the return of the instrument to the owner at the end of the lease in the condition in which the instrument then happens to be." The difference amounts to "nearly the whole of the deferred benefit which would be conferred upon the instrument." However, the private net product does not necessarily fall short of the social net product by the whole of this deferred benefit,

because a tenant, who is known to leave hired instruments in good condition, is likely to obtain them more easily and on better terms than one who is known not to do this. So far, careful tenancy yields an element of private, as well as of social, net product. Since, however, separate contracts are often made at considerable intervals of time, this qualification is not especially important.[22]

Long-Term Leases.—Another qualification relates to differences between the effects of long and short leases. If the lease is long, the products of improvement and maintenance works which are undertaken by the occupier in the earlier years of the term will accrue to him, and the private net product will not fall short of the social net product to any considerable extent. However, the difference will tend to increase as the end of the lease term draws near. Hence, during the later years of a long lease and during the whole period of a short lease wasteful exploitation of the land will be the rule; "a farmer, in the natural and undisguised endeavour to get back as much of his capital as possible, takes so much out of the land that, for some years afterwards, the yield is markedly reduced."[23] While long leases do not remove all difficulties, they will, in many cases, enable the tenant to reap the fruits of improvements. However, it has been said that annual leases establish the closest and most human relations between landlord and tenant, and it is somewhat difficult to frame a long lease

that without hampering the tenant will practically make it his interest to treat the land in the best way; and, where the tenants are poor, a

[20] *Ibid.*, p. 192.   [21] *Ibid.*, pp. 174-75.
[22] *Ibid.*, p. 175.   [23] *Ibid.*

long lease is open to the further objection, in view of the landlord, that the benefit of an unforeseen rise in the value of the land will accrue entirely to the tenant for the period of the lease, while the landlord is likely to bear a considerable share of the loss due to an unforeseen fall, through the actual or threatened insolvency of the tenants.[24]

Moreover, the history of land tenure in Ireland has illustrated that leases for twenty years and longer did not prevent the worst exploitation of the tenants. A long lease does not change bad terms into good ones. It merely alleviates to some extent the inherent difficulties of a separation of land ownership and cultivation.

Compensation for Improvements.—Pigou then goes on to analyze a second class of contracts, where the deficiency of the primitive type is mitigated by compensation schemes.[25] Such arrangements may merely provide that the tenant shall be compensated for injury and benefit when he leaves the holding. Negative compensation for injury is practically everywhere provided in the lease. Compensation schemes of this type often assume the form of penalties for the failure to return the rented holding in "tenantable repair." The legal basis of compensation payments for benefit and injury may be an explicit provision of the lease contract, a statutory or customary enforcement of the rules of husbandry, or a modification of these rules as provided in the English Agricultural Holdings Act of 1906 where the tenant is given freedom of cropping but is held liable for damages.

Moreover, positive compensation payments may be extended to cover future increments in value. The difficulties which a scheme of this type has to encounter arise from the fact that

some improvements do not add to the enduring value of the estate the equivalent of their cost of production. If the compensation for these improvements is based upon their cost, the private net product is raised above the social net product. In practice this danger is largely overcome by the rejection of initial cost as a basis of compensation value, coupled with the requirement of the landlord's consent to some kinds of improvement. . . . But even on this plan the private net product may be slightly in excess. In order that private and social net product may coalesce, the value of an improvement, for compensation purposes, should in strictness be estimated subject to the fact that, at interchanges of tenants, the land may stand for a time unlet, and that during this time the improvement is not likely to yield its full annual value. If this is not done, it will pay a tenant to press investment slightly—very slightly—further than it will pay either the landlord or society to have it pressed.[26]

[24] Sidgwick, *op. cit.*, p. 480.
[25] *Economics of Welfare*, pp. 177 ff.   [26] *Ibid.*, pp. 178-79.

Moreover, if improvements can be made without the landlord's consent, landlords will refrain from letting land. On the basis of this analysis, Pigou criticizes the provisions in the English Agricultural Holdings Act of 1906 which defines the compensation for improvements as "such sum as fairly represents the value of the improvements to an incoming tenant." According to Pigou the standard ought to be "the value to the landlord." However, this defect is not of great importance, since most of the improvements are exhausted after a few years.

Compensation for Disturbance.—A general weakness of the compensation schemes rests upon the fact that the tenant is aware of the threat of an increase in rent and that he cannot claim compensation until he leaves the farm. As a result of these contingencies the private net product may still fall short of the social net product. Hence, it is necessary to improve the compensation schemes and to grant the tenant compensation for disturbance as provided in the English acts of 1906 and 1920. However, Pigou does not regard this remedy as sufficient. "Since a tenant quitting his holding under the conditions contemplated obtains no compensation for 'goodwill' or the non-monetary inconveniences of a change of home, he will still be very unwilling to leave, and the landlord will still possess a very powerful weapon with which to force him to consent to an increase in rent."[27] Moreover, there are exceptions to the rule that the landlord has to grant compensation for disturbance. If the land is wanted for building, or if the landlord intends to sell it, the tenant obtains no such compensation. Pigou endorses the exception in the case of an intended building activity. In such a case the payment of compensation for disturbance "would encourage the investment of resources in agricultural improvements at the cost of a more than equivalent social injury in postponing the use for building the land that has become ripe for it."[28] The value of the second exception is more questionable. Since the tenant, if he leaves, does not obtain compensation for disturbance, he will be inclined to stay and rent the farm from the new landlord. He then is liable to the rent on any improvement which he has executed without receiving any compensation.[29] "It is probably a recognition of this danger that has given rise to the growing demand among farmers for legislation permitting them, when the landlord wishes to sell, to purchase their holdings on the basis of the old rent."[30]

These are the shortcomings of a scheme of compensation arrangements. In view of these difficulties, it is an understandable attitude to doubt that it is possible to formulate statutes regulating the lease which could bring about a complete adjustment. As Jesse Collins

---

[27] *Ibid.*, p. 180.   [28] *Ibid.*

[29] *Report of the Committee on Tenant Farmers*, Cd. 6030, p. 6, quoted in Pigou, *Economics of Welfare*, p. 180.   [30] *Ibid.*, p. 181.

said, "There is a lot of foolish talk about giving a tenant security and permanence, but it can't be done. The man who is master over rent must in spite of everything always command the situation."[31] It is true that there are some landlords who arrange their affairs in a manner that alleviates the difficulties involved in the separation of ownership and cultivation of land. Professor H. C. Taylor states that "in the United States there is to be found the beginning of compensation for unexhausted improvements."[32] However, these cases are exceptions. There is no reason for expecting that a landlord will act against his economic interest, and if there were reasons for such an expectation, the landlord, indeed, would claim political and other privileges as reward for his conduct.

In view of this situation, "it is often contended, in effect, that for a really adequate adjustment, not merely compensation for tenants vacating their holdings, but legal security of tenure, coupled with legal prohibition of renting tenants' improvements, is required."[33] Since an absolute security of tenure would result in waste in many cases, it has to be made conditional upon the observance of the rules of good husbandry. Moreover, in the case of a conflict between the interests of the tenant and the public, the interests of the tenant would have to yield. He would have to leave the farm if the land is required for purposes which the public interest places higher than farming.

Fair Rents.—The security of tenure per se does not bring about the desired results as long as the tenant is threatened by an increase in rent. The landlord's lack of legal power to terminate the lease can most easily be replaced by his economic power, since he can force the tenant to give notice by arbitrarily increasing the rent. Hence, the enforcement of a fair rent is necessary. The pursuit of these objectives requires the establishment of a tribunal which fixes rents and settles rent disputes. The rent tribunal would have to cope with difficulties which are inherent in any institution making constitutive decisions upon private rights. A "tenant may be tempted deliberately to let down the value of his holding in the hope of obtaining a reduced rent," and experience in Ireland has shown that the courts, while authorized to refuse the revision of rents, refrained from the use of that power.[34] "Two brothers divided a farm into two shares of equal values—the good husbandman got a rent reduction from the courts of 7½ per cent, the bad one got one of 17½ per cent."[35]

[31] Collins to W. J. Ashley, Ashley, *W. J. Ashley. A Life,* p. 136.

[32] "Land Tenure and the Social Control of the Use of Land," *Proceedings* of the Fifth International Conference of Agricultural Economists, 1938, special reprint, p. 3.

[33] Pigou, *Economics of Welfare,* p. 181.

[34] *Ibid.,* pp. 181-82.

[35] M. J. Bonn, *Modern Ireland,* tr. by T. W. Rolleston (Dublin, Hodges, Figgis, 1906), p. 113; quoted *ibid.*

In view of all these implications and effects of government intervention on behalf of tenants, it is understandable that Pigou's concluding remarks on the subject disclose a somewhat sceptical attitude towards fixity of tenure and "fair rents." He states,

It is not by any means obvious that the policy of fixity of tenure and judicial rents will really bring marginal private net product and marginal social net product more closely together than they are brought by simple compensation laws. The gap between the two marginal net products can only be completely closed if the person who owns the land and the person who makes investments in it are the same. But this arrangement is frequently uneconomic in other ways.[36]

If the rent is fixed, new implications arise. The rent is a price, and the fixing of prices in defiance of the laws of the market results in certain dislocations of demand and supply, dislocations which, however, are not necessarily undesirable. If rents are fixed below the level which the forces of the market tend to bring about, landlords will be inclined to abstain from renting their land to tenants. While the measures providing for security of tenure would prevent the landlords from terminating those leases which are in existence when the rent-fixing measures are enacted, it is to be expected that the supply of new leases will fall short of the demand. Now, if the landowners are not willing to enter into new leases because the rent is not high enough to cover their opportunity costs, they can do various things. They can either manage the farm themselves, or they can employ managers, or, if they are unwilling to do either, they can sell their farms, possibly to their tenants. Hence it is safe to say that measures of the described type would, in the long run, result in an increase in owner-occupancy, since the terminated leases would not completely be replaced by new ones. In England, where the most severe type of protective legislation has been enacted, the events have taken this course. Making renting unprofitable for the landlord puts an end to the expansion of tenancy.

The situation might be different in countries where the operation of farms by managers is a significant component of the tenure system and where there is a wide social discrepancy between tenants and landlords. In such countries the fixing of rents might result in an increase in manager-operated and owner-operated farms, the owner-occupiers being identical with the former feudal or semifeudal landlords. Under such a system the tenants might become farm laborers. In some countries in Eastern Europe, it has, therefore, been found necessary to enact provisions for compulsory leases.

AMERICAN FARM TENANCY POLICIES

A farm tenant program for the United States can follow two lines of approach. The attempt can be made through education or legal

[36] *Ibid.*, pp. 182-83.

provisions to modify and improve the prevailing terms of the lease contracts. The other approach would be through government action aiming at an increase in ownership in place of tenancy. The two policies are not mutually exclusive but may supplement each other. So far, action of the first type has been almost completely reserved to the several states. It is said that there is no constitutional basis for federal regulation of landlord-tenant relationships, though this view has never been tested in the light of recent court decisions. It was held in 1936 that the regulation and control of agricultural production is a "purely local activity," beyond the powers of the federal government.[37] However, later decisions have arrived at a broad interpretation of the Interstate Commerce clause[38] and the General Welfare clause.[39] In view of these decisions constitutional difficulties do not now seem to be so overwhelming as to justify complete federal passivity with respect to the regulation of landlord-tenant relations by legislative action.

State Action.—With a few exceptions, the state laws adhere to the rules of the common law which does not secure adequate protection for the tenant and, in England, has been supplemented by the Agricultural Holdings Acts. Only a few similar attempts have been made in the United States, and the practical importance of these attempts is almost negligible.[40] After unsuccessful efforts to set maximum rentals, legislation was enacted in Texas regulating rentals by making the landlord's lien conditional upon the rent's remaining within certain limits. However, the specified rents are the prevailing ones, and sharecroppers are not protected. A very comprehensive farm tenancy bill was introduced into the Texas legislature in 1939, but failed to pass. In Kansas two statutes were enacted which grant the tenant a moderate security for improvements erected by him and void leases which contain "harsh, burdensome, oppressive and extortionate" terms. Such leases "are entered into by necessitous persons only because of the scarcity of other rental lands"; they are "against the public policy of the State, illegal and unenforceable." Tenants under such leases have to pay only a fair and reasonable rental, and the landlord's lien is restricted to the crops and livestock actually produced on the land, and to the sums

[37] *United States* v. *Butler et al., Receivers of Hoosac Mills Corp.,* 297 U. S. 1 (1936).

[38] *National Labor Relations Board* v. *Jones and Laughlin Steel Corp.,* 201 U. S. 1 (1937); *Mulford* v. *Smith,* 307 U. S. 38 (1939).

[39] *Helvering* v. *Davis,* 301 U. S. 609 (1937).

[40] Vernon's *Texas Statutes,* 1936, art. 5222; *General Statutes of Kansas,* 1935, §§67-501, 501a, 531, 532, 533; *Iowa Acts and Joint Resolutions,* 48 G. A., Regular Session (1939), p. 347; *Oklahoma Laws,* 1937, S. B. 272 (repealed in 1939, S. B. 82). The information pertaining to the Kansas and Oklahoma statutes is based, in part, upon a communication to the author from Mr. H. A. Hockley, of the United States Department of Agriculture.

received by the tenant for pasturage. Among the burdensome requirements which void the lease are excessive tax payments by the tenant, excessive liens of the landlord, excessive duties of the tenant to make improvements, and laborious restrictions on his freedom of cropping. The practical significance of both these statutes is not great, since the first applies only to landlords who own more than 5,000 acres, and the second can be avoided by omitting a single one of the recited burdensome terms. The statutes were designed originally to protect tenants on Scully-owned land, which was rented by Scully agents with no improvements, buildings, or equipment. The tenant was obligated to construct any improvements which he needed to operate the farm successfully, and the lease practically gave a mortgage on these improvements to the landlord. During lean years, these provisions became so oppressive that legislation was necessary to curb them.

In Iowa a statute was enacted in May, 1939, which requires written notice by either landlord or tenant to terminate leases on forty or more acres of farm land. The statute extends leases one year on the same terms on which they were negotiated unless notice is given by either party before November 1. Iowa farm leases usually take effect March 1. During the legislative debates the fear was expressed that the measure might result in a greatly increased number of one-year leases. However, this fear seems unfounded, since most of the leases used in Iowa are one-year leases anyway.

Some other state laws provide for research and education. In Oklahoma additional provisions were made in 1937 for state assistance in the preparation of equitable lease contracts, in the formation of landlord and tenant organizations, and in the arbitration of differences between landlords and tenants. These functions were to be carried out by the Department of Landlord-Tenant Relationships, and $25,000 was appropriated for the biennium, 1937-38. In 1939, upon recommendation by the Governor, the department was abolished, ostensibly as an economy measure and because, apparently, the results were not sufficient to justify the expenditure. Considerable research had been accomplished by this department, and innumerable meetings were held separately with landlords and tenants, and in conjunction with each other, to discuss the various problems affecting them. The report of these meetings has been published by the Extension Service, which has decided to continue the functions of the department, using funds from some other source.

Upon the basis of this survey, it seems safe to say that state action did not succeed in improving the lease terms to a noteworthy extent. Hence, federal action seems necessary. Thus far, Congress has chosen the alternative approach—making owners out of tenants, with the exception that there is federal supervision of the leasing arrangements of rehabilitation clients.

Federal Action—The Bankhead-Jones Farm Tenant Act.—In 1936 the platforms of both major political parties promised action to cope with the farm tenancy problem. During his reëlection campaign in the same year, President Roosevelt made two definite pledges: to ameliorate housing conditions and to reform the farm tenancy situation. In December, 1936, the American Institute of Public Opinion, on the basis of a typical cross section of the voting public, reported that 83 per cent of the people would approve a government program to enable tenants to buy farms that they now rent.

On November 16, 1936, the President instructed the Secretary of Agriculture to serve as chairman of a special committee on farm tenancy. The report of this committee was sent to Congress by the President on February 17, 1937.[41] On the same day the President, in a message to Congress, asked for enactment of a nation-wide farm tenancy program. The Bankhead-Jones Farm Tenant Act, approved on July 22, 1937, marks the beginning of such a program.[42] The act authorizes the Secretary of Agriculture to make loans to farm tenants, farm laborers, sharecroppers, and other persons who obtain, or who recently obtained, the major portion of their income from farming. Only citizens are eligible to receive these loans, which are granted to enable the applicants to acquire farms.

Preference is given to persons who are married, or who have dependent families, or, wherever practicable, to persons who are able to make a down payment, or who are owners of livestock and farm implements. No loan is made unless the farm is of such size as the Secretary of Agriculture determines to be sufficient to constitute an efficient farm-management unit and to enable a diligent farm family to carry on farming of a type which the Secretary deems can be successfully carried on in the locality in which the farm is situated. Applications for loans are filed with the county agent and examined by a county committee composed of three farmers residing in the county. If the committee finds that an applicant is eligible to receive a loan and that the farm is suitable, it so certifies to the Secretary. The committee also certifies to the Secretary the amount which it finds is the reasonable value of the farm.

If and when certification has been made, the Secretary grants a loan not in excess of the amount certified by the county committee. The loan is made in such amount as is necessary to enable the borrower to acquire the farm and to make necessary repairs and improve-

[41] *Farm Tenancy.* Report of the President's Committee. Prepared under the Auspices of the National Resources Committee (February, 1937). The President's message and the report, without technical supplement, is also published as H. D. 149, 75th Cong., 1st Sess. (1937).

[42] Pub. No. 210, 75th Cong., 1st Sess., 1937.—50 Stat. 522-533.—7 U. S. C. A. §§1000-1029.

ments thereon and is secured by a first mortgage on the farm. The instrument under which the loan is made provides for repayment of the loan in installments not exceeding forty years. The Secretary may provide for a system of variable payments under which a surplus above the required payment will be collected in periods of above-normal production or prices and employed to reduce payments below the required payment in periods of subnormal production or prices. The interest on the loan is 3 per cent per annum. The instrument provides further that the borrower shall pay taxes and assessments on the farm and insure and pay for insurance on farm buildings. It also contains such covenants as the Secretary prescribes to secure the payment of the unpaid balance of the loan; and to assure that the farm will be maintained in repair; that waste and exhaustion of the farm will be prevented, and that such proper farming practices as the Secretary prescribes will be carried out.

The instrument contains the following additional provisions:

1. Without the consent of the Secretary, no final payment is accepted, or release of the interest made, less than five years after the making of the loan.

2. The Secretary may declare the amount unpaid immediately due and payable: (a) if the borrower transfers the farm or any interest therein, without the consent of the Secretary; (b) if the borrower is in default of, or fails to comply with, any condition of the instrument; (c) upon involuntary transfer or sale.

The loans are to be distributed equitably among the states on the basis of farm population and the prevalence of tenancy. In carrying out the act, the Secretary is to give due consideration to the desirability of avoiding the expansion of production of basic commodities for market where such expansion would defeat the policy of "agricultural adjustment" and is, so far as practicable, to assist beneficiaries of the program to become established upon lands now in cultivation.

The act contains authorizations of $10,000,000 for the fiscal year 1937-38, $25,000,000 for 1938-39, and $50,000,000 for each year thereafter.

Experiences under the Program.—The act met with widespread newspaper comment. It has been said that 85 per cent of that comment was friendly. Investigations of more recent date have confirmed the observation that a tenant program appeals strongly to the public. Six hundred and sixty-four questionnaires containing over forty questions were sent to owner-operators, tenants, and landlords in Iowa in 1938. Some of the questions and answers are presented in the following table. Of 628 persons commenting upon the question of how programs for helping tenants to buy farms should be financed, 348 persons declared themselves in favor of the federal government, 109 preferred private credit agencies, and 93 chose the state government.

The votes against the several institutions were 37, 73, and 121, respectively.

TABLE 15

SUMMARY OF SELECTED QUESTIONS FROM THE "LONG QUESTIONNAIRE" ON THE IOWA FARM TENANCY PROBLEM*

	Affirmative answers, per cent		
	Owner-operators	Tenants	Landlords
Should the policy of the Bankhead-Jones Farm Tenant Act be expanded?.......................	59	74	26
Do you consider a high proportion of tenancy undesirable?....................................	80	72	53
Do you believe that the average renter would take better care of the soil and improvements if his tenure would be more secure?.................	95	98	70
Would greater security of tenure on rented farms lead to higher farm returns to both landlord and tenant?..	90	94	77
Should long-term leases (3 or 5 years) be encouraged?.	85	90	66
If one of the parties wants to terminate the lease should the other party be entitled to compensation for inconvenience and loss?..	64	68	38
Should the tenant be entitled to compensation within certain specified limits, for unexhausted improvements he has made, in case he should leave the farm?..	88	94	69
Do you believe that arbitration could successfully settle many difficulties between landlord and tenant?..	94	86	64

*Iowa State Planning Board, *Report* and Recommendations of the Farm Tenancy Committee (Des Moines, 1938), pp. 56 ff.

Similar observations have been made in Oklahoma. They were confirmed by an investigation of the United States Department of Agriculture, which takes regional differences into account and covers a wider ground.[43]

Appropriations, loans, and the number of counties in which loans were made under the provisions of the tenant purchase program are indicated in Table 16.

The budget estimate for 1938-39 was only $15,000,000—$10,000,000 below the authorization. The department had requested the full amount. Congress finally approved the full authorization, largely on account of the efforts of the Southern members of the appropriation committees who wanted the program to go ahead. For matters of budgetary policy, the budget estimate for 1939-40 was only $25,000,000. The House voted for this sum, the Senate for the full authorization of

[43] E. A. Schuler, *Social Status and Farm Tenure. Attitudes and Social Conditions of Corn Belt and Cotton Belt Farmers*. Farm Security Administration and Bureau of Agricultural Economics, Social Research Report No. 4 (1938).

TABLE 16

APPROPRIATIONS, NUMBER OF LOANS, AND NUMBER OF COUNTIES IN WHICH LOANS WERE
MADE UNDER THE PROVISIONS OF THE TENANT PURCHASE PROGRAM OF THE
BANKHEAD-JONES FARM TENANT ACT, 1937-38 TO 1939-40*

Fiscal year	Appropriation, dollars	Number of loans	Number of counties
1937-38	10,000,000	1,840	332
1938-39	25,000,000	4,330	732
1939-40	40,000,000	6,677 (a)	1,289 (a)

*Agricultural Appropriation Bill for 1941. Hearings before the Subcommittee of the Committee on Appropriations, United States Senate, 76th Cong., 3rd Sess., p. 410 (1940).
(a) Estimated.

$50,000,000. Finally, $40,000,000 was appropriated. The budget estimates for 1940-41 reduced the appropriation to $25,000,000. The House bill eliminated the item entirely. Under the provisions of the bill as amended by the Senate, a new method of financing the tenant purchase program was adopted. The direct appropriation was limited to $2,500,000 which should be disbursed for administrative expenses in connection with the making of loans. Loans are to be financed upon the basis of a $50,000,000 loan from the Reconstruction Finance Corporation to the Secretary of Agriculture. The amount of obligations which the Reconstruction Finance Corporation is authorized to have outstanding was increased by a corresponding amount. The Secretary of Agriculture is directed to make repayment of the loan out of all moneys collected by him representing payments of principal and interest on the loans made out of the funds so borrowed. This method of financing was chosen to keep down direct appropriations out of the general fund which would necessitate an expansion of the statutory debt limit.

In appraising the effects of the program from a fiscal point of view, one has to keep in mind that "the annual repayment due on a farm tenancy loan, on a 40 years' amortization basis, including 3 per cent interest is in the majority of cases less than the amount these people have been paying as rent for the same type of farm, so that for the amount which they have been paying as rent they can now become owners of the farms through this program."[44] "The collection figures show that 99.9 per cent of the amount due has been paid, that is as of January 31 [1940]."[45] Substantial payments have been made in advance. The program has been self-liquidating, with the exception

[44] Agricultural Department Appropriation Bill for 1940. Hearings before the Subcommittee of the House Committee on Appropriations, 76th Cong., 1st Sess. (1939), p. 1165.
[45] Agricultural Appropriation Bill for 1941. Hearings before the Subcommittee of the Senate Committee on Appropriations, 76th Cong., 3rd Sess. (1940), p. 415.

of administrative expenses, which are limited to 5 per cent of the appropriation.

Down payments which are required from the borrowers are so small as to be insignificant.[46] The annual repayment on a forty-year amortization basis, including 3 per cent interest, amounts to 4.3 per cent. Under the terms of the act borrowers may repay their loans under a variable payment plan. They may pay each year a fixed percentage of their net income, based perhaps on a share of the crop during such year. If the amount paid is larger than the one called for under straight amortization payments, it is applied as prepayment on subsequent installments, so that in years of below-normal prices or yield the amount of such prepayment will be available to make up any deficit.

Loans vary from $1,800 to $12,000. The average loan is slightly higher than $5,000. Though the county committees often ask for more, the administration has limited the loan for a single farm to $12,000. Twelve per cent of the farms cost less than $3,000; 42 per cent from $3,000 to $5,000; 28 per cent from $5,000 to $7,000; 12 per cent from $7,000 to $10,000; and 6 per cent from $10,000 to $12,000. This includes the cost of land, repair of houses and other buildings, and protective measures against erosion, as terracing and the like. On a per-acre basis, about $30 is spent for land and $10 for improvements. Thirty-three per cent of the farms had to have new houses; 60 per cent had to have the houses repaired; 70 per cent had to have some of the land terraced; and 92 per cent of the farms needed additions, building of barns, or outbuildings. The cost of all these improvements is included in the average loan of $5,000. The average farm size is about 135 acres. Since diversification of crops is promoted, the acreage is somewhat larger than would be necessary otherwise.[47]

According to the act, the loans are to be distributed among the states on the basis of farm population and the prevalence of tenancy. Within the states, funds are distributed among the counties by state advisory committees who use the same device. These committees are composed of farm leaders, Extension Service representatives, and some businessmen, who are nominated to the Secretary of Agriculture by the Extension Service and the Farm Security Administration State Director. They are appointed by the Secretary. The Secretary also appoints the members of the county committees from a list of twelve persons originally suggested by the County Extension Agent and the county representative of the Farm Security Administration. After these names have been passed on by the state advisory committee, six names are submitted to the Secretary of Agriculture, who selects three

[46] *Ibid.*, p. 417.

[47] *Amending the Bankhead-Jones Farm Tenant Act.* Hearing before the House Committee on Agriculture, 76th Cong., 3rd Sess., on S. 1836 (H. R. 6768), Serial H (1940), pp. 14-15.

out of the six. The names of these committeemen are announced in the county, and applications from prospective borrowers are received by them. When an agreement is reached as to man, price, and farm, the Secretary of Agriculture approves the loan and advances the money to the borrower, who purchases the farm from the seller.[48]

Many of the purchases have been made by men who have been operating the same farm as tenants. If there is an applicant who has lost his farm and wants to buy it back, the county committee can recommend him. A small amount of land has been taken over from insurance companies; some tracts are bought from the Federal Land Banks. It is not the policy of the Farm Security Administration to encourage transactions extending over large tracts of land which would have to be subdivided into a number of small farms. It has also not been their policy to move people from county to county, though the law would permit it. The Farm Security Administration has also discouraged county committees from helping heirs who would be able to buy farms from their relatives. The committees have instructions not to make loans to people who do not need help.

Tenants who become farm owners receive guidance by the county representative of the Farm Security Administration. They work out with him a plan for the operation of the farm, which, among other things, provides for the constant improvement of the soil.

Congressional Attitudes toward a Farm Tenant Program.—The congressional hearings which preceded the Bankhead-Jones Farm Tenant Act present an instructive picture of the resistance which the program had to meet and the problems which are involved in it.[49] There was general scepticism with respect to the advisability of the program in view of unsatisfactory prices and income in agriculture.

Mr. Jones: "Tenancy is not the problem. It is but an outcropping of the problem. Behind the tenant question is the problem of price and income."[50]

Mr. Pierce: "Now, is it not a question rather of what price the farmer can get for his product, than a question of tenancy, that confronts us?"[51]

Mr. Fulmer: "It is my belief that before we should have this type of legislation we should give to the farmers some assurance, under a definite program, that they would have some assurance next fall that cotton would bring a reasonable price or that tobacco will bring a reasonable price."[52]

[48] *Agricultural Appropriation Bill for 1941.* Hearings before the Subcommittee of the Senate Committee on Appropriations, 76th Cong., 3rd Sess. (1940), p. 416.

[49] *Farm Tenancy.* Hearing before the Committee on Agriculture, House of Representatives, 75th Cong., 1st Sess., on H. R. 8, Serial A (1937).

[50] *Ibid.,* p. 10.

[51] *Ibid.,* p. 18.   [52] *Ibid.,* pp. 17-18.

Other legislators questioned the fundamental assumption of the tenant program—that ownership is preferable to tenancy. It was claimed that tenants are better off than owners, and that the separation of ownership and cultivation of land is a symptom of a general trend which can be observed in all lines of industrial activity,

Mr. Pierce: "During the last five years has not the tenant been better off than the landlord?"
Mr. Jackson: "I have heard that."
Mr. Pierce: "Is not that generally true the country over; haven't you heard those suggestions generally?"
Mr. Jackson: "I rather think so. I do not know how true it is. There are so many ways to take that. That is a pretty general statement. You can find many cases where the landlord is losing and where the tenant has the best of it."[53]
Dr. Gee: Landlords who become tenants "can, in some instances, secure more efficient sizes of farming units as renters rather than owners, and it does seem to make for better farm operation in such cases; but I think those instances are exceptional."[54]
Mr. Kinzer: "Is not about the same thing going on in the industrial world, so far as production is concerned, that is going on in agriculture; that is are there not hundreds of more people working for somebody else every year?"[55]

On another occasion, the late Senator Copeland referred to the fact that the people in the cities are not owners of their homes.

Senator Bilbo: "Roughly speaking, 50 percent of the people engaged in the agricultural life of this country are tenants."
Senator Copeland: "That may be. But you said they were nomadic and were roaming around?"
Senator Bilbo: "Well, that is the situation."
Senator Bankhead: "The census figures show that the whole tenant population moves once in three years."
Senator Copeland: "If that is the case, 97 percent of the people in my city are homeless; they are living in rented quarters."
Senator Bankhead: "But the farmer makes his living in his quarters."[56]

City-country differences came up on another occasion, when some legislators referred to the large federal expenditures for such items as urban housing and mortgage insurance, which justify an expansion of the farm tenant program.[57]

If the tenancy situation is admittedly bad, why not improve it instead of making owners of the tenants?

[53] Ibid.
[54] Ibid., p. 28. [55] Ibid., p. 41.
[56] Agricultural Appropriation Bill for 1939. Hearings before the Subcommittee of the Committee on Appropriations, Senate, 75th Cong., 3d Sess., p. 573.
[57] Hearings before the Senate Subcommittee of the Committee on Appropriations, 76th Cong., 1st Sess., on H. R. 5269 (1939), pp. 645 f.

Mr. Lucas: "Well, is that not more a matter of cooperation and education between the landlord and tenant?"
Mr. Wilson: "Yes."
Mr. Lucas: "Instead of for federal action?"
Mr. Wilson: "Yes."[58]

If the desirability of a tenant program is granted, would a program be feasible which is large enough to lead to substantial results? Taking care of the annual increase of 40,000 tenants would require $160,000,-000 per year.[59] However, if only a small fraction of the annual increase in tenancy could be taken care of, such a measure might set a good example.

Mr. Jones: "If a program of this kind is started, there will be a lot of individual help stimulated. I know that even the discussion of the problem has caused a few big landowners to realize that they can do some work along this line and one or two of them I know have done that in breaking up their tracts and giving real opportunities. The very talking of the program will itself stimulate a move that will be helpful, just as the landbanks did not, at the beginning, refinance anything like all of the land in the country that needed refinancing; but they have materially reduced the rates of interest charged by private institutions."[60]
Mr. Wilson: The program "will influence a great many people who have lands to sell them," especially lands which belong to institutional owners.[61]

A similar stimulation could be achieved if the government would enter into lease contracts and improve their terms. If that were done, other landlords might likewise improve their renting arrangements.[62]
How can the land requirements of a tenant program be met?

Dr. Gee: "We have a tremendous amount of absentee landlordism in this country and I think ample supplies of good land available, and I think that is the sort of land that these tenants ought to be put on."[63]

Would not a tenant program stimulate production?[64] According to Secretary Wallace, it would be a "very slight" encouragement of the back-to-the-land movement.[65] However, the land required for the program is already under cultivation.[66] The production might increase if the landlord whose land is bought would take up farming somewhere else.[67]

[58] *Farm Tenancy*. Hearing before the Committee on Agriculture, House of Representatives, 75th Cong., 1st Sess., on H. R. 8, Serial A (1937), p. 47.
[59] *Ibid.*, p. 243.
[60] *Ibid.*, p. 30.
[61] *Ibid.*, pp. 39-40.
[62] *Ibid.*, p. 206.
[63] *Ibid.*, p. 29.
[64] *Ibid.*, p. 32.
[65] *Ibid.*, p. 255.
[66] *Ibid.*, p. 52.
[67] *Ibid.*, p. 30.

How should the tenants who will be helped through the program be selected?

Mr. Jackson: "We do not believe that every tenant, just because he is a tenant, can become a farm owner."[68]

Should tenants at the top or at the bottom be helped to become owners?[69]

Mr. Gilchrist: "I think that all inheres in the question as to who this selection is to be made by."[70]

Should the program be handled by the AAA or by the Soil Conservation Service? These agencies enjoy a well-deserved reputation.

Mr. Gee: "But if you attempt to handle this problem as a part of those administrations my judgment is that you are going to make it so complicated and delay its operation and make it so cumbersome that it will break of its own weight."[71]

The county committee which H.R.8 proposed to establish for the local administration of the program was to consist of one farmer, one businessman, and one credit expert.

Mr. Jackson: "No sharecropper and no agricultural worker has ever been represented on any such committee. These classes are supposed to be the beneficiaries under this legislation. It seems pretty definite to my mind that they ought to have representation, as a matter of common justice and democratic procedure."
Mr. Lucas: "Are they organized?"
Mr. Jackson: "They are getting organized quite extensively."[72]

The bill's lack of provisions for coöperative holdings was criticized.[73] Coöperative settlements would be able to carry on large-scale production.[74] However, it might be possible to compensate for the advantages of large-scale farming by permitting lower taxes for small farms.[75] The formation of tenant communities is advocated by some, opposed by others.

Mr. Jackson: "We know that big plantations or large tracts of land may be purchased at prices per acre that are lower and more nearly in line with the per-acre prices usually required to purchase smaller,

[68] *Ibid.*, p. 15.   [69] *Ibid.*, pp. 22 ff.

[70] *Ibid.*, p. 27. At a later time the complaint was made that not the neediest men were selected under the Bankhead-Jones Act but men who are already self-sustaining and able to proceed under their own power.—*Agricultural Department Appropriation Bill for 1940.* Hearings before the Subcommittee on Appropriations, House of Representatives 76th Cong., 1st Sess., 1939, pp. 1166 ff.

[71] *Farm Tenancy.* Hearing before the Committee on Agriculture, House of Representatives, 75th Cong., 1st Sess., on H. R. 8, Serial A (1937), p. 22.

[72] *Ibid.*, pp. 179-80. The American Farm Bureau Federation proposed a non-salaried committee (p. 316).   [73] *Ibid.*, p. 145.

[74] *Ibid.*, p. 181.   [75] *Ibid.*, p. 204.

family size farms. We therefore recommend that the law should give the administrators of the act authority, when it seems to them advisable, to purchase and control such large tracts of land as are suitable for subdivision into family size farms, thus affording opportunity for locating groups of prospective farm owners together where their joint ambition for the attainment of ownership may have all the benefits of organized community and cooperative efforts."[76]

Mr. Gee: "I think we want to continue the worthwhile things in our American life. The settlement of tenants upon farming units so that they become segregated into communities apart does not appeal to me. But that they continue as an integral part of the community in which they live, translated into owners of land, I think, is very important and will result in an improved attitude toward citizenship."[77]

Mr. Cooley: "Do you approve of that idea of putting the farmers into a group; collecting them into a group so that they will live in a community entirely separated from the community in which they formerly lived?"

Mr. Wilson: "Well, I regard this instance that you speak of as an experiment . . . rather than as a national program."[78]

On whose land should the tenants be settled? Congressman Binderup made the proposal that the federal government should purchase the lands on which the Land Bank Commissioners have made second mortgage loans, and which are now under foreclosure, or have been foreclosed, or which may thereafter be under foreclosure. The government should then resell these lands, and the purchasing price should be amortized in forty years.[79] Mr. Wearin proposed that the lands which at present are owned by the Land Banks should be transferred to the government. The government, in return, should transfer its stocks of the Land Banks to the latter. Thereupon the lands should be leased by the government to tenants.[80] However, land acquisition by the government was opposed by some legislators:

Mr. Doxey: "Going in the land-purchasing business—that is dangerous."[81]

Mr. Lord: "What I am getting at is, if you cannot buy from the owners, how can you buy from the government? How is he ever going to pay for it?"[82]

With respect to the tenure of the settlers it was recognized that long-term leases of land owned by the government would be superior to fee simple ownership since land speculation would be prevented thereby.[83] However, since the government would not acquire land, but would grant loans to the tenants which would enable them to purchase farms, should there be restrictions on the title after the farm

[76] Ibid., p. 16 .
[78] Ibid., p. 56.
[80] Ibid., pp. 317 ff.
[82] Ibid., p. 28.
[77] Ibid., p. 24.
[79] Ibid., pp. 281 ff.
[81] Ibid., p. 175.
[83] Ibid., p. 197.

has been paid for? On the part of the legislators there was an outspoken disinclination against any restrictions on the property right of the farmer when full payments were made. Proposals to restrict the right of alienation, for instance, were rejected for the following reasons:

Mr. Jones: "I do not think you can get the more ambitious type of man."[84]
Mr. Cooley: "In other words, we are just taking tenants and making them wards of· the government; is that what you mean?"
Mr. Marshall: "That is right."[35]

Alienation of land for speculative purposes should be prevented by providing that the borrower could pay off all but the last installment, or by prohibiting him from making advance payments unless he also pays interest.[86]

The inflation of land values through low interest rates and tax exemptions was held to be avoidable if the advantages are limited to small owner-operators.[87]

One of the major issues was the time which the contract should run before the tenant would acquire full title. The technical committee of the President's Committee had proposed a period of forty years. The whole committee finally agreed on twenty years.[88] H. R. 8 provided that the tenant should live on the land for five years and, during these five years, pay 25 per cent of the original cost of the land. Thereafter he should receive title to the land, or a contract to purchase it for the balance. The American Farm Bureau Federation proposed that the Secretary should buy land and lease it for a probationary period. Thereafter the tenant should purchase the land, pledging himself to good farm-management practice, and turning over every year a definite percentage of his gross income. This money, above a reasonable rental, should accumulate to his credit until it would equal 25 per cent of the farm value. Then the purchaser should receive full title, while the balance would be provided by the Farm Credit Administration. The "reasonable" rental was defined as the customary rental in the community; if it were too large or too small, "a tremendous effect upon land values and community life" would be the result.[89]

Criticism of Farm Tenancy Reform.—In a recent paper T. W. Schultz has drawn attention to the fact that the supply of resources which the farmer is permitted to hire in the capital market is rationed.[90] A farmer with restricted assets who is confronted with the alternatives of renting a farm or of borrowing money to buy a farm

[84] *Ibid.,* p. 226.   [85] *Ibid.,* pp. 157, 308-9.
[86] *Ibid.,* pp. 256-57.   [87] *Ibid.,* pp. 255-57.
[88] *Ibid.,* p. 300.   [89] *Ibid.,* p. 315.
[90] "Capital Rationing, Uncertainty, and Farm Tenancy Reform," *Journal of Political Economy,* XLVIII (1940), 309 ff.

cannot buy as large a farm as he can rent. The farm which he is able to buy might be below the optimum size. This, in turn, would prevent the maximization of the returns on the farmers' labor and management. Professor Schultz also points out that the incidence of uncertainty in the farm business falls most heavily upon encumbered owner-operators, and more heavily upon owners than upon tenants. Upon the basis of these arguments, a farmer who goes from tenancy to ownership seems to be in a position which, on strictly economic grounds, compares unfavorably with his previous situation. However, this conclusion is based upon the tacit assumption, "other things being equal," and holds true only if institutional arrangements guarantee the tenant the same opportunities which the owner enjoys. In general, the unfavorable implications of ownership which are stressed by Professor Schultz are outweighed by such common characteristics of tenancy as high returns on outside capital, short and burdensome leases, and lack of compensation for improvements.

A Farm Tenant Program as Public Works Program.—The expansion of government credit under the Roosevelt administration has undoubtedly facilitated the launching of a federal tenancy program of the described type. The program has been self-liquidating. It has created employment inasmuch as it has strengthened the purchasing power of its beneficiaries and has led to repair and construction works on farms. Because of these features of the program a considerable expansion of its scope was proposed within the framework of the self-liquidating projects bill, which was considered by the House in July, 1939.[91] The program was to be financed by notes and bonds issued by the Reconstruction Finance Corporation. The House bill as reported by the Committee on Banking and Currency provided that of the proceeds of these notes an amount of $400,000,000 was to be diverted to the Department of Agriculture for rural security projects such as facilities for farm tenants, farm laborers, and sharecroppers, including rural rehabilitation loans, projects for the provision of additional water facilities, and farm-tenant loans as provided in Title I of the Bankhead-Jones Farm Tenant Act. The Senate bill as reported by the Committee on Banking and Currency provided for $600,000,000 for loans to farm tenants, sharecroppers, and farm laborers for the purchase of farms, livestock, feed, seed, farm implements, and other necessary equipment. Of this amount at least $300,000,000 was to be available under Title I of the Bankhead-Jones Farm Tenant Act. The remainder was for rural rehabilitation. Repayments would go into a revolving fund, thus enabling the Reconstruction Finance Corporation to issue new notes and bonds up to the limits set up in the various bills. None of these measures was passed by Congress.

[91] H. R. 7120. The corresponding Senate bills were S. 2759 and S. 2864, in 76th Cong., 1st Sess.

Their adoption would have resulted in a long-term program exactly along the lines of the present Bankhead-Jones Farm Tenant Act, with the only exception that the new program would have authorized the government to charge interest rates slightly lower than 3 per cent, the rate charged under the provisions of the Bankhead-Jones Act.

Proposals for Expansion of the Program.—The county committees have received twenty-four applicants for each loan they could make under the terms of the act. They limit the period for receiving applications; otherwise the number filed would be far in excess of the present number.[92] Only about 13,000 tenants have been helped thus far. Amendments to the act have been introduced in every succeeding session of Congress. Most of them provide for an expansion of the program along the lines of Senator Bankhead's earlier proposal to establish a corporation with power to issue government-guaranteed bonds to the extent of $1,000,000,000.[93] An extension of the program without drain on the Treasury is proposed in S. 1836, a bill passed by the Senate in 1939 and reported by the House Committee on Agriculture on February 26, 1940. It expands the present program by authorizing a system of mortgage insurance, by which private funds would be made available to finance farm ownership and to refinance the indebtedness of present owners. Since the insured mortgages are expected to be self-liquidating, contingent losses of the government would be negligible. The bill provides a $350,000,000 program for the next three fiscal years. The insurance provisions follow closely those of the National Housing Act. The Secretary of Agriculture is authorized to insure farm mortgages to secure loans. The proceeds of the loans are to be used for purchasing farms or for refinancing existing mortgages on farms. The mortgagor and the farm must be approved by the county committee. To be eligible for insurance, a mortgage cannot exceed 90 per cent of the appraised value of the farm unless the mortgagor has unencumbered livestock, farm supplies, or farm equipment equal to at least 15 per cent of the value of the farm. The interest rate payable on the loan secured by the mortgage will be limited to 3 per cent per annum. In addition to the interest and principal on the loan secured by the mortgage, each borrower will be required to pay an insurance premium of .5 per cent per annum on the unpaid balance of the loan. The premiums would be held by the Secretary of Agriculture in a special fund available for meeting any losses. In addition, the borrower will be required to pay an additional .5 per cent per annum on the unpaid balance of his loan to cover the cost to the government of servicing the loan.

[92] *Agricultural Appropriation Bill for 1941.* Hearings before the Subcommittee of the Senate Committee on Appropriations, 76th Cong., 3rd Sess. (1940), p. 416.

[93] 79 *Cong. Rec.* 1782 (1935). See, for example, H. R. 3247 by Mr. Whelchel, H. R. 5410 by Mr. Johnson, in 76th Cong., 1st Sess.

The Secretary of Agriculture is authorized to make direct loans on farms in a state where the insurance provisions will not be utilized and in amounts equal to the unutilized portion of the allocation to the state. These loans are to be made with debentures of the fund, or with the proceeds of debentures issued by the fund. As soon as a market is found for the mortgages made under this provision, they are to be sold by the Secretary. The proceeds are to be deposited in the fund and used to retire an equivalent amount of debentures.

This program would be in addition to the one already under way. The borrower must be one who would be eligible for a farm tenant loan under the provisions of the present law. However, the new bill gives direct authority to insure mortgages to enable borrowers to refinance existing mortgages. The provisions of existing law relating to the functions of county committees are made applicable to the new bill.[94]

[94] 76th Cong., 2rd Sess., House of Representatives, *Report* No. 1675 (1940).

V

ENGLISH LAND TENURE POLICY

AGRICULTURAL CONDITIONS IN ENGLAND

THE ENGLISH and German land tenure policies which are analyzed in the following pages can only be understood when they are regarded as part and parcel of the current agricultural policy of these countries. No attempt has been made by the author to appraise the ultimate objectives of the agricultural policies in both these countries. Maximization of the national dividend has ceased to be the goal and has been replaced by the strife for a larger domestic output of food or by policies which are based upon the belief in the absolute superiority of the agricultural occupation over others. The resulting pauperization is illustrated in the following table, which contrasts the consumption of selected foodstuffs in European countries with that in the United States. The difference between consumption in the United States and England is only slight; France is in the middle; Germany's consumption is far below that of the United States; and Italy is at the bottom.

Protectionism and trade restrictions have pushed the prices of virtually all agricultural staples above the prices in the United States. In 1929 the highest wheat price in Europe was 59 per cent higher than in the United States; in 1932 and 1936 the difference rose to 209 per cent and 114 per cent. In 1938 the maximum difference was 179 per cent. "To speak of a world price for wheat has now become an absurdity."[1]

TABLE 17

CONSUMPTION OF VARIOUS FOODSTUFFS PER HEAD OF POPULATION IN VARIOUS COUNTRIES, 1934*

Country	Milk and cream, gallons	Butter, lb.	Total meat, lb.	Eggs, No.	Imported citrus fruit, No.	Bananas, No.
United States...	37	17.4	140	184	....	....
Great Britain...	..	25.2	139	172	28.8	15.0
France.........	23	14.0	75	143	18.5	9.0
Germany.......	23	16.3	119	117	11.2	3.1
Italy..........	8	2.3	34	120	....	.7

*League of Nations: *The Problem of Nutrition*, Vol. IV, Statistics of Food Production, Consumption and Prices. Documentation prepared by the International Institute of Agriculture. 12 (c). 1936, II. B., pp. 43 ff.

[1] Robbins, *The Great Depression*, p. 67.

TABLE 18

DOMESTIC PRICE OF WHEAT IN SELECTED COUNTRIES, IN PER CENT OF UNITED STATES WHEAT
PRICES, 1929, 1932, 1936-38*

Country	January 1929	January 1932	1936 (average)	1937 (average)	1938 (average)
United States....	100	100	100 (a)	100 (a)	100 (a)
Great Britain....	102	91	102 (b)	128 (b)	148 (b)
Germany.......	112	253	204 (c)	185 (c)	279 (c)
France........	136	309	172 (c)	146 (c)	190 (c)
Italy..........	159	260	214 (c)	154 (c)	257 (c)

*1929-32: L. Robbins, *The Great Depression* (London, Macmillan & Co., 1936), p. 66; 1936-38: International Institute of Agriculture, *International Yearbook of Agricultural Statistics, 1938-39* (Rome, 1939), pp. xxv.
(a) No. 2 Hard Winter, (b) No. 1 Manitoba, (c) Home grown.

The differences are greater when other agricultural products are taken into account. While English prices are only slightly higher than those in the United States, German prices, on the average, are 200 per cent above the American. Italian prices, which were higher during the preceding years, have receded on account of the devaluation of the lira.

TABLE 19

DOMESTIC PRICES OF PRINCIPAL AGRICULTURAL PRODUCTS IN SELECTED COUNTRIES, IN
PER CENT OF UNITED STATES PRICES, 1938*

Country	Wheat	Rye	Barley	Oats	Butter	Eggs
United States.........	100	100	100	100	100	...
Great Britain.........	148	...	141	120	92(a)	100(b)
Germany.............	279	352	319	335	181	166
France..............	190	...	...	166	...	...
Italy................	257	...	...	...	...	...

*International Institute of Agriculture: *International Yearbook of Agricultural Statistics, 1938-39* (Rome, 1939), pp. xxv ff.
(a) Dutch, (b) Danish.

It is only with horror that the economist can look at these figures. He who is accustomed to identify progress with the decline in the proportion of consumers' expenditure devoted to foodstuffs must interpret them as a return to the time when mankind spent most of its time and energy on the production of the elemental necessities of life.

English Farming Under the Impact of Changing Policies.—When the English refer to a "farmer," it is the tenant whom they have in mind. In spirit and outlook a businessman, the English farmer has little in common with the continental peasants. Correspondingly he lacks a great deal of that romantic glamor which is attributed to agriculture on the Continent. It has been only within the last few years that the sacrifices which have been made in behalf of the farmer have become a substantial burden on the rest of the population. In the past there was no really effective protective tariff in England, except from 1815 to 1853. Since 1931 British agriculture has been protected to a degree of completeness never before attained. In addition, the government subsidizes it to the extent of £32,000,000 a year. The subsidies amount to 12.8 per cent of the value of the domestic food production.

TABLE 20

STATE EXPENDITURE ON AGRICULTURE IN GREAT BRITAIN IN 1938-39*

	£
A. Direct expenditures	
Commodities specifically aided by grants from the Exchequer	
Sugar beet	2,550,000
Barley and oats	203,000
Cattle	4,575,000
Milk	438,000
Contribution toward the cost of lime and basic slag	1,282,000
B. Votes of the Ministry of Agriculture and the Department of Agriculture for Scotland	3,500,000
C. Votes of other departments	200,000
D. Agricultural Research Council	61,000
E. Contribution in respect of derating land:	
Allowance in block grants to local authorities	17,000,000(a)
F. Wheat subsidy (levy on imports)	2,000,000

*R. J. Thompson, "State Expenditure on Agriculture in Great Britain in 1938-39," *Journal of the Royal Statistical Society*, CI (1938), 736-37.
(a) 1929-30. In 1929-30 agricultural land was finally relieved from the liability to assessment for local rates.

These are heavy subsidies for agriculture at the expense of the nation. However, the burden is not nearly so heavy as in Germany, for example, where the regressive effect of high food prices is experienced to a much greater degree. In both countries, indeed, the social costs of the inflated domestic food production are terrific. However, in England a much larger part of the social costs is contributed by the government in the form of subsidies which are shifted to the taxpayer through a wise and progressive taxation system. In Germany no attention is paid to the principle of ability to pay, and the high prices for food are paid by the poor and rich alike.

The effect of the governmental policy upon British agricultural production has been astonishing. The agricultural returns for England and Wales for the year 1938 show that the acreages under wheat and barley were the largest since 1922 for wheat and 1932 for barley; in each case, the yields per acre were the highest recorded since returns were first collected in 1885. The total production of wheat and barley was the greatest since 1921 and 1929 respectively. "The [agricultural] output per head (at the prices of 1930) rose by some 40 per cent between 1924 and 1935 (the greater part occurring in the last five years) and has further increased subsequently." A comparison with the increase in productivity per head in other lines of industrial activity shows that "the sometimes despised agriculture has done best of all."[2]

It is recognized in England that "there will certainly be no return to the old conditions under which the prosperity or adversity of the different branches of agriculture was regarded as lying outside the proper functions of the state. In the sphere of agricultural economics, at least, the dethronement of laissez-faire is final, and there is no real possibility of restoration. For the fundamental economic conditions which made laissez-faire a workable principle in the nineteenth century have passed away."[3] The structural change in the economic conditions which necessitates government interference with agriculture is attributed to the decline in population growth. The expansion of agricultural production which was desirable as long as there was a strong upward trend in population has to be checked. It is the strange paradox of British agricultural policy that its present aims are not directed toward meeting these changes but toward an increase in the domestic production which, in the long run, can only aggravate the structural maladjustments which are in existence on the international scene. To be sure, there is not much response in England to the arguments of those who claim that rural life, in general, is distinctly superior to urban life. During the Great Depression, however, it was possible to advance fantastic schemes of land settlement which, while alleviating the immediate distress of the unemployed, would have resulted in the permanent decline of the standard of living of the whole populace.

Today unemployment is not so overwhelming a problem as it was during the depression, but the fear of creating new unemployment is still strong enough to prevent any policy which calls for a transfer of agriculturists to industrial activities, the products of which would meet a more expansive demand. As in the United States the advocate of such a policy, which in the case of England would also uphold the international division of labor, is answered by the helpless outcry: "What, also, are the people going to do who would be put out of work by this policy? . . . Where are they going to live? Presumably in the towns where in many cases there are already more people than can be found work for."[4]

However, the want of confidence in an economic system which cannot stand the application of the principle of comparative cost and where workers are forced to remain in uneconomical or inflated occupations does not explain the present tendencies of British agricultural policy. Its primary aim is an increase in agricultural production, not in agricultural population. That is why the small-holdings program is only cautiously continued. Small holders, persons with holdings

---

[2] J. M. Keynes, in the London *Times*, September 13, 1938.
[3] Astor and Rowntree, *British Agriculture*, p. 10.
[4] Addison, *A Policy for British Agriculture*, p. 17.

of less than fifty acres or of less than £100 annual rental value, amount to half the total number of farm operators, but produce no more than one sixth of the domestic food output.

The requirements of the war which are the cause of the British food policy will certainly become less pressing sometime. Then the return to a policy which heeds the secular trend towards international overproduction in agriculture will probably be attempted. England's interests "are bound up with the maintenance of close and friendly relations with the agricultural countries overseas."[5] However, the obstacles to such a policy are obvious. Agriculture lends itself more easily to expansion than contraction. Planning for war purposes is more easily accomplished than the mere reversal of changes which were stimulated by that well-defined and simple objective. Moreover, who would dare to trust that there will be employment opportunities for those whom the reversal will directly concern?

The British Farmer.—Hence, the present tendencies of British agricultural policy may have long-lasting effects. The land tenure policies are part and parcel of that policy and are dominated by the quest for greater efficiency. To be sure, the English farmer does not have to be cured of an aversion to modern methods of farm management and capitalistic business spirit, an aversion which still prevails among a large number of continental peasants. While the role of agriculture on the English economic scene gradually declined, England did not cease to be the leading agricultural country which it had become at the turn of the nineteenth century. At that time the coöperation between landlord and tenant was excellent. Landlords resided on their estates; they often needed the electoral vote of the tenantry. Parts of the rent used to be spent on the county. The landlord, moreover,

took . . . a personal interest in the cultivation of his land. He would either improve it himself or would watch his tenant closely. Sometimes when a lease expired he took over temporarily the management of the farm, put it in order, erected more spacious and healthier buildings, renewed the stock, and radically altered the methods of cultivation. After this he would lease the farm to new tenants, who, being better provided than their predecessors, could pay a higher rent. Sometimes he was content to reserve one of his farms, which he transformed into an "experimental farm." Perhaps this farm would cost him more than the profits he derived from it, but it served as a model to all the tenants on the estate. Agriculture was at once the great source of revenue and the great luxury of the English aristocracy. The King, and the heads of the great families . . . agreed in their zeal for agriculture.[6]

[5] Astor and Rowntree, *op. cit.,* pp. 7, 16.
[6] Halévy, *A History of the English People in 1815,* p. 197.

The landed gentry, proud of their estates, willingly increased the amount of capital sunk in the farm in order to push technical progress forward and reap the benefits of innovations.

To erect buildings, to make roads, to drain the fields, to put up fences: all this was the business of the landlord. It was the farmer's business to supervise the ploughing and manuring of the land, to select the seeds, and to decide what rotation of crops he should best adopt. This was a difficult task which required intelligence, experience and technical knowledge.[7]

The English tenants meet these requirements. As a French observer recently said in emphasizing the contrast between French and English farming,

the British tenant is a business man, who administers his capital funds, conducts an industrial enterprise, strives methodically to improve his production, controls the market, visits the fairs and exhibitions; his views go beyond the local horizon.[8]

LAND TENURE IN ENGLAND

English landholding which gave rise to the classical theory of distribution still presents a threefold division of capital and incomes. The various shares present a striking symmetry. It has been estimated that about one third of the capital engaged in the farm belongs to the tenant,[9] and that agricultural wages amount to about one third of the whole product of the industry.[10] Moreover, the tenant's income, on the average, was held equal to the rent in 1912-14.[11]

Recent events seem to disturb this symmetry seriously. During the past century various measures have charged the landlords with burdens which were gradually increased. At the same time the system of primogeniture, one of the basic foundations which petrified the existing system of land tenure, began to decay. Various regulations for lease contracts have completely changed the landlord's position. Today he resembles an administrator or trustee of publicly-owned land.

The Trend Towards Owner-Occupancy.—During the last quarter of the nineteenth century rents fell about 30 per cent, remaining at this level until the outbreak of the World War. From then until the twenties the trend was reversed; but between 1925 and 1931 rents again fell 13 per cent.[12] Owing to the increase in maintenance cost,

---

[7] *Ibid.,* pp. 202-3.

[8] A. Demangeon, *Les Îles Britanniques* (Paris, 1927), p. 265.

[9] Astor and Rowntree, *op. cit.,* pp. 359-60.

[10] Clapham, *An Economic History of Modern Britain,* III, 100, quoting from A. L. Bowley.

[11] *Ibid.,* p. 96, quoting from Lord Stamp.

[12] R. J. Thompson, "An Inquiry Into the Rent of Agricultural Land in England and Wales during the Nineteenth Century," *Journal of the Royal Statistical*

the decline in rents does not even show to the full extent the deterioration of the landlord's position. The costs of proper estate management which requires the services of a scientifically trained expert were estimated before the war as 30 per cent of the rent; they have increased in the meantime, since such experts earn as much as £1,000 per year.[13] There are many landlords who cannot afford these expenses. Moreover, the landlords are more urban-minded than they used to be, partly on account of the rise of institutionalized research and experimental work which now take the place of the landed gentry in pushing forward agricultural progress. Their political influence in the county has also gradually declined. Finally they had to resign themselves to the fact that agricultural enterprise had become a liability rather than an asset. There was no protection against competition from overseas. Death duties loomed, and their payment often made it necessary to sell part of the estate or mortgage the whole. Correspondingly many landlords turned away from land ownership and sold their holdings to tenants. Until recently not much attention was paid in England to this development which, if it continues, may change the whole structure of British land tenure. The century-old trend toward cultivation by tenants seems to be reversed, and the proportion of land operated by the owner increases rapidly.

TABLE 21

OWNER-OPERATED FARMS AND FARM LAND, PER CENT OF ALL FARMS AND FARM LAND, ENGLAND AND WALES, 1908, 1913, 1919-24, 1926-27*

Year	Owner-operated farms, per cent	Owner-operated acreage, per cent
1908 (a)	13.09	12.4
1913	11.19	10.65
1919	11.68	12.32
1920	13.7	15.5
1921	16.8	20.0
1922	15.1	17.8
1923	21.4	24.2
1924	23.0	25.4
1926	....	28.0
1927 (b)	36.6	36.0

*Board of Agriculture and Fisheries, *Agricultural Statistics*, 1908 (London, 1909), Pt. 1, pp. 70, 74; Ministry of Agriculture and Fisheries, *Agricultural Statistics*, 1919 (London, 1920), Pt. 1, p. 7; 1924 (London, 1924), p. 13; 1926 (London, 1927), p. 28; 1927 (London, 1928), p. 28.
(a) England.
(b) A part of the increase is the result of improvements in statistical technique.

As Table 21 indicates, the amount of rented land decreased most rapidly during the postwar years. Between 1919 and 1927 the acreage

---

Society, LXX (1907) 595 ff.; Ministry of Agriculture and Fisheries, *The Agricultural Output of England and Wales, 1930-1931* (London, 1934), pp. 50-53.

[13] Addison, *op. cit.*, p. 29; Astor and Rowntree, *op. cit.*, p. 391.

of owner-operated land increased from three to nine million acres. It is generally held that many tenants were unwilling to acquire ownership and did so only in order to prevent the sale of the holding to a new landlord. There are no figures available indicating the indebtedness of the new owner-occupiers. However, it is known that many who bought their farms at the inflated prices of the postwar years lost them through tax sales and foreclosures. English tenants, in general, have no desire to become owners, nor do they have the financial means to undertake those improvements which the landlords used to make.

The Agricultural Holdings Act.—The fact that many of the landlords have ceased to be improvers as J. S. Mill wanted them to be, but have become sleeping partners in the Marshallian sense, is aptly illustrated by the chain of the Agricultural Holdings Acts.[14] The problem of improvements forms the center of that legislation. The first step in a direction which finally had to lead to a protective legislation was taken during and after the Napoleonic Wars. At that time it had become necessary to shorten the customary long-term leases. They had acquired a speculative character on account of violent fluctuations in the prices of agricultural products. Moreover, rapid progress in farming technique increased the capital required for improvements. At the same time, the growth of capitalistic calculation led to a disappearance of the old patriarchal bonds. It became necessary to replace the old local customs, which had protected the tenants, by a rigid system of Agricultural Holdings Acts, which opened the way to a system of dual ownership of landlord and tenant. Many of the reforms brought forth by this legislation were also Irish issues. It is significant that the English landlord-tenant relationship became tense enough to demand the application of remedies which originated from the national demands of Irish tenants directed against the English absentee owners.

The chain of the Agricultural Holdings Acts began in 1875 and ended during the twenties. In order to show the aims and ends of the various reforms, it is preferable to discuss them systematically. The principal issues were security and freedom of tenure, better farming in general, and betterment of the tenants' position with respect to fixtures and the landlords' right of distress. Except the latter, all these subjects had been dealt with already in the law of 1875. The subsequent laws established compulsory rules which could not be modified by agreement of the parties.

Security of Tenure.—Security of tenure was accomplished by restrictions on the landlord's right to terminate the lease and by provisions for compensation for "unreasonable disturbance." At the time when the one-year term had replaced the long-term lease, notices to quit

[14] Karl Brandt, "The English System of Regulating Landlord-Tenant Relations," *Journal of the American Society of Farm Managers and Rural Appraisers,* II (1938), 3-14.

could be given semiannually. In 1875 annual notices were substituted. In 1883 the parties were permitted again to provide for semiannual notices in the contract, but by written agreement only. Since 1920 landlords generally may not terminate the lease earlier than twelve months from the end of the current tenancy year. A notice to quit is also required if the term was fixed by contract for a certain number of years.

Compensation for Disturbance.—An essentially new feature was introduced in 1906, when compensation for unreasonable disturbance was provided for. If the landlord gives a notice to quit without good reasons, or if he does not renew the contract, or if he demands a highei rent because of improvements effected by the tenant without compen·sation as noted below, the tenant who thereupon leaves the farm may claim compensation for expenses and losses caused by his moving from one farm to another; for example, losses caused by sales of implements or costs of transportation. The obligation of the landlord cannot be abrogated by contract. These rules change the one-year lease to an almost hereditary one because they prevent the landlord from terminating the contract, if he is unwilling or unable to pay the compensation. In the historical development of farm tenancy this compensation signifies an almost revolutionary change. While there existed in feudal times various forms of fees which had to be paid by the tenants for a transfer of the lease to a new holder, the landlord now has to make a payment if he wishes to effect a change in the management of the farm.

There are not many examples of such payments in other legislations. Originally compensation was to be paid in England only if the landlord had no good reason for terminating the lease, a reason which had to concern the management of the farm. In Germany the special rules regarding the suburban lease contracts of small gardeners' associations provide for similar payments, even if the landlord has a good reason for giving notice; the compensation must be paid whenever the termination of the lease involves a special hardship to the tenant. In practice the courts often forget this restriction and charge the landlords with considerable burdens which even exceed one year's rent. There was a similar provision in a German farm tenancy reform bill of 1930 which has never been enacted. There the landlords were not required to show any other special reason for terminating the lease if they were willing to pay compensation.

To return to the English legislation of 1906—there was no obligation to pay compensation for unreasonable disturbance if the landlord's notice to quit or his refusal to renew the contract was issued within three months after a tenant's death. This is the principal reason why the English lease cannot unqualifiedly be called hereditary.

In the following years the concept of unreasonable disturbance was broadened in favor of the tenants. Special provisions regarding notices to quit in case of sale of the farm were enacted. Originally they provided only for compensation. They were modified in 1914: in the case of a lease from year to year the notice to quit is void if the farm is sold partly or wholly before the termination of the lease. The notice is valid if the tenant agrees upon it by written consent.

The provisions were changed again in 1920. The form they received then is still in force. The new regulations set forth that compensation for unreasonable disturbance must always be paid unless there is one of certain enumerated exceptions present, as mismanagement by the tenant, arrears in rent, violations of the contract, decline of the tenant's property, and the tenant's refusal to agree to an arbitration of the future amount of rent. There are county agricultural committees which upon the landlord's request decide whether there is a mismanagement. Either party may appeal to an arbitrator from their decision. The amount of the compensation shall, in general, not exceed a year's rent which is prima facie regarded as appropriate compensation. However, the tenant may claim up to twice that amount if he proves such damages.

If the County Agricultural Committee holds that the tenant "is not cultivating according to the rules of good husbandry," a certificate of bad husbandry is issued, and the landlord is freed from his liability for compensation. As the following table indicates, only a few of these certificates are applied for. The committees seem to be inclined to refuse a larger number of certificates than they are willing to grant. Applications and grants have steadily declined throughout the last ten years. Only eleven certificates were issued in 1936.

TABLE 22

APPLICATIONS FOR CERTIFICATES OF BAD HUSBANDRY, ENGLAND AND WALES, 1926-36*

	1926	1928	1930	1932	1934	1936
Applications................	114	71	63	51	43	45
Granted...................	52	30	24	24	15	11
Refused...................	47	28	22	20	19	24
Withdrawn................	15	13	17	7	9	10

*Ministry of Agriculture and Fisheries, *Reports* on the Work of the Land Division, 1929 (London, 1930), p. 43; 1930 (London, 1931), p. 44; 1932 (London, 1933), p. 37; 1934 (London, 1935), p. 46; 1936 (London, 1937), p. 35.

As previously, there are time limits set for the declaration and the claim to compensation. Furthermore, no compensation is granted if a railroad or similar corporation has rented land which it wants to use for its own purposes; if permanent pastures are rented; if the landlord operated the land for at least twelve months before leasing it and if the contract excludes compensation in case the lease is terminated within seven years or less; or, finally, if the landlord gives notice within three months after the tenant's death. There is no such exception any more for leases for years. The renewal of these leases cannot be refused without compensation if the tenant dies. This means a further approach to a hereditary lease.

Fair Rents.—The decision concerning the compensation is subject to arbitration. The right to compensation has also an effect on the determination of the rent. Both the landlord and the tenant may request an arbitration for the purpose of an adjustment of the rent in each second year; if one party fails to agree to that procedure, the other may terminate the lease. The landlord then has to pay compensation if it was he who refused to submit; he is not liable if the refusal was the tenant's. The number of rent arbitrations is extremely small and has steadily declined throughout the years. Only eight cases came up for arbitration in 1937. In the large majority of the cases, rent reduction was granted. At first glance it seems that the provisions are too complicated and obscure to be of much practical importance. However, it may be true that the mere existence of the arbitration provisions increases the bargaining power of the tenant and prevents the landlord from refusing reductions in rent since he is conscious of the fact that the tenant is able to obtain them by applying for arbitration. The annual number of rent arbitrations is as follows:

TABLE 23

RENT ARBITRATIONS, ENGLAND AND WALES, 1931-37*

	1931	1932	1933	1934	1935	1936	1937
Number of cases....	36	44	38	35	15	16	8
Rents reduced......	33	43	35	32	13	14	6
Rents increased.....	2	0	2	2	0	2	2
Rents unaltered.....	1	1	1	1	2	0	0

*Ministry of Agriculture and Fisheries, *Reports* on the Work of the Land Division, 1935 (London, 1936), p. 45; 1936 (London, 1937), p. 34; 1937 (London, 1938), p. 31.

Compensation for Improvements.—Besides the compensation for unreasonable disturbance, which was created by statute, the customary law of some regions, such as the Lincolnshire and Evesham customs, has for long provided for some compensation for improvements made by the tenant, especially for such improvements as were made during the last year of the lease. Under the "Evesham custom" a tenant who wanted to leave the farm could sell the improvements to his successor. If the landlord did not accept the successor chosen by the tenant, then he himself had to pay the price for the improvements. The reform legislation standardized and extended these provisions. The law of 1875 did not prove successful because its rules could be modified by party agreements. They were, therefore, made compulsory in 1883. A study of the change in the compensation system effected by the various acts is highly instructive. Its development is indicated below. The most striking difference between the law of 1875 and that of 1883 concerns the abandonment of the rigid time limits imposed upon the compensation claims, which were replaced by a more appropriate method of calculating the amount to be paid. The principles underlying the system of 1883 have not since been changed. The contents of the three classes are, however, somewhat different today.[15] In 1890 the liabilities of the landlord were made applicable to mortgagees who entered into possession of the farm. Some other changes of less im-

TABLE 24

COMPENSATION FOR IMPROVEMENTS IN ENGLAND, 1875

Class of improvements	Number of years after which the improvement is regarded as depreciated	Requirements	Amount of compensation	Deductions	Procedure
I Permanent improvements, as buildings and drainage	20	Landlord's consent	The tenant's expenses, reduced by a depreciation allowance for every year. Upper limit: increment in rental value due to the improvement	(a) Taxes and charges to be paid by the tenant (b) Rents due (c) Contributions of the landlord to improvements (d) Negative compensation for waste and other violations of the contract within the last four years. As regards Class I (e) Expenses for necessary repairs. As regards Class III (f) Value of manure to be produced by feeding stuff sold within the last two years	Compensation is to be claimed within one month before expiration of the lease. Deductions must be announced within two weeks after this date. In case of disagreement, decision by arbitration; appeal, if compensation claim exceeds £ 50.
II Semipermanent improvements, as chalking and liming of the soil	7	Notification of the landlord. Improvements to be made after landlord has given notice require his consent.			
III Temporary improvements, as manure and artificial fertilizer	2	. . . .	Value of the improvement for a new tenant. Upper limit: average expenses for the last three years		

[15] Cf. Table 26.

TABLE 25

COMPENSATION FOR IMPROVEMENTS IN ENGLAND, 1883

Class of improvements	Requirements	Amount of compensation
I 1. Erection or enlargement of buildings..... 2. Formation of silos.................... 3. Laying down of permanent pastures..... 4. Making and planting of osier beds ...... 5. Making of water meadows or works of ir- rigation..... 6. Making of gardens................ 7. Making or improving of roads or bridges. 8. Making or improving of water courses, ponds, wells, or reservoirs, or of works for the application of water power or for sup-ply of water for agricultural or domestic purposes.................... 9. Making of fences.................... 10. Planting of hops.................... 11. Planting of orchards or fruit bushes...... 12. Reclaiming of waste land .... 13. Warping of land.................... 14. Embankment and sluices against floods ..	Landlord's consent	Value of the im-provement for a new tenant. In computing the amount "inherent capabilities of the soil" must not be taken into cal-culation. The parties may agree upon a different method of cal-culating the com-pensation. As re-gards Class III, this method must be "fair and reasonable." De-ductions are like those of the law of 1875.
II 15. Drainage.......................	Notification of the landlord, who, then, can himself carry out the work. In this case the tenant has to pay 3 per cent interest on the expenses, and an-nuities.	
III 16. Boning of land with undissolved bones.. 17. Chalking of land.................... 18. Clay-burning.................... 19. Claying of land.................... 20. Liming of land.................... 21. Marling of land.................... 22. Application to land of purchased artificial or other purchased manure............. 23. Consumption on the holding by cattle, sheep, or pigs of cake or other feeding stuff not produced on the holding........	No consent required, unless work is to be done during the last year of the lease. In this case compensa-tion is granted, if the landlord was notified and did not refuse consent, or if notice was given after the work had started.	

portance were enacted in the same year. Class III was enlarged and the old local customs abolished in 1883 were revived. They are of some importance with respect to improvements which are made in the last year of the lease. The procedure was, in the first instance, left to the parties. If no agreement was reached, the issue was submitted to arbi-tration. The arbitrators were appointed by the parties or by the Sec-retary of Agriculture and had to make an award within twenty-eight days. On appeal the award was subject to reversal only with reference to questions of law and not of fact.

Some minor changes were introduced in 1906. Compensation for building repairs was no longer conditional upon the landlord's consent. The prohibition to take into account the "inherent capabilities of the soil" in calculating the value of an improvement was abolished. The procedure was changed again. In the first place, a single arbitrator should decide.

The law of 1920 authorized the Secretary of Agriculture to provide that improvements within Class I (except No. 1, Buildings) should make the landlord liable to compensation even if they were made without his consent. Arbitration was extended, and the Secretary was authorized to issue new rules concerning the procedure. The most important feature was embodied in a general clause which enabled the arbitrator to award compensation for improvements not enumerated within the three classes. If the continuous adoption of a special standard or system of farming results in an increase in the value of the farm for an incoming tenant, the tenant may claim compensation for this amount, whatever the improvement might be. The new cultivation must be superior if compared to the previous one and to one which the tenant might contractually be required to provide. The conditions have to be proved by records and the compensation is conditional upon information of the landlord about the intended improvement. These provisions impair very much the practical value of the newly-arranged compensation. In calculating it, compensations which have to be paid for other improvements have to be taken into account.

The law of 1923 did not establish any changes, but codified the several reforms laws. The present contents of the three classes are shown in Table 26. The amount of money to be paid for the various improvements can be calculated relatively easily by means of tables published by technical experts.

Freedom of Cropping.—Tenants have been subjected to many restrictions in England. When the provisions for compensation for improvements proved to be a sufficient bar to a predatory cultivation of the land, the tenant could be afforded a greater freedom of cropping in order to attain that optimal system of tenancy "which will avoid the evils of soil robbery without involving the evils of too great restrictions."[16] Thus the freedom of management was secured by the law of 1906 which had also introduced compensation for unreasonable disturbance. The landlord's control became less necessary, the more the position of the tenant improved through various compensations which induced him to employ better farming practices. Now the tenant obtained the right to apply a system of cropping at his discre-

[16] H. C. Taylor, *Outlines of Agricultural Economics* (New York, Macmillan Co., 1925), p. 360.

TABLE 26

COMPENSATION FOR IMPROVEMENTS IN ENGLAND, 1923

Class of improvements	Requirement
I	
1. Erection, alteration, or enlargement of buildings...........	
2. Formation of silos.......................................	
3. Laying down of permanent pastures......................	
4. Making and planting of osier beds.......................	
5. Making of water meadows or works of irrigation..........	
6. Making of gardens.......................................	
7. Making or improvements of roads or bridges..............	
8. Making or improvement of watercourses, ponds, wells, or reservoirs, or of works for the application of water power or for supply of water for agricultural or domestic purposes...	Consent of the land-
9. Making or removal of permanent fences..................	lord
10. Planting of hops.......................................	
11. Planting of orchards or fruit bushes......................	
12. Protecting young fruit trees.......	
13. Reclaiming of waste land.......	
14. Warping or weiring of land......	
15. Embankments and sluices against floods..................	
16. Erection of wirework in hop gardens......................	
17. Provision of permanent sheep-dipping accommodation......	
18. In the case of arable land the removal of bracken, gorse, tree roots, boulders or other like obstructions to cultivation......	
II	Notice to the land-
19. Drainage...	lord
III	
20. Chalking of land......	
21. Clay-burning...	
22. Claying of land or spreading blaes upon land..............	
23. Liming of land...	
24. Marling of land...	
25. Application to land of purchased artificial or other purchased manure...	
26. Consumption on the holding by cattle, sheep, or pigs, or by horses other than those regularly employed on the holding, of corn proved by satisfactory evidence to have been produced and consumed on the holding......................	The tenant, before beginning to execute any such repairs, shall give to the landlord notice in writing of his in-
27. Consumption on the holding by cattle, sheep, or pigs, or by horses other than those regularly employed on the holding, of corn, cake, or other feeding stuff not produced on the holding...	tention. He shall not execute them unless the landlord fails to execute them within a
28. Laying down temporary pasture with clover, grass, lucerne, satin-foin, or other seeds, sown more than two years prior to the termination of the tenancy in so far as the value of the temporary pasture on the holding at the time of quitting exceeds the value of the temporary pasture on the holding at the commencement of the tenancy for which the tenant did not pay compensation....................................	reasonable time.
29. Repairs to buildings, being buildings necessary for the proper cultivation or working of the holding, other than repairs which the tenant is himself under an obligation to execute........	

Nos. 1-15 and 19-26 were already stated in the law of 1883. Nos. 16 and 27-29 were added in 1900, and Nos. 17 and 18 in 1920. The compensation for improvements of market gardens is dealt with separately since 1900.

tion and to dispose of farm products according to his own wishes, except during the last year of the lease. However, the freedom of cropping may be modified by the provisions of the contract and by regional customs, and the tenant is obligated to omit injury and deterioration of the farm. If the tenant violates his duties, the landlord may claim damages, and he may also prevent the tenant from further mismanagement by means of an injunction. Since 1920 the landlord's claim for waste or deterioration can be referred to arbitration.

Fixtures.—The tenant's position was improved also with respect to fixtures and to the landlord's right of distress. At common law, fixtures annexed by the tenant and crops sown but not harvested belong to the landlord when the tenant leaves the farm. As soon as the fixtures are connected with the land, they become the property of the landlord and may not be removed by the tenant. In order to eliminate this inequity, a law of 1851 had already provided that the tenant might remove buildings and machinery if they were set up with the landlord's written consent. This measure was supplemented by the law of 1875 which provided that the title to the fixtures remained with the tenant, with the exception of those fixtures for which he may claim compensation or which he is obliged to erect. There was a special arrangement with respect to steam engines which should, as before, become the landlord's property if erected without his consent.

If the landlord wished to retain the fixtures, he could do so, as before, but only against payment of the value which they have for an incoming tenant. The importance of these provisions increased when they were made compulsory by the law of 1883 which mentioned hedges, fences, and buildings as examples of fixtures and repealed the exception concerning steam engines. The provisions were made applicable in 1900 to fixtures not erected but otherwise acquired by the tenant. There were no essential changes later on. The growing number of improvements for which compensation can be claimed by the tenant rendered the provisions concerning fixtures unimportant. Those fixtures for which compensation can be claimed may not, of course, be removed by the tenant when he leaves the farm.

Right of Distress.—The landlord's right of distress for arrears of rent for the last six years covered literally all stock on the land, to whomever it might belong. The harshness of this provision was mitigated in 1883, when the distress was restricted to arrears of the last year and to goods of the tenant. This enabled the latter to improve the equipment of the farm with implements rented or bought by installments, because the renting or installment-buying of machinery was possible now without such property becoming subject to encumbrances. Goods for personal use and of little value were exempted from the distress in 1888.

Effects of the Legislation.—Under the protection of this legislation the tenant was expected to provide for improvements to a sufficient extent and to relieve the landlord from the functions which he could not properly fulfill any longer. However, if the landlord has no financial means to provide for improvements, he can hardly be expected to be able to pay the tenant for the making of such improvements. The tenant himself has been hit by the same blows which have struck English agriculture and the landlord as well. If sufficient financial means are at his disposal, he may supply the working capital and a large part of the fixed capital. If not, his outlay on fixed capital will curtail the necessary working capital. However, even if the farmer were able to supply fixed capital, the incentive to do so is not strong enough in many cases. The same secular trend which has curtailed the landlord's rent has also curtailed the tenant's profits. Why should he sink money in an enterprise which does not pay?

When the rate of return on landlords' capital averages over the long period something well below the return on Government Stock, it needs a quixotic farmer (just as it needs a quixotic landlord) to undertake long-term improvements, especially when the future course of agricultural prices remains so uncertain.[17]

RECENT REFORM PROPOSALS

The disinvestment which is the result of the lack of fixed capital in many cases has been eloquently described in the following terms:

The truth is that the system of land tenure is breaking down. It has never been sufficiently recognized that the fixed capital, so-called, of British farming (i.e., buildings, drains, fences, roads, etc.) is really a wasting asset, to replace which reserves should have been created. And so it is hardly an exaggeration to say that the majority of farms have an equipment which has fallen into disrepair or one which is obsolete in the changing circumstances of modern agriculture. On most farms much-needed repairs and improvements have been postponed owing to the difficulties of financing them; it would be easy to find farms cumbered with buildings no longer needed, while lacking those essentials for the efficient farming of the land today. The tenant farmers are only in part responsible for this state of affairs. For a variety of reasons, the landlords have been unable to fulfill their economic function of supplying the capital needed.

Even with the cheap credit readily available, even with the extension into the sphere of land-owning of the joint-stock principle, it is extremely doubtful whether this state of affairs could be remedied within the framework of private ownership of the land.

What is needed is the assumption by the state of the power to acquire land compulsorily.[18]

[17] Astor and Rowntree, *op. cit.,* p. 395.

[18] *The Next Five Years. An Essay in Political Agreement* (London, Macmillan & Co., 1935), pp. 163-64.

Extension of Credit.—This diagnosis stated by nonpartisan observers contains references to a number of possible remedies. Some of them are rejected, others are approved. It is generally recognized that greater liberality in extending governmental credit facilities is not likely to overcome the obstacles to a more efficient and increased production. Under present tenure conditions, the mobility of the managerial units is insufficient to bring about the best approach to the perfect combination of the productive agents and factors, even if ample credit is at hand. Public opinion in England is not inclined to subscribe to a permanent system of controlled production like that in Germany which would have to complement the credit facilities. "It is difficult to believe that, short of the emergency of war, it would be possible to persuade our fellow countrymen to adopt an arbitrary system of this kind, in the control over what is still regarded as 'private' property."[19]

Joint-Stock Companies.—Another proposal is directed toward the establishment of corporate units which would manage larger holdings than the individual farmer can do. The most eloquent advocate of this proposal, E. P. Weller, is bursar of Gonville and Caius College in Cambridge University and has a wide experience in the management of the large number of estates owned by that college.[20] So far, private estate companies have been used merely as devices to deal with the inheritance tax. Joint-stock companies, Mr. Weller holds, should be formed to purchase and manage agricultural land as an investment. Instead of renting from the landlords, tenants would rent from the companies. The overwhelming difficulties of a scheme along these lines have been most forcibly indicated by Professor Henry Clay. The landholding companies would have to compete with industry and commerce for capital not only for agriculture but for people who are trying to get out of agriculture. Agriculture is based on huge subsidies, and the increase in agricultural prices during the last few years has been brought about by the new marketing organizations. "If an industry, for the time being at any rate, was based on subsidies on that scale and an organization of producers of that type, and at the same time was paying wages about one-third less than those which were general in industry, he [Professor Clay] thought there was a political risk attached to agriculture . . . which might quite well deter many who might otherwise be attracted by that new investment from putting their money into it."[21]

[19] Addison, *op. cit.*, p. 94.

[20] *The Future of the Ownership of Rural Land in England.* Published by the Chartered Surveyors' Institution, London, 1935; *Investment Companies and Rural Land*, reprinted from the *Journal of the Chartered Surveyors' Institution*, March, April, 1936.

[21] Weller, *Investment Companies and Rural Land*, pp. 33 ff.

Land Nationalization.—Under present conditions the nationalization of agricultural land is advocated by an increasing number of Conservatives, Liberals, and members of the Labour Party. While the liberal and socialist proposals date far back, the Conservatives have been converted only in recent times. This factor throws light upon new aspects of a land nationalization policy. It has ceased to be the goal of radical reformers, and it has lost, or is not based only upon, an ethical foundation. Population growth has declined, and the emphasis of the reformers upon "unearned increment" is not too vigorous. Land nationalization now has been admitted to the realm of *Realpolitik.* Land should be nationalized not because one wants to expropriate the owners, but in order to attain a higher output of domestic foodstuffs. As Sir Daniel Hall said in his address to the British Association at Nottingham on September 7, 1937:

It is easy to envisage the planning of the land of Great Britain to ensure an increase in its productivity and population if it could be treated as a great estate managed by a business corporation with ample capital to enable it to take a long view about development. Such a plan can only be attained under the national ownership of the land. A plan is necessary not only in the broad national interests of production, but also to prevent the short-sighted destruction of the most valuable agricultural land and of the amenities of the countryside which is everywhere going on to satisfy immediate urban requirements. British land is too limited and too precious to be left to the unrestricted play of commercial exploitation.[22]

Many advocates of public ownership of agricultural land propose only a gradual nationalization. They support their claim by references to a number of factors. Government financing of the necessary adjustments and improvements is said to be cheaper than that through private capital. In many respects nationalization would mean rationalization. Present subsidies are held unjustified if they finally accrue to the landed interests without securing improvements. It is said that farms would continue to be operated by tenants, and that the government is better able to control the farming operations of the tenant than a private landlord who is hampered by the provisions of the Agricultural Holdings Acts. The tenant would enjoy full security of tenure since no more sales of estates would take place. Finally,

it might also be of advantage to the state that a larger proportion of the capital expenditure of the community should come in this way under its control. In recent years the idea of regulating or stimulating public works so as to offset the fluctuations of industrial activity or to promote recovery from depression has become a major question of economic policy both in this country and abroad. In the event of another serious depression, it is virtually certain that this question will come again into the foreground of discussion. . . . It might in these

[22] Quoted in Addison, *op. cit.*, p. 99.

circumstances be of some assistance to public policy, if there was a considerable amount of work that could be put in hand by our proposed Land Improvement Commission for the better equipment of agriculture.[23]

The fact that the nationalization proposals have not materialized so far is due to the fear of many people that the nationalization of agricultural land, while justified per se, may open the way toward the socialization of other forms of property. However, the recent nationalization of British coal has proved that this fear is not insurmountable. More important, perhaps, is the fact that government expenditures for military purposes have brought about a budgetary situation which would make land nationalization extremely difficult. Compensation for the landowner is provided in virtually all schemes.

Fair compensation should, of course, be paid. But in assessing the value of land, no account must in future be taken of any increment in value arising directly out of public action or expenditure. The large annual sum which the State is spending on agriculture must not be allowed to accrue solely to the landlords, while public works and town planning schemes must not be rendered expensive by the inflated claims for compensation.[24]

The English tenure policy offers a perfect example of the dynamics which are inherent in governmental action. Once the path of intervention is chosen, each step necessitates the next, and a retreat becomes unfeasible. It is a far cry from radical Thomas Spence to conservative Viscount Astor, both of whom plead for public ownership of land. The English doctrine of tenure which denies the proprietor an absolute right has facilitated the growth of government interference with the landlord-tenant relationship, and it helps to explain the present tendency toward national ownership. There can be hardly any doubt that the infringements of the rights of landlords introduced by the Agricultural Holdings Acts have prevented some landlords from sinking funds in land which is only nominally their own. There can be even less doubt that the propaganda for public ownership which has been going on for decades has worked in the same direction. Yet the history of the acts is a fascinating example of the political instinct and social stability of the English. As Élie Halévy rightly says,

in no other country of Europe have social changes been accomplished with such a marked and gradual continuity. The source of such continuity and stability is . . . not to be found in the economic organization of the country . . . [or] in the political institutions of England. . . . To find it we must pass on to another category of social phenomena—to beliefs, emotions and opinions.[25]

[23] Astor and Rowntree, op. cit., pp. 396 ff., 431-32.
[24] The Next Five Years, p. 164. Compensation schemes have been drawn up by Lord Addison (op. cit., pp. 96 ff.), Viscount Astor, and Seebohm Rowntree (op. cit., pp. 399 ff.).   [25] Op. cit., I, 335.

VI

LAND TENURE UNDER THE SWASTIKA

GENERAL CHARACTERISTICS OF THE NEW AGRICULTURAL POLICY

AMONG THE objectives of the agricultural policy of the Nazi regime are "liberty of food" or autarchy, and the reëstablishment of the peasantry as the backbone of the nation. The land tenure policy is used as a means towards the attainment of these objectives. In the totalitarian state all policies and programs are interrelated and coördinated so as to attain the goals set by the government, and all policies serve some definite political purpose. So do all sciences and arts. Agricultural economics as well as the natural sciences concerned with agriculture have become political science. The title of a recent book, *The Political Tasks of German Plant Breeding*,[1] illustrates the new aspect.

Agricultural life in Germany is supervised and controlled by the authorities of the government and of the Nazi party, and by a vast public corporation, the Reich Food Corporation, which embraces all German agriculturists and controls every phase of German agriculture. The corporation has 12,000,000 members, and its annual expenses amount to 60,000,000 marks.[2] Public investigations into the productive capacity of all German farm land, which recur at regular intervals, enable the authorities to tell the farmer what to produce, how much to produce, to whom to sell, and at what price.

The Structure of German Agriculture.—In the United States the average size of a farm is 155 acres according to the Census of 1935. It is considerably less in England. In Germany the average size of a farm is only one fifth of a farm in the United States; it was 13.5 hectares, or 33.3 acres in 1933.[3] Table 27 indicates the size distribution of farms in Germany.

Of all farms 27.4 per cent are smaller than two hectares, or five acres. There are many part-time farmers among the operators of these small holdings. Most of them are located in the highly industrialized western parts of Germany. The farmers work in the industrial plants, devoting their spare time to their farms. Farms like these are neither completely self-sustaining, nor can the farmer produce a considerable amount for the market. The farm is merely a means of improving the

[1] W. Rudorf, *Die politischen Aufgaben der Deutschen Pflanzenzüchtung* (Goslar, 1937).
[2] Membership: *Recht des Reichsnährstandes*, Vol. II (1934), No. 3. Expenses: *Neue Zürcher Zeitung*, October 12, 1934.   [3] 1 hectare = 2.4 acres.

TABLE 27

NUMBER OF FARMS AND FARM AREA, WITH PER CENT DISTRIBUTION,
BY SIZE OF FARMS, 1933*

Size group, hectares (1 ha = 2.4 acres)	Number of Farms		All Land In Farms and Forests	
	In thousands	Per cent	Thousand hectares	Per cent
.5 to 2 hectares...	834	27.4	934	2.3
2 to 5 " ...	788	25.9	2,584	6.2
5 to 20 " ...	1,070	35.1	10,630	25.6
20 to 100 " ...	321	10.6	11,567	27.9
100 hectares and over.	34	1.0	15,709	38.0
Total..........	3,047	100.0	41,424	100.0

*Statistisches Reichsamt, *Statistik des Deutschen Reichs*, Vol. 459 (Berlin, 1936), Pt. 1, p. 36.

diet of industrial and other wage earners, who become more independent of the fluctuations of the labor market.

The area covered by this 27.4 per cent of small farmers amounts to only 2.3 per cent of all land in farms. Together with the operators of farms of from two to five hectares, these farmers account for 53.3 per cent of all German farmers. The area covered by these farms amounts to only 8.5 per cent of all land in farms. The farm of two to five hectares may be self-sustaining in some cases, particularly in the fertile regions of the Rhine Valley and the tributaries of that river. When the operator is a part-time farmer, the importance of the agricultural occupation is greater than that of his outside job.

The next group of farms of five to twenty hectares is the largest of all. It is composed of family farms, most of which are self-sustaining. The following group employs hired help and represents the transition to the large estates. These, while only 1 per cent of all farms, utilize 38 per cent of all farm land. The size distribution of the large estates is shown below.

Of more than three million farmers, 2,797, or less than one tenth of 1 per cent, operate farms which amount to 18 per cent of all farm

TABLE 28

NUMBER OF FARMS OVER 100 HECTARES, AND PERCENTAGE OF FARM AREA,
BY SIZE OF FARM, 1933*

Size group, hectares (1 ha = 2.4 acres)	Number of farms	Per cent of all land in farms and forests
100 to 200 hectares...........	16,542	5.5
200 to 500 "	10,593	8.0
500 to 1,000 "	3,911	6.5
1,000 hectares and over...........	2,797	18.0
Total....................	33,843	38.0

*Statistisches Reichsamt, *Statistik des Deutschen Reichs*, Vol. 459 (Berlin, 1936), Pt. 1, p. 36.

land. However, large parts of these "farm" lands are covered by forests.

The figures do not fully indicate the concentration of land ownership. The census only enumerates the farms but does not give any information on the amount of land or number of farms held by one person. For political reasons the census bureau has never attempted to collect such information. It is said that such a census is forthcoming at the present time, largely on account of pressure by that faction of the Nazi party which demands greater activity in the matter of land settlement.[4] The most outstanding instances of concentration of land ownership are as follows:

TABLE 29

CONCENTRATION OF LAND OWNERSHIP, SELECTED LARGE ESTATES*

Owner	Amount of land, hectares (1 ha = 2.4 acres)
Wilhelm von Hohenzollern	97,000
Prince von Hohenlohe-Oehringen	48,000
Prince von Hohenzollern-Sigmaringen	46,000
Prince von Stolberg-Wernigerode	36,000
Duke von Ratibor	31,000
Duke von Dessau	30,000
Duke von Ahrenberg-Nordenkirchen	28,000
Reich Count Schaffgotsch	28,000
Reich Count von Brühl	23,000
Former King of Saxony	22,000
Count Fink von Finkenstein	21,000

*Theodor Habich, *Deutsche Latifundien* (2nd ed. Königsberg, 1930).

These heavily-endowed owners are spread over the whole country, though they are more prominent in the east. There is more concentration of land property in Germany than in any other country within the realm of western civilization.

TABLE 30

SIGNIFICANCE OF "LARGE" FARMS (a); SELECTED COUNTRIES*

Country	Year	"Large" farms, per cent of all farms	"Large" farms, per cent of farm area
Denmark	1933	.5	6.6
France	1929	.8	15.9
England	1924	3.1	22.8
United States	1935	1.3	29.4
Italy	1930	.5	35.1
Germany	1933	1.1	37.9

*Denmark, France, Italy, and England: International Institute of Agriculture, *International Yearbook of Agricultural Statistics*, 1935-36 and 1936-37 (Rome, 1937), pp. 982, 983; *ibid.*, 1934-35 (Rome, 1936), p. 853. Germany: *Statistisches Jahrbuch für das Deutsche Reich*, 1937 (Berlin, 1937), p. 76. United States: *Statistical Abstract of the United States*, 1938 (Washington, 1939), p. 590.
(a) France, Italy, Germany: farms over 247 acres; Denmark and England: farms over 300 acres; United States: farms over 1000 acres. The minimum size of a "farm" is different in the various censuses.

[4] *Frankfurter Zeitung*, September 5, 1936.

The Junkers.—The large farms are an important factor in German agricultural and political life. The historical development of these estates, their rise and growth out of medieval feudalism, and their increase during the nineteenth century explain many chapters in the history of Germany. The present land tenure organization in Germany is to a large extent the result of political changes which took place after the French Revolution. When the peasants were liberated from the relics of feudal servitude during the first part of the nineteenth century, the protective measures were also abolished which had hindered the complete expropriation of the peasants and the taking over of their holdings by the large landowners. The paternalistic bonds which had supplied the peasants with small additional earnings and had enabled them to overcome times of depression were likewise abolished. The newly won freedom did not prove advantageous to many of those who were expected to be benefited by the change. Many peasants who used to work on the lord's estate became landless laborers or acquired unrestricted ownership of their small holdings. After a short interlude many of the new owners lost their holdings to the lords, who were not prohibited any longer from enlarging their estates through additional purchases. Thus the *Junkers* were able to increase their holdings from 140-400 acres to 600-1,800 acres in the course of the nineteenth century.

By enlarging their estates the *Junkers* tried to overcome the economic changes which happened during that time—the growth of industries and the rise of agricultural competition in foreign countries. They were supported therein by the willingness of the credit organizations to grant loans to the members of the politically mighty class. Small farmers were unable to obtain credit and had to rely upon coöperatives which they had founded themselves. The prewar distribution of credits granted by the landbanks is indicated in the following table.

TABLE 31

PER CENT DISTRIBUTION OF FARM MORTGAGES GRANTED BY LANDBANKS, BY SIZE GROUPS, PRUSSIA, 1905*

Size group, hectares (1 ha = 2.4 acres)	Mortgaged farms, per cent of all farms of specified size
5 to 20 hectares..............................	5.8
20 to 100 ”	21.3
100 hectares and over...........................	66.3

*Hermann Mauer, *Das landwirtschaftliche Kreditwesen in Preussen* (Strassburg, 1907), p. 189.

The need for changes in the social and economic organization of the eastern part of Germany was constantly expressed by the leading social scientists of the time. "Our East must gradually become like the West; it needs it in every respect," said G. F. Knapp, the outstanding historian of German land tenure.[5] Max Weber spoke of the "process of chronic putrefaction of the East."[6] The economic changes of the time had forced the landed gentry to spend cash in order to maintain their social and political status, to buy farm machinery, and to pay wages to the huge number of their farm hands. The nexus of the money economy made them more dependent upon the market, which, at the same time, reflected the greater efficiency of the competing smaller farms and the producers beyond the seas. In this situation Max Weber advised a policy which would have resulted in a change from commercial farms which produce for the market, a task to which the east proved unequal, to smaller farms. "That farmer who puts his products there where world prices play only a negligible role, namely into his own stomach, can now make his living in the East best."[7] So moderate a social reformer as Gustav Schmoller proposed that the government purchase all the large estates; he held that this sacrifice of the public would be more tolerable than a permanent increase in the cost of living which would take place were the East to remain the main source of commercial crops in Germany.

These proposals were made when the tariff was moderate and when international trade was still guided by the principle of comparative advantage. When the World War came, nobody dreamed any longer of abandoning the capacity of the East to supply the domestic market with agricultural products. At the end of the war, General von Hindenburg promised to grant land to the soldiers, and strong demands for an active settlement policy were heard. When the Republic was established, many believed that the historical moment had come to abolish the economic and social basis of the disastrous power of the *Junkers* and shape a just and equitable distribution of land. But the *Junkers* were saved again, this time by a settlement legislation which did not work.

There are no substantial amendments to this settlement legislation under the Nazi regime. Though Point 17 of the party platform had promised the "expropriation of land, without indemnification, for the public benefit," Adolf Hitler was forced in 1928 to reassure his sponsors and followers among the landed gentry by adding a comment which virtually annulled the promise contained in the platform. R. Walther Darré, secretary of agriculture, declared: "It is strongly to be warned against playing with the idea of expropriation by the state."[8] He also issued the following statement, in which, he said, Hitler accorded

[5] "Landarbeiter und innere Kolonisation (1893)," *Ausgewählte Werke* (Munich and Leipsic, 1925), I, 142.

[6] "Die ländliche Arbeitsverfassung (1893)," *Gesammelte Aufsätze zur Sozial- und Wirtschaftsgeschichte* (Tübingen, 1924), p. 456.

[7] *Ibid.*, p. 464.

[8] *Neuadel aus Blut und Boden*, p. 97.

completely: "I shall not infringe upon any property, the latter being as large as it might be; nor shall I infringe upon any indebted large estate."[9]

Settlement Activity.—Since these promises have been kept, there is no land available for new settlements. "The new formation of German peasantry has nothing to do with breaking up the estates."[10] As Table 32 indicates, the settlement activity under the Nazi regime has rapidly fallen off. Only 1,400 new holdings were established in 1938, as contrasted with 9,082 in 1931. The amount of land acquired for settlement purposes in 1938 was considerably lower than in any year during the preceding decade, as was the number and acreage of the newly established holdings. Only the land grants to established holdings have not decreased to a considerable extent. They are favored by the government since they can be used as a means of changing subsistence farms into commercial farms.

TABLE 32

LAND SETTLEMENT, 1927-38*

Year	Land acquired for settlement, hectares (1 ha=2.4 acres)	New Holdings			Land grants, hectares
		Number	Area, hectares	Average size, hectares	
1927........	85,948	3,372	36,704	10.9	5,700
1928........	78,468	4,235	50,616	11.9	6,816
1929........	117,115	5,545	61,213	11.0	10,531
1930........	127,112	7,441	79,833	10.7	15,862
1931........	111,995	9,082	99,624	11.0	24,618
1932........	81,737	9,046	01,926	11.3	17,767
1933........	107,058	4,914	60,297	12.3	17,047
1934........	148,113	4,931	74,192	15.0	27,056
1935........	122,848	3,905	68,338	17.5	23,145
1936........	82,225	3,308	60,358	18.2	22,044
1937........	63,859	1,849	37,596	19.8	21,400
1938 (a)....	61,000 (b)	1,400	26,600	18.9	15,400

*Statistisches Jahrbuch für das Deutsche Reich, 1938, p. 90; Wirtschaft und Statistik, 1939, p. 414.
(a) Preliminary.
(b) Including Austria.

The average size of the newly established holdings has risen considerably under the Nazi regime. The significance of this increase becomes more clear if one considers the development of the different size groups during the whole period since the enactment of the settlement legislation as indicated in Table 33. This legislation was sponsored to provide small holdings for the many farm laborers without land. The new holdings were small in size to enable the land proletariat to acquire them and to settle as many as possible. While only 40 per cent

[9] *Deutsche Allgemeine Zeitung,* July 20, 1933.

[10] Fritz Nonhoff, "Das Recht der Neubildung deutschen Bauerntums," *Zeitschrift der Akademie für Deutsches Recht,* September, 1936, p. 779.

of all new holdings were over ten hectares during the first ten years of the legislation, this percentage is twice as high now. The new regime is more interested in "crop factories" than in the improvement of the social and economic status of the farm workers.

TABLE 33

NEW HOLDINGS, PER CENT DISTRIBUTION BY SIZE GROUPS, 1919-38*

Year	SIZE OF NEW HOLDINGS		
	Under 2 hectares, per cent	2 to 10 hectares, per cent	Over 10 hectares, per cent
1919-1930..............	38.5	20.6	40.9
1931................	13.2	33.0	53.8
1932................	5.8	38.2	56.0
1933................	5.3	34.1	60.6
1934................	4.8	24.9	70.3
1935................	5.7	16.2	78.1
1936................	5.1	15.0	79.7
1937................	3.4	12.5	84.1
1938 (a)...........	5.5	16.9	77.6

Statistisches Jahrbuch für das Deutsche Reich, 1938, p. 91; Wirtschaft und Statistik, 1939, p. 415.
(a) Preliminary.

It has become customary in Germany to predict a greater settlement activity for the future. The year 1934 was called a "pause,"[11] and in 1937 the journal of the Census Bureau spoke of a "certain reserve" with respect to settlement activities, caused by "the general prosperity of the German economy, the consolidation of national defense, and the fulfillment of other, more important tasks. . . . The increase in land prices, too . . . might have influenced the development towards a limitation of settlement activities."[12] High land prices were again emphasized in a statement in 1938.[13] In 1939 the necessity to divert human and natural resources to military uses was emphasized.[14]

Land Reclamation.—In order to compensate for this obvious inactivity, the Nazi regime has always propagated a strong reclamation policy. According to the Census Bureau there are about 700,000 hectares of waste, swamp, and littoral land available for cultivation, though much higher figures are quoted by politicians and other "experts."[15] However, the reclamation of this land is so expensive that it "must lead to a fiasco." If the waste land were to be reclaimed, "a capital investment must be made which would be much more useful on the older and better soils."[16]

[11] *Die Wirtschaftskurve,* XIII (1934), 292-95.
[12] *Wirtschaft und Statistik,* 1937, p. 745.
[13] *Vierteljahrshefte zur Statistik des Deutschen Reichs,* 1938, No. 3.
[14] *Wirtschaft und Statistik,* 1939, p. 415.
[15] See the references in P. Hävel, *Grundfragen deutscher Wirtschaftspolitik* (Berlin, 1935), pp. 104, 178.   [16] Aereboe, *Agrarpolitik,* pp. 576-77.

All in all, the Nazis have improved an area of 536,000 hectares for cultivation, as compared with 650,000 hectares which have been apportioned for airports, roads, buildings, and other military purposes.[17] Reclamation costs did not reach a high level, since unpaid labor of the Labor Service Corps and of political prisoners was used. However, the production costs on the new holdings are still extremely high, and they increase rents of other holdings. It is held, however, that the principle of differential rent does not apply in Germany.[18]

Professor Aereboe, one of the most realistic students of German agriculture, once expressed the opinion that "only a confused mind can wish or hope to attain an increase in the number of farmers without breaking up the large estates."[19] Under the Nazi regime the *Junkers* have been enabled so far to maintain their estates. They are protected from the consequences of the principle of comparative advantage, and their holdings have become more profitable, this at a price level which competes with Italy's for being the highest in the world. Since Germany's agricultural policy aims at increasing agricultural production, the relatively small group of large owners who produce a large part of the market supply are favored by most of the German farm programs. This aspect of the matter has to be taken into consideration when it is now maintained that

until the outbreak of the Great Depression, the small farms, sometimes also the middle sized, had the highest net return. Since then the larger farms distinctly have the advantage over the former. The price policy established since 1933 has, indeed, restored the profitableness of all farms whatsoever, but it could not abolish the reversion of the profitableness-relation between large and small farms. Under present conditions one can expect that in Germany, as in England, the land settlement policy sponsored by Bismarck will dwindle away entirely.[20]

Increased prices of farm products do not benefit the small farmer who raises crops and animals mainly for his own use.

FARM TENANCY POLICY

Because of a highly-developed farm-credit system, farm tenancy is nowhere near so important in Germany as in many other countries. Only 10.7 per cent of all land in farms and forests was rented in 1933. As Table 34 shows, the tenancy situation has been virtually stationary

[17] H. Backe, "Der Stand der Erzeugungsschlacht," *Der Vier-Jahresplan*, November, 1938.

[18] See, for instance, E. Carrell, "Bäuerliche Siedlung und Entwicklungsmöglichkeiten der deutschen Industrie," *Schmollers Jahrbuch*, LX (1936), 598.

[19] Aereboe, *op. cit.*, p. 581.

[20] Max Sering, "Die agrarischen Grundlagen der Sozialverfassung," in *Probleme des deutschen Wirtschaftslebens* (Leipsic, 1937), Essays in Honor of Dr. H. Schacht, p. 855.

for many years. The slight changes in the last twenty years are the results of changes in statistical techniques.

TABLE 34

PER CENT OF ALL LAND IN FARMS AND FORESTS UNDER LEASE, 1895-1933*

Period and area	Per cent of land under lease
1895.	12.4
1907, prewar territory	12.8
1907, postwar territory, excluding the Saar	12.6
1925, postwar territory, excluding the Saar	12.4
1925, all land in farms and forests over .5 hectare.	10.8
1933, all land in farms and forests over .5 hectare.	10.7

*Statistik des Deutschen Reichs, Vol. 459 (Berlin, 1936), Pt. 1, p. 55.

The Census of 1933 does not cover holdings under .5 hectares (1.24 acres), which include a large number of rented "farms." Moreover, the figures for the earlier years represent the percentage of all land in farms, which comprises also the acreage of forest property in so far as such property includes farm land. The second figure for 1925 and the figure for 1933 represent the percentage of all land in farms and forests. Recently an official of the Reich Food Corporation maintained that it is not correct to take the percentage of rented land from a total which includes land in forests, because forest land is seldom rented. Thus he takes the percentage of rented land from a total which includes only agricultural land proper. On this basis, the land under lease amounted to 16.6 per cent in 1933.[21] Much may be said in favor of this method because it compares better with the large number of tenants who rent the relatively small area under lease. As a matter of fact, almost 50 per cent of all farmers rent some land.

The difference between the amount of rented land and the number of farmers who rent land indicates not only a large number of small tenants, but also of part-owners in particular. The distinction between the renting of farms, which means leasing a complete productive unit including buildings and all other improvements on the land, and the supplementary renting of certain tracts of bare land, which are used by farmers with adjacent land, is of great importance. The distribution of owner-operated farms, tenant farms, and partly owned farms is shown in Table 35. As this table indicates, 92 per cent of all farm operators own their land, partly or wholly; 51 per cent own all their land; and 41 per cent have farms composed of owned and rented land. Only 6 per cent of all farmers are tenants proper.

[21] Sauer, "Agrarpolitik und Landpachtproblem," Recht des Reichsnährstandes, V (1937), 213.

Again the changes in the figures from 1925 to 1933 do not represent real changes, but rather the exclusion of the holdings smaller than .5 hectare from the 1933 census. These "farms" include a large number of tenant holdings, but relatively fewer owner-operated and partly owned farms. Thus the percentage of both these types has risen and that of the tenants has decreased.

TABLE 35

FARMS, BY TENURE GROUPS, PER CENT DISTRIBUTION, 1895-1933*

| Year | Owner-operated farms, per cent | Tenant farms, per cent | PARTLY OWNED FARMS | | | Other (allowances etc.), per cent | All farms, per cent |
			All, per cent	Less than ½ of land rented, per cent	More than ½ of land rented, per cent		
1895	40.7	16.4	30.5	20.9	9.6	12.4	100
1907	42.9	17.2	29.9	20.2	9.7	10.0	100
1925	42.0	17.0	29.0	20.0	9.3	12.0	100
1933	51.3	6.2	41.0	(a)	(a)	1.5	100

*1895-1907: K. Grünberg, "Agrarverfassung," in *Grundriss der Sozialökonomik* (Tübingen, 1922), Pt. VII, p. 149; 1925: *Statistisches Jahrbuch*, 1927, p. 53; 1933: *Wirtschaft und Statistik*, 1934, p. 370.
(a) Not reported.

We shall pass now to the distribution of tenant, part-owner, and owner-operated farms within the various size groups. Table 36 indicates that the tenants and the part-owners are more significant among the small and medium-sized holdings than among the larger. The comparatively large percentage of tenants within the class of 200-500 hectares is caused by the renting of the large holdings of the mortmain

TABLE 36

FARMS BY TENURE AND SIZE GROUPS, PER CENT DISTRIBUTION, 1933*

Size groups, hectares (1 ha = 2.4 acres)	Owners, per cent	Tenants, per cent	Part-owners, per cent	All farm operators (in thousands)
.5 to 1......	50.4	12.6	33.1	360
1 to 2......	46.9	8.9	42.1	474
2 to 5......	42.2	5.9	51.0	788
5 to 10......	46.7	3.7	49.4	619
10 to 20......	59.9	3.5	36.6	451
20 to 50......	74.1	3.9	22.0	267
50 to 100......	77.0	5.7	17.3	54
100 to 200......	75.3	9.8	14.9	17
200 to 500......	76.2	12.4	11.4	11
500 to 1,000.......	79.8	8.0	12.2	4
1,000 and over.......	91.1	.8	8.1	3
Total..........	51.3	6.2	41.0	

*H. Krause, "Pachtland und Betriebsgrössen," *Berichte über Landwirtschaft*, XXI (N. s. 1937), 735.

corporations and the public institutions. Among the largest estates, which often contain big forests, the percentage of tenants becomes negligible. Similar conclusions can be drawn from Table 37, which shows the per-cent distribution of the land under lease by size groups.

The number of tenant farms of 2-5 and of 5-20 hectares has increased since 1925 faster than owner-operated holdings of this size.[22] One observer has maintained that this development may be a forerunner of a general trend in size of all farms and that, perhaps, owner-operated farms, too, will move from the larger to the middle- and small-sized groups.[23] If this occurs, the government, whose policy is directed toward maximization of the agricultural output for the

TABLE 37

LAND UNDER LEASE, BY SIZE GROUPS, 1933*

Size group in hectares (1 ha = 2.4 acres)	Per cent of all land in farms and forests
.5 to 2	27.5
2 to 5	23.4
5 to 20	14.2
20 to 100	8.5
100 to 1,000	12.6
1,000 and over	.7

*Wirtschaft und Statistik, 1934, p. 370.

market, will have to check the new trend, for smaller farms mean less commercial farms.

Three Tenancy Regions.—About fifteen years ago the tenancy situation in Germany was investigated by Max Sering and his associates in order to collect the facts upon which reform legislation could be based.[24] According to the work of these men, three different regions of farm tenancy are to be distinguished: the region of the small farmers in the south and west; the region of large estate owners east of the Elbe; and the region of the medium-sized farms between these regions.

In South and West Germany the favorable climate, the fertility of the river valleys, and the division of inherited farms have resulted in a

[22] "Die Besitzverhältnisse der land- und forstwirtschaftlichen Betriebe," *Wirtschaft und Statistik,* 1934 pp. 371-72.

[23] Krause, "Pachtland und Betriebsgrössen," *Berichte über Landwirtschaft,* XXI (N. S. 1937), 733 ff.; XXII (N. S. 1937), 252 ff.

[24] Max Sering, R. Seiff, and C. von Dietze, "Die wirtschaftliche und soziale Bedeutung der Zeitpacht," *Berichte über Landwirtschaft,* Vol. I (N. S. 1924), Nos. 3-4; II (N. S. 1925), 1 ff. The following description of the three tenancy regions draws much from this valuable source. See also Karl Brandt's "Untersuchungen über Entwicklung, Wesen und Formen der landwirtschaftlichen Pacht," *Landwirtschaftliche Jahrbücher,* LXVI (1927), 535-634, and his "Die Lehre von der landwirtschaftlichen Pacht," in *Handbuch der Landwirtschaft,* eds., Friedrich Aereboe *et al.* (Berlin, 1930), I, 524-91.

large number of small farms. Farming is based upon family labor, and there are only a few hired men, who are, in general, much better paid than in the east. The density of the population, the adjacent cities with their industries, and absentee ownership of large holders have brought about keen competition for farm land. There are many small holdings, part-time farms which consist of a house with a strip of land that would represent several city lots, which do not have the capacity to provide a livelihood for a family without additional income. On the other hand, these smallest holdings include also the vineyards and the horticultural holdings which are so labor-intensive that frequently they have to employ a considerable amount of hired labor. In that region public and private corporations own vast areas, especially in the Rhine province, where more than one third of the farm land proper is rented. A large proportion of these farms consist of vineyards which are leased in small units. The growth of cities near by has brought about absentee owners—townspeople who let the land to small tenants. One big owner lets his estate sometimes to a thousand tenants. Many industrial corporations have invested their money in land which they rent in small parcels on reasonable terms. These corporations are more willing to lower the rent in times of depression than are the small owners who are more dependent upon the rent as a source of income. Because of the competition for land, it is more profitable to divide the land into small parcels and rent it thus, than to operate it as an owner or rent it as a whole.

The customary division of inherited land led to a peculiar mechanism of the social life. The inherited holding is equally divided among the children. The son who gets the buildings remains a farmer. However, because the buildings are too big for the inherited farm after its division, he looks around for enlargements. Besides a clever marriage policy this is effected in the main by additional leases and purchases. A second son goes into the city to work as a laborer, craftsman, or small official, until he has saved enough money for taking up farming again on his own inherited land, which he, meanwhile, has let to a tenant. The daughter enlarges the husband's farm with her inherited land. In this manner, every division of inherited land brings many new small owners and tenants. Among the lessors there are laborers, craftsmen, small officials, minors, and women.[25]

This admirable description was written fifteen years ago when there was no Entailed Farms Law in Germany.[26] This law was enacted in 1933 and applies to 25 per cent of all German farms which it has entailed. There was thereby established a form of tenure which turns out to be inflexible because the farms cannot be subdivided, cannot be

[25] Seiff in Sering, Seiff, and von Dietze, op. cit., I (1924), 17.
[26] See below, pp. 136 ff.

sold or mortgaged, and because of a compulsory rule as to the succeeding heir.

The small farmer lets his land for personal reasons only; there is no institutional landlordism in this class. The agricultural ladder works only through the renting of additional land.

The medium-sized farms are located between the western regions and the Elbe River. Throughout this area the state and the nobility own large estates which are operated by tenants. The conditions are good because of the high training of the farmers and the satisfactory size of the farms.

There is not so much tenancy in the East where the population is sparse and where large landed property still prevails. Closed inheritance keeps the land distribution stationary. If large estates are rented, the tenants enjoy a position which is hardly inferior to that of an owner-operator. Small tenants, on the other hand, have little opportunity for social advancement. Many workers on the large estates receive allowances in land which give them a tenant-like status. These allowances are a part of the wage in the labor contract which specifies the various forms of payment which the farm laborer receives, including cash, wage in kind, and the usufruct of a certain stretch or patch of land, which may consist of a garden plot; as a rule it amounts to a larger area sufficient for cultivating potatoes or providing food for hogs, for example.

The Rent.—With some insignificant exceptions the rent is always flat cash. Unlike the farmer in the United States, where, in 1930, only 7.8 per cent of all farms were operated by cash tenants, the German tenant does not take refuge in a share lease. The typical diversification of farming in Germany, which is most intensive on small farms but is also prevalent on the larger estates, makes them less susceptible to the financial collapse that is typical for specialized one or two commodity farming. Furthermore, since there is so much renting of adjacent lots of bare land in Germany, it is economically impracticable to divide the products raised with the help of the additionally rented land. Moreover, German farming is not only less specialized than American farming, but has also been for a long time much less risky than American farming because the state used to mitigate price fluctuations at a time when such help was unknown in the United States. If the state does so, it is not necessary to take refuge with the landlord. Finally, the landlord does not want to share the various products raised for home consumption of the tenant.

Rents are high. Rents for a farm amount to 4 to 5 per cent, and rents for parcels of land amount to 6 to 10 per cent of the so-called "basic value,"[27] a value which is, in general, much higher than the

[27] Sauer, *op. cit.*, pp. 215-16.

market value of the holding. Other estimates speak of a return of 4.5 to 6 per cent on the landlord's capital.[28] Rents were much higher before the depression than before the war. It is now reported that "the rents will probably once more reach the peak of 1928."[29] The development up to the depression is as follows:

TABLE 38

RENTS IN BRANDENBURG AND POTSDAM, 1910-17 AND 1925-30*

Type of soil	Rent per hectare (marks)		Increase, per cent
	1910-17	1925-30	
Medium soils...........	29	40	38
Good soils............	38	46	21

*W. Rothkegel, "Die Entwicklung der Kauf- und Pachtpreise für Landgüter und Stückländereien," in *Deutsche Agrarpolitik*, p. 421.

The increase in rent may be in a line with the general price level or, what is the same, with the purchasing power of the mark. However, it is interesting to note that keener competition has brought about a considerably greater increase in rent for medium than for good soils.

There is an inverse relation between rent and the amount of rented land. The most outstanding authority in this field states that the rent (per hectare) for holdings of 10 to 20 hectares is twice as high as the rent for holdings over 100 hectares, and that the rent for holdings under 10 hectares is even three times as high as that for holdings over 100 hectares.[30] The reason for this high price of smaller tracts is, in the first place, that often the price is not determined by capitalistic calculations, but by the tenant's vital desire to use his working power. Thus the amount of the rent is related rather to the intensiy of his personal needs than to objective conditions. But occasionally objective conditions justify such high prices of small parcels, particularly when additional land is rented. Here the return of the parcel may be higher if it is rented than if it is owner-operated. "If, for instance, a large estate contains much pasture land while the near-by peasants have only little pasture, then, if the peasants rent this pasture land, the productive capacity of their farms is much higher." They may raise cattle now and increase the production of barnyard manure needed so urgently on sandy soils. "But even if the lease term is long, the peasants depend a great deal upon the landlord . . . and their situation, after the expiration of the lease, is perhaps worse than as tenants of the whole farm, when at least they would have the possibility of terminating the lease" and moving away.[31]

[28] W. Rothkegel, in *Deutsche Agrarpolitik*, ed., Friedrich List-Gesellschaft (3 vols., Berlin, 1932), I, 421.   [29] Sauer, *op. cit.*, p. 216.

[30] Rothkegel, *op. cit.*, p. 420.   [31] Aereboe, *Agrarpolitik*, pp. 212-13.

Characteristics of the Landlords.—There is no doubt that a class of permanent landlords exists in Germany.[32] We have mentioned the large landowners in the west who let their land to thousands of tenants. Although these landlords, in the main, belong to the nobility, many industrial corporations and townspeople, such as officials, businessmen, "retired colonels," and the like, are absentee owners. All these permanent or institutional landlords may amount to one quarter of the total number of landlords.

Of more importance is the second class of institutional landlords which is composed of the public authorities, the states, railroads, municipalities, churches, and charitable trusts. They may likewise amount to 25 per cent of all landlords, but about 50 per cent of the rented land belongs to them. The amount of farm land rented by Prussia is reported as 350,000 hectares, that of the Reich Railroad Corporation as 70,000 hectares, and that of the various churches as 850,000 hectares.

Where the landlord is a farmer, tenancy is mainly temporary. Likewise, almost all landlords who belong to the non-permanent landlord class are farmers who, for managerial or personal reasons, let part of their holdings to tenants. Finally, there are many temporary landlords among those who have bought land for the erection of buildings or for other nonfarming purposes.

Retired farmers, who rent their farm to a son, are few in number. In recent times an increase in this lease type has been recorded; entailed farmers who want to retire have rented the farm to a son instead of transferring it to him. They did this because they tried to avoid the *Altenteil* as provided by the Entailed Farms Law of 1933 which allows the retired farmer only scanty means. The authorities frown upon leases of this type which supply the retired farmer with better means at the cost of the farm, and they do not permit the conclusion of leases as a method of retirement.[33]

The Functions of Tenancy.—One often finds the statement that tenancy enables the passing of the land to the best farmer; in particular, many poor, but efficient, farmers are supposed to become farm operators by means of tenancy. This opinion probably was correct in earlier times, but today tenancy fulfills such a function only in a very limited sense.[34] A tenant does need some capital. As a rule he has to take over implements and occasionally buildings, also. A new tenant has to pay cash for the livestock, equipment, stocks of fertilizer, and

[32] Sauer, *op. cit.*, pp. 217-18.
[33] Sauer, "Erbhof und Pacht," *Recht des Reichsnährstandes*, II (1936), 287. Cf. Henry W. Spiegel, "The Altenteil—German Farmers' Old-Age Security," *Rural Sociology*, IV (1939), 215-16.
[34] In connection with the following passages see Aereboe, *Agrarpolitik*, pp. 203-6.

whatever else he may find on the farm. It is either the landlord or the predecessor who demands these payments, and, in addition, landlords often ask for a security payment and the like. "Thus the farmer, if he rents a farm, needs as much cash as he does for buying an equal-sized holding, and often he needs much more." These opinions may be slightly exaggerated; however, they have been advanced by Professor Aereboe, the most realistic student of German farming who is very familiar with existing conditions. He also has pointed out that the main function of tenancy is to "permit the estate owners, who do not know farming, to use the knowledge and ability of the generally efficient tenantry. . . . Thus the latter is an important means of maintaining the status of the large landowners."[35] However, with regard to the many lands held by public authorities and the like, farm tenancy is the best method of using them, as long as the authorities regard it as necessary to hold the land. Administration and management by the authorities themselves often failed.

Where the renting of whole farms is done for personal reasons of the landlord, a capable farmer without money may occasionally become a farm operator. However, the main function of farm tenancy rests upon supplementary renting of bare land. This function serves highly-useful purposes, but it also increases the dependence of the tenant upon the landlord. As for the great majority of German farmers, additional renting is the only thing which could be compared with the "agricultural ladder" in the United States.

A special type of tenancy should be mentioned, namely, the work lease, which is an allowance in land given to farm hands on the large estates. The Nazis have applied the work lease on a large scale in order to establish more paternalistic bonds between estate owners and farm hands, and in order to keep the latter on the farm. We cannot deal here with this type of remuneration but shall pass on to the measures applied to farm tenancy by the government.

Protective Legislation.—Before we deal with the new measures brought about by the Nazi regime, we shall briefly discuss what has been done by former governments. Since 1920 a system of protection was established which safeguarded the tenants against harsh eviction and the evils of rackrenting. This was not the result of particularly vicious tenancy conditions, but a consequence of the currency inflation after the war which disturbed the landlord-tenant relationship. Landlords were forced to shorten the term of the lease and frequently to change the amount of rent in order to follow the rapid decrease in the value of money. We must remember that there were virtually only flat cash rents in Germany. Many landlords had recourse to rents in kind or in money expressed in commodity prices. Later on the rents again became flat cash rents.

[35] *Ibid.*, pp. 206-7.

Originally intended as a temporary measure, the legislation has been renewed time and again. Special courts which are formed by one jurist and by representatives of the landlords and tenants were authorized to adjust the rents to the changing conditions and to annul notices of eviction. It should be emphasized that the first provision benefited both tenants and landlords.

Farm Tenancy under the Swastika.—Tenants of farms larger than 300 acres (125 hectares) were made exempt from the protection in 1934 because by then their position had greatly improved. They had suffered more from the decline in prices than had the small tenants who raise crops for their own use only and do not depend so much upon hired men and machinery. The increase in farm prices and the cancellation of debts had bettered the situation of the large-scale tenants, who enjoy a long lease term. Even if they must leave the farm, they will find another much easier than will the small tenant. There is a large enough supply of big farms whose owners are often occupied in new positions in the army, the party, or the government. On the other hand the supply of small- and middle-sized farms is scarce, and an abolition of the protective measures would have resulted in mass evictions because of the desire of the landlords to get higher rents. It has been said that "changes in the management of rented farms are now particularly undesirable . . . because every change necessarily results in a temporary decrease in the yield."[36]

Besides the partial abolition of the protective measures, the new agrarian policy of the Reich affected the landlord-tenant relationship in various ways. The rent is not only subject to adjustment by the courts, but is controlled also by the Reich Commissioner of Prices who supervises the formation of all prices and brings them in line with the objectives of the Four-Year Plan which is directed toward economic autarchy. So far the Commissioner has prohibited the raising of rents[37] and has restricted the auctions of lease contracts.

The two price controls aim at different ends. Whereas the courts purport to settle the conflicting interests of private parties—this was, at least, the underlying conception when the protective measures were enacted—the Commissioner's task is to help achieve the general political objectives by holding down prices. In addition to that double price control, lease contracts of land of more than five acres and all lease contracts of land belonging to an entailed farm may not be entered into without official permit which is necessary for every sale of land as well as for agreements concerning the utilization and transfer of land. Through these permits the government regulates all transactions in land and makes them dependent upon the approval

[36] *Frankfurter Zeitung,* August 13, 1935.
[37] Decree of May 22, 1937, *Recht des Reichsnährstandes,* V (1937), 452.

of the local authorities.[38] Furthermore, tenants, like all farmers, may
be dispossessed if they do not live up to the commands of the authorities.[39]

The Model Lease Contract.—These four restrictions were supplemented in 1937 by a series of model lease contracts for the three main
types of tenancy. The models are prescribed by the powerful Reich
Food Corporation, and it is expected that they will be used by the great
majority of landlords and tenants. Predominance of the model forms
is attained through public pressure, such as has already occurred in
the case of the urban lease contract where a model form has been
substituted for the old contracts.[40] This method is a repetition of the
Italian example where "collective contracts" have likewise been de-
creed. In effect they convert the landlord and tenants into public
functionaries. What is valuable in these German model contracts has
been taken from the plans for a permanent tenancy reform discussed
since the war. The government had issued a draft for a new farm tenancy law in 1930, but because of the political unrest during the following years this draft never became law. In many instances its proposals
were based on the English reforms. Most of the proposed provisions
were of a compulsory nature. Moreover, where the landlord refused
to consent to certain acts, as, for instance, to the making of improvements, the tenant, in his place, could be authorized to make them by
a court decree which was based on vague rules, such as "principles of
good husbandry," and the like. The new contracts are not law. They
have been drafted by the Reich Food Corporation, which is authorized
to regulate the social and economic relations between all agriculturists.
The contracts are stronger than a law which could be modified by an
agreement of the parties. On the other hand, the disadvantages of
compulsory legislation are avoided, for the provisions of the model
contract can be changed in special cases.

According to an authoritative source, the model contracts are to
be regarded as "an important advance in the battle of production."[41]
The individual landlord-tenant relationship is not regarded any more
as a balance of private interests, not as "regulated conflict," but as a
regulation within the framework of collective order. The goal of the
totalitarian state expresses itself even in the contractual relationship
of private law, and the parties to such contracts have to adjust their
intentions to the uniform regulation enacted by the state.[42]

[38] *Grundstücksverkehrs-Bekanntmachung,* January 26, 1937.
[39] *Verordnung zur Sicherung der Landbewirtschaftung,* April 23, 1937.
[40] Henry W. Spiegel, "Der deutsche Einheitsmietvertrag im Lichte der Rechts-
vergleichung," *Zeitschrift für Schweizerisches Recht,* 1936, pp. 293 ff.
[41] Sauer, "Pachtpolitik in der Praxis," *Recht des Reichsnährstandes,* V (1937),
616 ff. In the following analysis ample use is made of this authoritative statement
of policies.
[42] Hans Merkel, "Grundfragen des ständischen Rechts," *Zeitschrift für die gesamte Staatswissenschaft,"* XCVII (1937), 602.

There are three such model contracts. One (Model A) is used for the temporary lease of an entailed farm; another (Model B) for that of another farm; and the third, for the lease of parcels and tracts of land. All contracts have a motto which briefly expresses the new ideas. The motto of the lease contract of an entailed farm reads as follows:

The German people, for the sake of their maintenance, need a healthy peasantry in healthy units of life. Blood, soil, and labor, in organic cooperation, shall cooperate on the entailed farms and be responsible to the whole people. However, if it becomes necessary to separate temporarily labor and land ownership by means of renting the entailed farm, then social justice in the conditions of the lease contract and a just rent are necessary to maintain the tenancy peace within the general order of the people, the estate, and the land. This will possibly increase the productive capacity of the entailed farm, as is due to the community. It is likewise necessary to return the farm intact to the family when the lease term has expired.

Thus landlord and tenant are joined by a community of duties which have to be fulfilled so that the ends of the national policy may be attained.

The lease term has been extraordinarily lengthened. To be sure, in the past lease terms were much longer in Germany than in this country. If a farm is rented, the term is now eighteen years, and the tenant has an option to renew the contract for eighteen years more. If single parcels or tracts of land are rented, the term is nine years. Here the tenant has similar options for two succeeding terms of nine years. There are no such options if the landlord or a member of his family wishes to operate the farm or the parcel of land, or if he is entitled to give notice because of the tenant's inefficiency or dishonesty, for instance.

Another important change is the provision giving the tenant the right to claim compensation for improvements. Compensation has to be given for those improvements which, according to the principles of orderly husbandry, are helpful ameliorations, such as the change of grass land into crop land, drainages, reclamation of waste and swamp land. There are, however, some restrictions to the right to compensation. The improvements still have to represent an increment in value when the lease expires. Furthermore, compensation is given only if the payment can be reasonably expected from the landlord. This is a characteristic feature of the German provisions which cannot be found in the English. If the tenant wants to make improvements, he has to inform the landlord of the intended measures. Within two weeks after such information is given, the landlord may ask the District Leader of the Peasantry, an official of the Reich Food Corporation, for his intervention. The district leader then appoints a referee who decides whether or not the improvements may be made.

If the landlord does not ask for intervention at this time, the referee may still decide at the end of the lease term whether or not the improvements are in accordance with the provisions of the contract, and whether or not they deserve compensation. The same referee also estimates the value of the improvements to be paid by the landlord. The provisions of the contract, especially the requirement that payment of compensation is due only if it can be expected from the landlord, are vague enough to render the decision discretionary.

Two years before the lease expires the tenant is entitled to ask the landlord for a security for his compensation. If the landlord does not pay the security, the tenant may retain a corresponding amount of rent. The provisions regarding compensation for improvements were necessary to enable the tenants to establish silos and the like. Within the last few years the number of silos has risen from 19,000 in 1931 to more than 200,000.

There are other provisions of the model lease which probably sound somewhat strange. The contract expressly provides that the parties submit themselves to all conditions and changes commanded by the authorities who decide on the validity of the lease. Thus it is somewhat dangerous to enter into a lease contract. The contract might be established in accordance with the intention and the purpose of the contracting parties. However, the authorities to whom the contract has to be submitted may change it at will, and the parties are bound to the changed conditions. The authorities know that many farmers try to evade the regulations and regimentations by secret agreements not written in the contracts. Thus it is expressly stated in the model contracts that agreements of this type are void.

The rules referring to the formation of rents are laid down in an appendix to the model contracts, which fills two large pages. These rules state that each deviation from the standard conditions as laid down in the contracts shall result, respectively, in an addition to, or subtraction from, the rent. If, for instance, the prescribed lease term is shortened in an individual case, the rent will increase, if the shortening benefits the tenant; or it will decrease, if the shortening benefits the landlord.

The standard rent is computed according to the following principles: (1) the rent has to be paid from the net return; (2) increases in rent are prohibited—if an exception to this rule is urgently necessary, the Reich Commissioner of Prices must be asked for his permission; (3) the rent, as an economic rent, should be the same percentage of the landlord's investment throughout the whole country—family and financial conditions of the individual landlord or tenant should not be taken into account; (4) the rent does not have to take into account demand or supply—contrariwise, the computation of the rent should be based upon the national-socialistic economic order, or upon a rent which has been regarded as reasonable in similar cases by the Reich Food Corporation; (5) in determining the rent, accounts of similar farms have to be consulted—relying only on the account of the concerned farm is prohibited.

In addition, some principles are enumerated which are not regarded as appropriate: (1) the rent which is or was usual in a certain region, inasmuch as it is determined by demand and supply; (2) interest on the purchase price of the farm or on a possible selling price, because the latter does not yet exclusively depend upon the economic value of the farm; (3) a rent which a particularly efficient farmer could pay; (4) where bare tracts of adjacent land are rented, the rent may not take away all advantages which the tenant may receive through the supplementary lease. As we have seen, such supplementary leases often result in a return on the land which is greater than the landlord could get out of it were he himself to operate the parcel. In conclusion, the regulations state that "the rent, from the point of view of the landlord, is an interest payment on a safe investment: the greater the security, the lower the interest rate."

Thus the tenancy reform of the Nazi regime, which was ushered in by interventionist measures of the preceding republican governments, has a degree of regimentation which can only be explained by the goal of their agricultural policy—economic autarchy. Farm tenancy has come to be regarded as a mere necessary evil. It is considered undesirable because of its capitalistic elements and because of the disturbance of the land-peasant relationship, which cannot entirely be avoided. It may be stressed that neither a tenant nor a permanent landlord can have an entailed farm. Thus both are excluded from the village gentry.

LAND INHERITANCE

The German Entailed Farms Law of 1933 has probably aroused more interest in foreign countries than any other part of the Nazi land policies. It gives preference to one heir who is called the *Anerbe*. His holding is called the *Erbhof*, or entailed farm, and the institution of entailed farms is expressed by the concept of *Anerbenwesen* or *Anerbenrecht*, which has been replaced by the somewhat plainer *Erbhofrecht*. Inheritance by one child is the outstanding feature of the entail. This type of inheritance is sometimes also called *geschlossene Vererbung*, or "closed" inheritance, in contrast with other systems where the farm is divided among the heirs.

Several investigations, initiated by the late Professor Max Sering, show the customary application of closed inheritance among the estate owners of eastern Germany and among the owners of large estates generally, especially among the nobility.[43] The division of real property predominated among the peasants of the Upper and Middle Rhine and its tributaries, where small holdings with very intensive cultivation are favored by climate and soil conditions. The German civil code of 1896 provided for free division of land among the heirs. As in France, the freedom to bequeath real property at will was accompanied by a system of "compulsory portions." Their amount, however, was smaller, and there was not an aversion to farm indebtedness comparable to that in France. Many farmers, therefore, preferred to keep the farm as a whole and pay off the other heirs in cash or by mortgage. Both methods resulted in indebtedness, but too unsound a degree of dispersion was prevented.

Even before the Nazi upheaval, closed inheritance was provided by statutes in the northwestern part of the Reich. Yet it was the farmer himself who ultimately decided whether or not his farm should become an entail, just as the closed inheritance in other parts of Germany was based on custom, but never on compulsion. The extent to which closed inheritance prevailed in Germany before the new legislation has been estimated at two thirds of all farm land.[44] Other estimates give four fifths for the Reich and thirteen fourteenths for Prussia,[45] but these figures are only rough estimates. An investigation by the Prussian Census Bureau shows the ratio of divided farms to undivided farms.

TABLE 39

INHERITED FARMS: DIVIDED FARMS AS PERCENTAGES OF UNDIVIDED FARMS, BY SIZE GROUPS, PRUSSIA, C. 1920*

Size group, hectares (1 ha = 2.4 acres)	Per cent
2 to 5 hectares	31
5 to 20 "	9
20 to 50 "	3
50 to 100 "	1.7
100 hectares and over	1

*Höpker, "Der Besitzwechsel in Preussen während der Jahre 1896 bis 1921," *Zeitschrift des Preussischen Statistischen Landesamts*, LXII (1922), 1 ff.

Although limited to holdings with over two hectares and not covering many parts of Germany where division of inherited land is prevalent, the data confirm the fact that closed inheritance prevailed among the owners of the larger farms, while there was a large number of small

[43] Max Sering (ed.), *Die Vererbung des ländlichen Grundbesitzes im Königreich Preussen* (14 vols., Berlin, 1897-1910); Max Sering and Constantin von Dietze (eds.), "Die Vererbung des ländlichen Grundbesitzes in der Nachkriegzeit," Verein für Sozialpolitik, *Schriften*, Vol. CLXXVIII (Munich, 1930).
[44] Friedrich Aereboe, *Agrarpolitik*, p. 259.
[45] Gustav Wagemann and Karl Hopp, *Reichserbhofgesetz*, p. 45.

holders who divided their farms. One quarter of all German farm holdings averages two to five hectares.

It should be emphasized again that the institution did not rest on compulsion and that the farmer could bequeath his farm to the son who appeared to be best fitted. Exclusive predetermination by birth existed only among the nobility. The following data relating to selected districts in Württemberg indicate the percentage distribution of heirs of farms by birth. They show that a growing number of farmers were abandoning the irrational selection of a predetermined heir.

TABLE 40

HEIRS OF FARMERS, PER CENT DISTRIBUTION BY BIRTH; SELECTED DISTRICTS OF
WÜRTTEMBERG, 1865-1935*

The heir was	1865-89, per cent	1890-1914, per cent	1915-34, per cent
the oldest son..........	57.8	54.5	49.3
the youngest son........	21.1	23.4	21.8
another son............	21.1	22.1	28.9
Total..............	100.0	100.0	100.0

*P. Brugger, "Der Anerbe und das Schicksal seiner Geschwister," *Berichte über Landwirtschaft* (N. s.), Sonderheft 121 (Berlin, 1936), p. 23.

The differences between closed inheritance and division of inherited land and the regional distribution of these systems are connected with the type of land settlement. Where the farms are separate, the inheritance is usually closed; and where the peasants are settled in villages, the inherited holdings are often divided.[46] Ultimately, the difference in the inheritance is of historical origin. The control of the manorial lords over the holdings developed differently in the various regions. The lords maintained control in the east and in the northwest for a longer period than in other parts of Germany where the rights of the peasants grew strong at a comparatively early time. In the present century the division of inherited land has taken place chiefly in central and southern Germany, where manorial control disappeared at an early date. Closed inheritance, on the other hand, continued in the regions where the peasants became owners comparatively late. "It is the good property right which makes the division of land possible. Property and free divisibility belong together, while closed inheritance was, in the main, intended to serve the manorial lords."[47] When the peasants were freed, they were given the right to distribute their newly-won property among their children.

Outstanding historians have drawn the further conclusion that

[46] C. J. Fuchs, *Die Epochen der deutschen Agrargeschichte und Agrarpolitik* (Jena, 1898), p. 17.   [47] *Ibid.*

closed inheritance is a product of the manor and feudalism. Much may be said in favor of this opinion, even though it was opposed by the romantic and reactionary faction of the German economists and historians. These scholars favored paternalistic bonds and dependencies and therefore sought to make closed inheritance more popular. They tried to prevent its savoring too strongly of feudalism and to revive it by discovering more attractive features. Thus, closed inheritance and primogeniture were heralded as ancient institutions of the Germanic tribes which had been established long before feudal times. To be sure, the old laws provided the contrary, as, for instance, the law of the Saxons, or the law of the Bavarians which said that "brothers divide equally."[48]

The vigorous efforts to reëstablish the entail during the nineteenth century were not successful. If the peasants used the scheme at all, it was only to a negligible extent. When the civil code for the Reich was enacted, there were many attempts to secure provisions for closed inheritance. They failed, however, for they were resisted by a large number of outstanding scholars like Lujo Brentano, Theodor von der Goltz, Adolf Buchenberger, Karl Bücher, and many others who combined social consciousness with a wide knowledge of economic history and advanced sharp opinions against the creation of inheritance legislation which was destined to separate a single estate from the national community.[49] At this time the defenders of closed inheritance did not ask for more than a legal scheme to which the farmer could have recourse if he intended to pass the farm over to one heir. There were, however, some who advocated the automatic application of such a scheme to all farms so that the farmer who did not want to apply it would have to state his intention in some legal form. This was, perhaps, the most extreme demand advanced at this time. It was based on the observation that the German farmer, in general, has an almost insurmountable aversion to making his testament or dealing with the authorities in matters pertaining to inheritance. Compared with the present legislation, the attempts of forty-five years ago were very moderate. Nobody dared to advocate compulsory entail. Professor Max Sering said: "I do not know of any living man who defends compulsory entails, who would want to fall back upon the medieval law of estates which made the peasant holdings closed units and which excluded the free disposal of the owner and testator."[50] Thus was prevented the fulfillment of wishes, which, according to Karl Bücher, were directed toward "the intruding of a compact class of satisfied people between the many who are not satisfied with their situation,—a class of people

[48] Lujo Brentano, *Agrarpolitik* (2nd ed., Stuttgart, 1925), pp. 216 ff.
[49] "Das bäuerliche Erbrecht," Verein für Sozialpolitik, *Schriften*, LXI (Leipsic, 1895), 239-404.   [50] *Ibid.*, p. 300.

who unconditionally lend themselves to be led by the classes hitherto authoritative."[51]

The attempts to revive closed inheritance were renewed in the twentieth century. After the Great War two German states enacted laws which, although voluntary, could be applied by the farmers. When the Nazis came to power, they could choose between various possible forms of entail. They could provide that the scheme was to be applied only after the farmer had declared his intention to entail his farm, as in Denmark, or they could raise the scheme to a law automatically prevailing in all cases of succession among the peasantry. Regarding the latter possibility, they could permit the farmer to exclude the application of the scheme by his will or by some other act, as in Switzerland and Czechoslovakia, or they could make it compulsory. They have chosen the latter way. In doing so, the government and the men behind the legislation have often stated that they regard the Norwegian legislation as the model for the German.

The Nazis evaluate Scandinavian institutions as precious relics of the Germanic spirit which they cherish so fondly, and they went so far as to give a new and leading magazine in the field of agricultural policy the title *Odal*, as a reminder of the Norwegian Odel law. This *Odels og Aasaetesrett* rests upon very ancient Norwegian institutions which were incorporated in a statute in 1821.[52] The *Odelsrett* provides for a redemption right which is given to members of a family, if the holding was in their hands at least twenty years. If such a holding is sold, close relatives of the former owner may repurchase it. The redemption right has the effect of an encumbrance on the holding, and *odel* holdings are sold at lower prices than other holdings because the buyer deducts the negative value of the risk that redemption may be claimed.

The *Aasaetesrett* is a mere primogeniture. The eldest son inherits the farm, which may not be divided unless the holding is sufficient to maintain several families. In this case the eldest son receives half of the holding, and the disinherited brothers and sisters have a right to liberal compensation. When the mortgage banks were established in Norway during the nineteenth century, many farmers began to suffer from heavy indebtedness, as they still do today, especially during the deflation after the Great War. Many Norwegians are anything but satisfied with these ancient institutions which drove many of their people across the Atlantic and which proved a check on the country's economic progress. Several attempts were made to do away with both institutions, but this proved impracticable, since they are protected by the Constitution of 1814 which prohibits their abolition.

[51] *Ibid.*, p. 333.
[52] J. Frost, *Das norwegische Bauernerbrecht* (Jena, 1938); Knut Robberstad, "Le droit successoral dans les héritages ruraux faites dans les différents pays," *Annales de la Commission Internationale d'Agriculture*, XVI (Paris, 1936), 137-50.

The Entailed Farms Law.—This law of September 29, 1933, was enacted by decree and replaced a corresponding Prussian law which had been enacted for Prussia a short time after the new regime had come to power. Later, similar measures were enacted in the Free City of Danzig. The drafters of the measure tried to provide a brief and popular law, and, as a result, it is one of "basic principles" which can be amended by executive decrees. No less than three such decrees became necessary within the first six months of the new legislation. In spite of many official statements to the contrary, the authorities were not well satisfied with many effects of the legislation, and they took refuge in two new executive decrees of December 21, 1936, which revoked the preceding three executive decrees. Every state intervention necessarily produces a new and wider intervention, so an increasing number of rules and regulations had become necessary. The new decrees cover a number of pages tantamount to about one sixth of the whole civil code. Even in Germany there are some critical comments on the form of the legislation: "The distinctness of the legislation has very much suffered from this inflation. Unfortunately the decrees are not understandable by themselves in many respects; even if one has recourse to the Entailed Farms Law, much remains obscure. . . . The form of the entailed farms legislation as placed before us now, is not yet satisfactory on the whole."[53]

Farms, according to the law, become entailed if they meet the following five requirements:

1. They must represent an *Ackernahrung;* that is, an amount of land sufficient to maintain a family independent of the conditions of the market and the general business situation and sufficient to maintain the management of the farm. The provision excludes, in general, all holdings which are under seven and a half hectares and which form the great majority of all farms in Germany. Likewise excluded are the so-called *Kleinsiedlungen* or small settlements, and the many part-time farms whose size does not meet the requirement. The size limit varies in accordance with the conditions of the land; while two hectares may be sufficient in the fertile Rhine Valley, ten hectares may be insufficient in the eastern parts of the Reich.[54]

2. The upper limit is expressly stated by the law: entailed farms must be under 125 hectares (309 acres). While the lower limit is an absolute requirement, several provisions enable the Secretary of Agriculture to raise the upper limit in special cases if he wishes to do so.

3. The same holds good with respect to the further requirement that the farm can be managed without *Vorwerke;* the farm has to be an administrative unit without "outworks." This requirement, too,

[53] Karl Blomeyer, "Neuerungen im Erbhofrecht," *Jahrbücher für National-ökonomie und Statistik,* CXLVI (Jena, 1937), 452-53.
[54] Wagemann and Hopp, *op. cit.,* pp. 50-51.

excludes the larger estates from becoming entailed, unless the Secretary of Agriculture makes an exception.

4. Furthermore, the holding which is permanently rented cannot become an entailed farm. The close connection between the peasant working on the soil which he owns and the land is missed here. Such permanent tenant farms, it is said, are nothing better than pure capital investments.

5. The owner of the holding must be a person "capable of being a peasant." He has to be a German citizen, also, in the racial sense; he has to be of good repute and must enjoy his full legal status; and he must be in a position to run the farm properly. The last requirement does not mean that the owner of the entailed farm has to be an agriculturist. The farm may be operated by a manager, but the owner must be the master who ultimately decides on the management.[55]

Recently a further requirement has been added according to which no holding can become an entailed farm in the future if the debts of the owner exceed 70 per cent of the taxable value of the farm. This requirement is interesting chiefly because of a significant exception. When farms over 125 hectares are admitted to become entailed, their indebtedness may amount to any percentage whatsoever. This provision again illustrates how much favor the Nazis show the large landowners. The creditor of an entailed farm can do virtually nothing to enforce his claim. As a result, an indebted member of the landed gentry can get rid of his debts from one day to another if the Secretary of Agriculture wishes to extend this favor to him.

If all these requirements are fulfilled, the farm is legally regarded as an entailed farm, whether the owner likes it or not. Once an entailed farm, always an entailed farm. The farmer has no authority to change the legal status of his holding. He is not permitted to deal with his land according to his wishes. "The entailed farm is not your 'free,' that is, desecrated property; you have to listen to the blood which rolls in your veins and which will roll in your children for the centuries."[56] Thus the owner of an entailed farm may neither sell nor otherwise alienate his land or parts of it unless the authorities permit him to do so. Likewise he must secure permission to rent his land. Entailed farms cannot be foreclosed; thus, nobody dares to mortgage them, and the farmers have to rely on government credit and personal loans.[57]

[55] H. Dölle, *Lehrbuch des Reichserbhofrechts*, pp. 24-25.

[56] R. Freisler in Wagemann and Hopp, *op. cit.*, p. 38.

[57] The farm credit problem is not considered in this book. For information on this subject see A. R. Herrmann, "Erbhof und Kredit," *Zeitschrift für die gesamte Staatswissenschaft*, XCV (1935), 719-41; Herbert Timm, "Zur Erbhofkreditfrage," *ibid.*, XCVIII (1938), 456-97; K. E. Mössner, *Das landwirtschaftliche Geschäft der Hypothekenbanken* (Berlin, 1937).

In addition, the freedom of the entailed farmer is further restricted by other provisions which threaten to deprive him of the rights and liberties still left to him. These provisions did not prove efficient, and they have been amended recently. Four different procedures can be followed by the authorities:

1. If they hold that the farmer's management is not satisfactory or that he does not meet his obligations, they may empower a neighbor or somebody else with the control of the management.

2. Instead of empowering the neighbor, the authorities may appoint a trustee who administers the farm for the owner. Both these types of interference with the management of the farm may be applied only temporarily. They can, however, be renewed. The transition to the definitive deprivation is represented by the next method which may be applied temporarily or permanently.

3. If the farmer has lost his "capability of being a peasant" or if he does not meet his obligations although able to do so, the authorities may deprive him of the administration and the revenue of his holding, and they may put one of his relatives in his place. The authorities may even go so far as to designate this person as the heir of the entailed farm. Such an expropriated farmer has no claim to maintenance on the farm unless he works under the new master's rule.

4. The same holds good when the *grosse Abmeierung* takes place. This is the harshest step to which the authorities may have recourse. It implies the definite transfer of ownership to a person appointed by the Reich Leader of the Peasantry without indemnification for the dispossessed farmer.

All these provisions, important as they may be, are not regarded by the sponsors of the legislation as the most outstanding feature of the statute. As contrasted with the German civil code of 1896, the new legislation prefers one heir and discriminates against the others. If the farmer dies, the entailed farm devolves on the *Anerbe,* while the remainder of his property passes to the heirs as determined by the civil code. In addition, these heirs have to pay the farm debts.

Who, then, is the *Anerbe?* In general, it is one of the sons; if there are no sons, the father, or one of the brothers, daughters, sisters, or other relatives of the deceased. No person virtually eligible to inherit the farm shall become the *Anerbe* if he already has another entailed farm. The legislation prefers that the youngest son become the *Anerbe* unless custom and tradition provide otherwise. This is done in order to enable the farmer to endow his older children, with whose interests the legislation interferes. To be sure, the children have a claim to maintenance on the farm and to education until they become of age. In addition, they may claim vocational training and an endowment, the claims, however, being restricted by the legislation to an amount the farm can bear. No figures are as yet available concerning the fate of the children disinherited by the new legislation. The results of earlier studies are indicated in the following table.

TABLE 41

OCCUPATION OF BROTHERS OF THE PRINCIPAL HEIR; SELECTED DISTRICTS OF WÜRTTEMBERG, 1915-34; POMERANIA, 1924-29*

Occupation	Württemberg per cent	Pomerania per cent
(Unmarried) on the home farm	10.7	16.2
Entrepreneurs........................	44.3	47.3
Public officials......................	10.0	12.5
Clerks...............................	6.1	....
Emigrated............................	3.4	3.6
Not known...........................	5.0	....
Wage earners........................	20.5	20.4
Total........................	100.0	100.0

*P. Brugger, "Der Anerbe und das Schicksal seiner Geschwister," *Berichte über Landwirtschaft* (N. s.), Sonderheft 121 (Berlin, 1936), pp. 60-62; W. M. Freiherr von Bissing, in Sering and von Dietze, "Die Vererbung des ländlichen Grundbesitzes in der Nachkriegszeit," Verein für Sozialpolitik, *Schriften*, Vol. 178 (Munich, 1930), Pt. 1, p. 95.

When these studies were undertaken, the children who left the farm received their share of the inheritance in cash or in mortgage; now their fate will be much worse. On the other hand, farmers no longer have to mortgage the farm in order to compensate the heirs who have gone away. However, as Professor Aereboe once said, this method of wiping out the farmer's debt "is like jumping out of the frying pan into the fire."[58] Before the new legislation, the brothers and sisters who had left the farm could rely upon their claims when they were in want. Now they are permitted to come back to the farm, where they have to work for their living. The law goes as far as to make this right dependent upon their "innocently" being in want.

The treatment of the children who leave the farm is a regression to the feudal time when the farmer had no property right in his land. The reason for this discriminatory treatment in feudal times has been explained by G. F. Knapp, the outstanding historian of land tenure in Germany:

The reason for not paying compensation was not to preserve the farm free from debt. It was not for reasons of expediency that the brothers and sisters had to go away empty-handed; it was so, because a compensation would have had no legal sense whatsoever. For the farm was not considered the property of the family like an amount of saved money. Legally the farm belonged to the feudal lord! All the peasant had was the right to use somebody else's land; and this right to use had become hereditary.[59]

[58] *Agrarpolitik*, p. 509.
[59] "Die Grundherrschaft in Nordwestdeutschland," in *Ausgewählte Werke*, I (Munich and Leipsic, 1925), 199.

Today the Nazi regime has taken over the role of the feudal lord. Many farmers tried to avoid the Entailed Farms Law, or sought recourse in illegal agreements which favored the disinherited children; many *Anerben* proved more righteous than the law and supplied their brothers with additional means.[60] The general feeling of the populace is illustrated by the fact that "there is an avalanche-like rise in complaints to the Reich Court for Entailed Farms."[61] In view of the well-known fact that there is no open criticism of government measures in Germany, the following veiled statement is not without interest: The Entailed Farms Law which "brings about harsh results in a great many individual cases had to give rise to many grievances of the peasantry; and it is natural that the great number of complaints which do not seem to be unjustified easily led to the conclusion that the whole legislation is a failure."[62] No wonder the number of entailed farms does not come up to the expectations of the government. The legislation was expected to establish 1,000,000 entailed farms. Later the estimates became more moderate, and the expected number was reported as 845,000 farms.[63] This estimate, however, still proved too high. There were only 685,000 entailed farms in 1938. That means that 22 per cent of all farms are entailed.[64]

The entailed farms cover 37 per cent of all farm land. The average size of an entailed farm is twenty-three hectares, or fifty-five acres. The size distribution of the entailed farms is shown in the following table.

TABLE 42

ENTAILED FARMS, PER CENT DISTRIBUTION BY SIZE GROUPS, GERMANY (EXCLUDING AUSTRIA AND SUDETEN-AREA), 1938*

Size group, hectares (1 ha = 2.4 acres)	Per cent of all entailed farms	Per cent of all land in entailed farms
Under 7.5 hectares	.9	2.9
7.5 to 15 "	19.5	40.2
15 to 25 "	24.1	28.3
25 to 50 "	31.9	21.2
50 to 125 "	22.3	7.2
Over 125 "	1.3	.2
Total	100.0	100.0

*"Die Erbhöfe im Deutschen Reiche," *Wirtschaft und Statistik*, 1939, p. 166.

[60] W. Herschel, "Geheime Nebenabreden und freiwillige Leistungen im Erbhofrecht," *Recht des Reichsnährstandes*, IV (1936), 283 ff.

[61] *Westdeutsche Zeitung*, July 20, 1935.

[62] Blomeyer, *op. cit.*, p. 469.

[63] The first estimate is from "Die deutschen Erbhöfe," Berlin, Institut für Konjunkturforschung, *Wochenbericht*, VII (1934), 56-58; the second from "Die Erbhöfe im Deutschen Reich," *Wirtschaft und Statistik*, 1934, pp. 806-8.

[64] *Ibid.*, 1939, pp. 166-68.

As the table indicates, 97 to 98 per cent of all entailed farms and entailed farm land are composed of farms below the maximum size limit of an entailed farm. Up to 1938 the Secretary of Agriculture had granted permission to 1,086 owners of farms over 125 hectares to have the farm entailed. These farms cover an area of 208,600 hectares.[65]

Figures concerning the number of cases where permission was granted to sell, mortgage, rent, divide, or otherwise alienate entailed farm land indicate that such permissions had to be granted not infrequently. In 1935, 54,591 selling permits, 13,091 mortgaging permits, 2,118 renting permits, and 5,769 permits to divide the farm were granted. Though most of the selling permits concern cases of retirement or of sales of parts of the farm for road-building and other public purposes, the number of permits indicates that more than 10 per cent of all entailed farms had to be exempted from the strict provisions of the law for one reason or another. During the same year, the authorities appointed trustees to administer the farm in 176 cases; 240 similar cases were settled without final decision. In most of these cases the farmers transferred their holding to the *Anerbe*.[66]

The old *Fideikommisse*, strict family settlements, have been abolished. The Entailed Farms Law provides for the institution of *Hofsatzung*, which represents a kind of combination of the old and the new entails. While the large landowners try to revive the strict family settlements,[67] the name of this institution is still in such bad repute that most of the writers who comment upon the entailed farms legislation feel it necessary to emphasize that this legislation has nothing in common with the strict settlements. However, Secretary Darré has admitted that there is no "fundamental difference" between both types of entails and has stressed the fact that the provisions of the Entailed Farms Law are sufficient to allow owners of large estates to have their holdings entailed.[68] The common features of strict settlements and new entails are, indeed, more significant than the differences. The main distinction is based on the fact that the settlements originated from a covenant or *Stiftung*, while the entails are created by law. The old settlements were used by the nobility only and by a few wealthy commoners; they served to maintain and increase the *splendor familiae ac nominis* and were established on estates much larger than the new entails.

Closed Inheritance vs. *Division of Estates*.—The defenders of undivided land inheritance assert that the division of inherited farms

[65] *Ibid.*
[66] Karl Hopp, "Erbhofrecht in Zahlen," *Deutsche Justiz*, 1936, p. 1567.
[67] Vollert, "Latifundien, Fideikommisse, Grossgrundbesitz," *Deutschlands Erneuerung*, 1937, pp. 188-98.
[68] "Blut und Boden, ein Grundgedanke des Nationalsozialismus," *Zeitschrift der Akademie für Deutsches Recht*, II (April, 1935), 198.

makes the holdings smaller and smaller, so that finally they are no longer manageable. This charge has never been proved; on the other hand, many experts have shown that it is not correct. As Professor Sering said: "Every marriage connects two heirs of land. Holdings are permanently broken up, and many heirs sell or rent their portion. Thus there is always opportunity to acquire land."[69]

Another reason which is often given in favor of closed inheritance rests upon the observation that the division of the holding depreciates the farm buildings. Why not alter the buildings, if in this way land utilization can become more intensive?[70] Division of inherited land encourages building activity; it restricts the use of pastures and forests; it increases the livestock on the farms, and, thus, the production of manure. Even if there is a rigid size limit below which farms cannot be managed, it is far from being reached in Germany. The deterrent examples which are often given are mostly the result of other factors, as, for instance, the breakdown of industries where the small farmers were additionally employed.[71]

Even if these economic reasons were justified, it seems that they are more than outweighed by disadvantages. If the government interferes with the liberty of parents to transfer their property at will, the government's will becomes the only basic title to inheritance.[72] Inheritance, then, is a means of distributing goods by order of the state. It is

socialism in the interest of the owners. No wonder when those without property are induced then to strive for power in the state in order to change this kind of socialism into one in the interest of those without property. They will draw the only logical conclusion which can be drawn from this type of legislation: they will demand the abolition of the right of inheritance.[73]

Instead of distributing property among as many as possible, a class of disinherited is created. The objection which was raised against the establishment of entails in France a hundred years ago holds true even more in our times: England is the only country where a party of considerable strength demands the abandonment of private property in land; in France, with her enormous number of small owners, such a party is impossible.[74]

As contrasted with the disinherited sons of the farmer, the heirs are supposed to form the new elite. The members of this elite are distinguished by the name *Bauer*, or peasant, which no other agriculturist

[69] Max Sering *et al.*, *Deutsche Agrarpolitik auf geschichtlicher und landeskundlicher Grundlage*, pp. 55-56.

[70] Aereboe, *Agrarpolitik*, pp. 258 ff.   [71] *Ibid.*, pp. 266-67.

[72] Lujo Brentano, *Erbrechtspolitik; Alte und neue Feudalität; Gesammelte Aufsätze*, I (Stuttgart, 1899), 402.

[73] *Ibid.*   [74] *Ibid.*, p. 75.

is permitted to have. As always, such classifications and titles are a means of privilege and exclusion. They discriminate against those who do not belong to the privileged group. Is it more than an accident that the same classification once started the fateful development which led German farmers to the edge of the abyss? When Prussia freed her peasants from the relics of feudal serfdom in 1816, the decree of the government distinguished between two classes of farmers: those whose holdings were too small to require a team of draught animals, and those who needed them. Only the latter were called "peasants" and were permitted to keep their holdings, while the former became landless and shifting labor. When the new elite was formed in 1933, the principle of selection was neither achievement nor blood, but property. The requirement of racial purity excluded only a negligible group which was not prominent in farming, and it proved rather deceptive, for the members of a Slavonic race were held eligible to become owners of entailed farms.

Due to the inalienability of the land and the lack of adequate settlement, the elite is renewed by marriage only, and, in a negative sense, by the ejection of those members who do not live up to the commands of the authorities. But there is no intrusion of newcomers, no social progress, no "agricultural ladder"; there is, in short, no selection by achievement. The abandonment of this principle is characteristic of the crisis of civilization in Germany. It has been described and analyzed by an able sociologist: "In their competitive struggle for power, individual groups in our society promise, as a reward for their followers in the social conflict, to drop the principle of selection on the basis of achievement."[75] The latter being thwarted, the members of the new village gentry are relieved from the struggle with new elements who could dispute the claims of this privileged aristocracy. They are relieved from this struggle as long as they appear faithful and loyal followers of the political power who gave them their privileges. Ultimately, the principle of selection is neither property, nor blood, nor achievement, but mere obedience which is rewarded by privileges.

The sponsors of the Entailed Farms Law expect that the families which form the new elite will become closely connected with the land. As a means to this end a high degree of immobility of tenure is attained. However, it is highly questionable whether such an inflexibility of tenure is desirable. While the mobility of American farmers is so tremendous that it would be desirable to make their tenure more fixed, too high a degree of immobility is already attained in the old countries, particularly in Germany. An inflexibility of tenure often is a symptom of the lack of social progress among the farm population.

[75] Karl Mannheim, "The Crisis of Culture in the Era of Mass-Democracies and Autarchies," *Sociological Review*, XXVI (1934), 114. See also Karl Brandt, "Junkers to the Fore Again," *Foreign Affairs*, XIV (1935), 130-32.

The following table indicates the changes in the possession of agricultural holdings in Prussia during 1920-1936.

TABLE 43

CHANGES IN POSSESSION OF AGRICULTURAL HOLDINGS, PRUSSIA, 1920-36*

Year	Number of holdings affected	Area in hectares (1 ha = 2.4 acres)	Per cent of total area
1920...................	15,712	493,670	2.45
1925...................	11,683	295,096	1.46
1930...................	23,542	285,175	1.41
1931...................	23,508	228,572	1.13
1932...................	23,716	239,661	1.00
1933...................	17,441	221,696	0.92
1934...................	12,271	179,327	0.75
1935...................	13,907	178,689	0.74
1936...................	16,166	192,225	0.80

*Statistisches Jahrbuch für das Deutsche Reich, 1938, p. 431.

These figures show that changes in the possession of agricultural holdings were extremely small even before the new legislation. The farms which were sold, rented, or otherwise alienated per year did not exceed 2 per cent of the total area in all the years since 1920. In the United States 34 per cent of all tenants and 6 per cent of all owners occupied their farms for less than one year in 1935. Even in Europe, an inflexibility like that of the German land tenure is extraordinary. Only about two thirds of the cases reported in the tabulation above are sales, as leases are also included. The figures do not include those changes in possession which are brought about by inheritance. If one estimates the distance between two generations as thirty years, at least 3.3 per cent of all holdings are concerned per year by a change in possession due to inheritance.[76]

The inflexibility of the distribution of land ownership in Germany is also supported by low inheritance taxes. While other taxes are extremely high, the death duties fall short of the rates prevailing in other countries. Though small estates carry a high tax rate, the rate does not increase in Germany as progressively as in England and in the United States. Thus there is no economic effect of the death duties in Germany, and the large estates are not broken up by this means which is so effective in England.

The inflexibility of the tenure as applied to the family deserves further analysis. The late Professor Karl Bücher once fervently contested the alleged strength of the farmer's family bonds. According to his opinion these ties are not stronger among the farm population

[76] "Der Besitzwechsel landwirtschaftlicher Grundstücke in Preussen," Zeitschrift des Preussischen Statistischen Landesamts, LXXII (1934), 195.

than among other groups, and they are, in particular, not so strong as to require entailed farms legislation.[77] Bücher also laid stress on one other point. He asked if the moral value of the ties between the land and the farmer would not be far greater if the land had to be acquired by means of the farmer's efforts than if it had been inherited by one who, happily enough, was predetermined by his birth. "Nothing binds stronger than the sweat of labor."

As to the effect of entailed farms upon family life, there is plenty of material which shows that they are anything but good. Writers and novelists have often pictured the family conflicts arising out of the entailed farm. The fact that the *Anerbe* is not necessarily better than his brothers, and that there are many chances that he is inferior to them, will cause many conflicts. The less happy and, perhaps, better-fitted brothers will envy or even scorn him, especially if they become wage earners on the father's farm, which is now under the command of the brother. Since there are many restrictions on migration into the cities, the number of these men, already high, will increase. This is an atmosphere out of which, as Max Weber once put it, "the most dreadful passions" arise.[78] Moreover, many *Anerben* will lack respect in the treatment of their parents. Under farm inheritance laws of the past, farmers often took refuge in the most desperate devices in order to avoid the fate of being inherited while still alive. Herr Glatzel, president of the Royal Settlement Court of Prussia, reported in 1894 that a part of the peasantry in Westphalia, where an Entailed Farms Law was in force, had entered concubinage in order to avoid legitimate children to whom that law could have applied.[79]

Effects Upon Population.—The time which has passed since the enactment of the German entailed farms legislation is too short to permit an appraisal of its effect upon population. In the past primogeniture and restrictions upon the free divisibility of farm land were invariably regarded as checks upon population growth. Many passages in the writings of the early British demographers illustrate this view. Josiah Tucker enumerates among others the following factors which have the "bad effects" that "the country grows thinner of inhabitants":

The power of entailing [estates] upon the male heir; the power of settling them all upon the eldest son at the marriage contract; and, lastly . . . the common law of the land, which gives all the landed estates of intestate persons to the first-born son, without showing the least regard to the rest of the children. These monopolies of land must occasion, according as they prevail, a great diminution of people.[80]

[77] "Das bäuerliche Erbrecht," Verein für Sozialpolitik, *Schriften*, LXI, 333 ff.
[78] *Op. cit.*, p. 446.   [79] Quoted in Brentano, *op. cit.*, p. 369.
[80] "The Elements of Commerce and Theory of Taxes," in *A Selection of His*

At the same time Robert Wallace referred to

the rules of succession, and the right of primogeniture, by which the eldest son, not only of the most opulent, but even of the middling and inferior families, carries off the greatest part of the father's estate, that the family may be supported in grandeur and affluence, while the younger children get but a small parsimony. [These rules] may justly be accounted another cause of the scarcity of people in modern times. [If this custom] becomes so extensive, as to produce a general inclination to raise and support families by such an unequal division of the father's estate, it will prove a source of idleness to the eldest, and prevent the other sons from marrying, since being born of the same parents, and educated in the same manner, they will naturally incline to live somewhat on a level with their elder brother; which they will seldom find possible, unless they keep themselves free from the embarrassments of a family.[81]

It was for these reasons that measures of this type were advocated during the era of Malthusianism.[82] When the French reaction tried to reëstablish the entails in 1825, the sponsors of the measure asserted that the legislation would induce the farm population to migrate to the cities.[83] It is difficult to see why similar measures should have different effects under present conditions. "The principle of hereditary estates . . . will in the long run operate to reduce the agricultural population unless industrial decentralization is carried through on a large scale, since it means that land can no longer be divided and hence younger sons must migrate to the cities."[84] Hence, the entailed farms legislation does not seem to be compatible with the many efforts to raise the birth rate in Germany. According to Secretary Darré, the rural exodus continues in spite of all restriction; at least 700,000 workers have left agriculture in favor of industry and trade from 1933 to 1938.[85] Every year brings growing multitudes of farm labor imported from foreign countries (especially from Eastern Europe and Italy), thus lowering the standard of living of domestic farm laborers; 120,000 seasonal foreign laborers employed in agriculture were re-

Economic and Political Writings (New York, Columbia University Press, 1931), pp. 65-66.

[81] *A Dissertation on the Numbers of Mankind* (Edinburgh, 1753), pp. 92, 93, quoted in R. R. Kuczynski, "British Demographers' Opinions on Fertility, 1660 to 1760," in *Political Arithmetic*, ed., Lancelot Hogben (London, Allen & Unwin, 1938), p. 309.

[82] See, for instance, Robert Mohl, *Die Polizeiwissenschaft nach den Grundsätzen des Rechtsstaates* (3 vols., Tübingen, 1833), II, 25 ff.

[83] Brentano, *op. cit.*, p. 53.

[84] H. Staudinger, "Germany's Population Miracle," *Social Research*, V (1938), 142-43.

[85] Address delivered before the National Socialist Farm Congress at Goslar, on November 27, 1938.

ported in 1937-38,[86] and the number has increased during the following years.

The entailed farms legislation and other parts of the German land tenure program tend to maintain the present size distribution of farms. Only a few small holdings are being established, and the ownership of a large amount of land remains concentrated in the hands of a few people. As to the effects of these aspects of German land tenure policy upon population, it is interesting to analyze them from the point of view of some recent findings of the German Census Bureau. It has been observed that "in all occupations, married couples who own land have more children than those without land."[87] This rule also applies to farm laborers who own small parcels of land as compared with other farm laborers. However, farm laborers in general have a few more children than farm owners. Among farm owners, the size of the farm has a definite effect upon the number of children. In the size groups under five hectares, the number of children increases together with the size of the holding. Owners of farms of 5 to 50 hectares have most children. "Already in the size group of 50 to 100 hectares the percentage of marriages with a higher number of children decreases, and there is a further and more rapid decrease of this percentage among the owners of 100 and more hectares."[88]

TABLE 44

RELATIONSHIP BETWEEN SIZE OF FARM AND NUMBER OF CHILDREN; ALL MARRIED FARM OWNERS, GERMANY, 1933[*]

Size group in hectares (1 ha=2.4 acres)	MARRIAGES WITH SPECIFIED NUMBER OF CHILDREN, PER CENT OF ALL MARRIAGES						All marriages, per cent
	0	1	2	3	4	5 or more children	
2 to 5	11.0	14.7	18.0	15.0	11.4	29.9	100
5 to 20	9.4	15.2	19.1	15.5	11.5	29.3	100
20 to 50	10.4	14.7	19.1	15.3	11.2	29.3	100
50 to 100	11.0	14.3	20.9	16.4	11.0	26.4	100
100 and over	13.0	14.4	21.3	18.4	11.9	21.0	100

*"Neue Beiträge zum Deutschen Bevölkerungsproblem," *Wirtschaft und Statistik*, 1935, Sonderheft 15, pp. 16-17.

A more complete discussion of the causes of these birth differentials is beyond the scope of this book. There is first the general rule that "groups and classes in less fortunate and favorable social and economic circumstances tend to exhibit higher fertility rates than do groups or

[86] *Statistisches Jahrbuch für das Deutsche Reich*, 1938, p. 362.
[87] "Neue Beiträge zum Deutschen Bevölkerungsproblem," *Wirtschaft und Statistik*, 1935, Sonderheft 15, pp. 16-17.
[88] *Ibid.*

classes more fortunately or favorably situated."[89] These differences in the birth rate are the result of the increasing age at marriage with advancing economic position and of the increasing prevalence and effectiveness of volitional restriction with advancing economic status. A recent study of a large sample of the population of the United States arrives at the conclusion that "in the absence of these factors there were but little if any fertility difference between economic classes."[90] Other factors of a more specific nature which explain the birth differentials of small and large farmers are possibly connected with varying needs for child labor. Small farmers are often inclined to have more children because of the importance of family labor. A special application of the general explanation of birth differentials can also be found in Professor Pigou's observation that "those persons . . . who have something to leave to their children are more affected by the fact that, if their family is large, what is left at their death must be divided into a number of small parts, than those who have nothing to leave and are apart from economic motives."[91] Of course, the psychological situation which confronts the owner of an entailed farm is different. His estate is not divided after his death, and all but one of the children will be virtually disinherited. It is safe to assume that this prospect does not induce him to welcome a large number of children.

There is also ample evidence relating to the large number of illegitimate births in the regions of closed inheritance.[92] Reference has already been made to the observation that farmers entered concubinage in order to avoid the fate of being inherited while still alive. Moreover, if the ownership of land is concentrated, and all but one son disinherited, the desire to marry cannot express itself in as many legitimate marriages as when all sons are enabled to found homes.

TABLE 45

DISTRIBUTION OF LAND PROPERTY AND ILLEGITIMATE BIRTHS, RURAL REGIONS IN BAVARIA, 1879-88*

Districts where specified per cent of births are illegitimate	In these districts specified per cent of the inhabitants own land
3.4 to 5	24.4
5.1 to 10	21
10.1 to 15	16.6
15.1 to 20	16.5
20.1 to 25	14.1
25.1 to 30	14.7

*Ludwig Fick, *Die bäuerliche Erbfolge im rechtsrheinischen Bayern* (Stuttgart, 1895), p. 314.

[89] Raymond Pearl, *The Natural History of Population* (Oxford, Oxford University Press, 1939), p. 18.

[90] *Ibid.*, p. 224.   [91] *Economics of Welfare*, p. 101.

[92] See the quotations in Brentano, *op. cit.*, pp. 435, 442.

Table 45 indicates the inverse correlation between the number of landowners in rural regions and the number of illegitimate births.

The German entailed farms legislation is combined with restrictions on the division of holdings. There are similar effects upon the number of illegitimate children in those countries where there are only restrictions on the divisions of holdings. In Sweden, for instance, an inherited farm may not be divided among heirs if the division is impracticable. In addition, every division of farm holdings requires a permit by the authorities, and the permit is granted only if the divided holdings are "manageable units." Saxony furnishes another example. There, a law of November, 1843, prohibited the separation of more than one third of the area of a farm at the time of the enactment of the law. The measure which was once called "the frothing horse of the chariot of reaction" applied to about 70 to 75 per cent of the total area. The vicious consequences of these measures are illustrated in Table 46. Saxony and Sweden have a much higher number of illegitimate children and of *"Brautkinder,"* children who are procreated before marriage, than other countries. If the rural population has no chance to become independent, marriage is avoided and delayed as long as possible.

TABLE 46

CHILDREN PROCREATED BEFORE OR OUTSIDE OF MARRIAGE, PER CENT OF ALL CHILDREN, SELECTED COUNTRIES, C. 1930*

Country	Per cent
Italy	11
France	13
Switzerland	14
Sweden	30
Saxony	37

*Federal Bureau of Statistics, Berne.

THE NEW FEUDALISM

It is only natural that the question has been raised whether a German farm, especially an entailed farm, may properly be called the property of its owner. If one means by property the absolute liberty of the owner to do with his real estate as he pleases, the German farmer certainly has no property in his farm. But such a type of property does not exist anywhere in the world. In all countries ownership implies nothing more than the liberty to dispose of the property according to the law, and it is real estate, in particular, which is more regulated by legal provisions than other forms of property. So the question hinges on whether or not the restrictions upon the German farmers' rights are so extensive as to amount to institutions which are different in kind from the types of restrictions applied in other countries. The totalitarian state has curtailed all rights and liberties so prodigiously that it does not seem appropriate to discuss the question only with reference to landed property. It has discarded, particularly, those rights which were ushered in by the era of liberalism: the liberty to alienate and acquire, encumber and utilize property at will. In present-day Germany "not only the legal acquisition, but, in addition, the legitimate use is the basis of property."[93] The concept of property, which was static and founded upon the mere act of righteous acquisition, has become dynamic. The legal title is permanently to be recuperated by a legitimate use. Only that use which is conformable with the commands of the men in power is legitimate, and it has been spoken of as a "politically responsible use."[94] Property has become a reward for obedience, like the privileges given to the new elites.

Restrictions upon Agriculture.—In his daily life the farmer is confronted with the vast marketing scheme. It restricts his liberty to produce what and how much he wishes, his liberty to dispose of the products, the price which he may demand, and the person to whom he may sell. If the farmer does not live up to the commands of the authorities, he is threatened by the loss of his holding or of its management. The authorities may transfer the property or the right to use it to someone else whom they regard as better fitted. Here the use is not changed. Another type of deprivation of property rights is the expropriation proper, which takes place if the use of the land is to be changed.

There is virtually no transaction in land which the farmer could proceed with at his own will. Recently an attempt was made to enumerate the legal provisions which require a permission by the authorities for various transactions in land. It was found that there are at least twenty-nine laws which require a permit in case of a sale thirteen in case of an acquisition, eight in case of a foreclosure, fourteen in case of a division, twenty in case of a mortgage grant, and ten in case of a lease of land.[95] The technical questions resulting from this regimentation have become very cumbersome, especialy if various permits have to be procured from different authorities guided by different points of view. It happens not infrequently that the one authority permits what the other prohibits. "Each authority reaches its decision entirely independently from the other. Each has to take into consideration entirely different points of view."[96]

[93] E. R. Huber, *Gestalt des deutschen Sozialismus* (Hamburg, 1934), p. 23.

[94] Hövel, *op. cit.*, p. 97.

[95] von Spreckelsen, "Genehmigungen im Verkehr mit inländischen Grundstücken," *Deutsche Justiz*, CI (1939), 1061-73.

[96] Kurt Münch, "Staatliche Genehmigungen im Wohnsiedlungsverfahren," *Zeitschrift für die gesamte Staatswissenschaft*, XCVIII (1937), 175.

Much of the stringency of the restrictions results from the fact that not only the farmer's legal rights are restricted but his economic liberty as well. If he is required to ask for the permission of the authorities before he sells or rents his land, he is limited with respect to the use of legal rights. Restrictions of this type are to be found all over the world, but nowhere outside of Russia are they as comprehensive as in Germany. The farmer is also restricted with reference to the acquisition of legal rights. Nobody can become an owner-operator or tenant farmer to whom the government objects. Restrictions of this type do not occur often in modern times. Restrictions upon the economic liberty of the farmer can be found in many countries; but where they are in existence they are of a negative nature and have the character of exceptions. What is meant thereby can be illustrated by such well-known instances as restrictions on the sale of sick cattle, or on the cultivation of certain crops. In Germany the farmer not only is prohibited from doing many things, but is also told what to do. The legal duties of omission are supplemented by duties of action. In other countries the farmer merely is motivated and induced to follow government programs, being given advantages if he does so. In Germany there is no motivation through the offer of advantages, but the rule of compulsion.

It is not the place here for a survey of all the newly formed authorities which have jurisdiction over the farmer. One man, R. W. Darré, heads them all. He is Secretary of Agriculture, President of the Supreme Court for Entailed Farms, Reich Leader of Peasantry, and Head of the Agricultural Department of the Nazi party.

Secretary Darré's Philosophy.—To understand Secretary Darré's philosophy it is necessary to know his background and training in the field of animal husbandry. The concepts, devices, and spirit of that science have determined his general outlook. He believes in strange parallels of the development of human civilization and of domestic animals. The pig is propounded as criterion of the Nordic race. Pigs were sacred animals of the Nordic tribes, while the economy of the nomadic Jews did not permit the keeping of pigs.[97] "In the conflict of the Nordic race with the Semites in the Eastern Mediterranean it was the pig which brought about the most violent struggle of opinions."[98] There is also a "parallel of the Nordic marriage customs and the customs of the animals in the forests of Northern Middle Europe."[99] Darré could blame the discovery of America for the intrusion of the Ostic (Eastern) race, for he "is inclined to think that it was the general introduction of the potato which enabled the Ostic race to gain ground

[97] *Das Bauerntum als Lebensquell der Nordischen Rasse*, pp. 20-21; *idem, Das Schwein als Kriterium für nordische Menschen und Semiten* (Munich, n.d.).
[98] *Das Bauerntum als Lebensquell der Nordischen Rasse*, p. 239.
[99] *Ibid.*, p. 236.

among the German peasants." Potatoes facilitated the decrease in the size of the holdings and the subdivision of inherited farm land. The close relation between the intrusion of the Ostic race and the introduction of the potato is supported by the fact that "the peasants regard an un-Nordic (Ostic) face as a 'potato face.' "[100] There is much reason for the belief that Thuringia (in Middle Germany) was the home of the Nordic race.[101] This race has a firm belief in fighting, keeps itself pure, and prevented the intrusion of foreign blood.[102] It probably has also controlled the individual's selection of his spouse and only permitted the mixing of socially desirable partners.[103] Darré wants to reëstablish this control and has set up "breeding estates," *Hegehöfe*, where persons who meet his standard of racial, physical, and mental fitness indulge in the breeding business.[104] "The Nordic peasant farm and its laws of descent which transfer the farm from one generation to the other" are another prerequisite of this type of control.[105] "The farm is nothing but the food basis of the sperms which one generation passes to the next."[106] Darré wants to revert the development from Christianity to the arrival of the third estate, and he preaches a return to the institutions of the Germanic tribes.

Darré's philosophy of *Blut und Boden*[107] has been a source of many conflicts and incompatibilities with another objective of German agricultural policy, the increased output of agricultural products. Under the Nazi regime the production of potatoes which Darré so angrily despises has increased more than any other crop. Family farms, which Darré seems to favor in his writings, supply less products for

[100] *Ibid.*, p. 256. Already a century ago romantic agrarians blamed America for the potato crop—it grows everywhere and has no character. Cf. F. Lenz, *Agrarlehre und Agrarpolitik der deutschen Romantik* (Berlin, 1912), pp. 80 ff.

[101] Darré, *Das Bauerntum als Lebensquell der Nordischen Rasse*, p. 227.

[102] *Ibid.*, pp. 227, 325. [103] *Ibid.*, pp. 366-67.

[104] Darré, *Neuadel aus Blut und Boden.*

[105] *Idem, Das Bauerntum als Lebensquell der Nordischen Rasse*, pp. 367.

[106] *Ibid.*, p. 113.

[107] The author has been told that this term has been coined by the Viennese historian of art, Josef Strzygowski, a man of wide repute in his field. Such an origin of the concept would be a most fitting illustration of the romanticism of the agricultural leader. His philosophy has also entered animal husbandry in Germany. It is said in a recent study that the superiority of the Nordic races is reflected in race differences among the chickens. The Nordic chick is better behaved and more efficient in feeding than the Mediterranean chick and less apt to overeat by suggestion. These differences parallel certain typological differences among human races. The Nordic is an inwardly integrated type, the Mediterranean an outwardly integrated type. The poultry yard confutes the liberal-Bolshevik claim that race differences are really cultural differences, because race differences among chicks cannot be accounted for by culture.—E. R. Jaensch, "Der Hühnerhof als Forschungs- und Aufklärungsmittel in menschlichen Rassenfragen," *Zeitschrift für Tierpsychology*, II (1939), 223-58 (*Psychological Abstracts*, October, 1939).

the market than large commercialized farms. Owners of large farms have fewer children than owners of small farms. An increase in the rural birth rate would produce more soldiers, but requires small holdings whose owners are free of the business spirit and outlook of the commercial farmer. It is this conflict between the various means and ends of the Nazi agricultural policy which has necessitated so many regulations.

The New Feudalism.—The new feudalism which has replaced the feudalism of the lords is different from all traditional types of interventionism. The interventionist measures were directed toward a mere protection of agriculture as an end in itself, while the measures applied in Germany are means to various ends—the preservation of the race, warfare, and, according to the totalitarian concept of the state, the support of all objectives of the government. This aspect of the new measures links them with one of the first instances of "protective measures" in favor of agriculture. When the old feudal powers became weak and the central government of the state grew more powerful, the state began to interfere with the feudal lords to prevent a complete breakdown of the peasants. The reason for this intervention was not the maintenance of the peasantry as such, but fiscal interest. The peasants had to pay a land tax which was one of the main revenues of the state. Thus it was provided that the peasants should not be overburdened with duties to the lords to an extent which would affect their ability to pay the tax. "The fiscal interest of the state speaks in favor of the peasants, long before humanity is allowed to speak."[108]

In accordance with the subsequent changes in the objectives of public policy, the goals of agricultural policy changed, too. When King Frederick II, of Prussia, prohibited the taking over of peasant holdings by the landed gentry, he did so less for fiscal reasons than for the strengthening of the reservoir out of which his army was filled. In our times the objectives of public policy have changed again. Other sources of taxes have been found, and the economy of war has undergone many changes. Warfare does not depend any longer upon paid mercenaries who maintain themselves by pillaging the enemy's country. The government has to make arrangements for feeding the troups and the civil population as well, for the older concept of war which did not interfere to a great extent with international trade and the supply by neutrals has ceased to exist. A government which is willing to go to war has to provide for sufficient supplies of foodstuffs produced at home. It must establish the autarchy of war times already in peace time.

It is difficult to classify the system of production which has been established under this form of war-autarchy. There are, in the main,

[108] G. F. Knapp, "Die Bauernbefreiung in Oesterreich und in Preussen," *Ausgewählte Werke* (Munich and Leipsic, 1925), I, 169.

three systems of unfree production: slavery, contract labor, and the so-called compulsory production. Compulsory production, which Werner Sombart calls "the most cunning type of exploitation,"[109] was to be found chiefly in the early capitalistic era. It is the system of indirect compulsion, under which the producers have to perform certain services, consisting of the delivery of a prescribed amount of their products. In modern times this system exists as a permanent institution only in colonial exploitation. The economy of modern warfare has led to its revival in Germany.

The Results.—Agricultural policy under the Nazi regime is full of tendencies which are often incompatible with each other. The gravest incompatibility seems to be the attempt to favor commercial farming for the market and to increase the agricultural output, while everything is done to strengthen the precapitalistic attitudes and dispositions of the farm population. Thus the concept of profitableness is neglected and even despised to an unbelievable extent. When Professor W. Seedorf, an agricultural economist of wide reputation, said: "What is efficiency? Not an output unconditionally as high as possible, but one which is proportionally high, if compared with the input," he was charged with "having maltreated our German battle of production so cruelly." He was accused of having "tried to oppose the German goal of liberty of food with the most scanty arms of expenditure accounting." "The liberal wants to make the national-socialist believe that the law of diminishing returns governs our Reich."[110]

Secretary Darré has often advanced similar opinions and has, in particular, contrasted German peasants with American farmers: "Some years ago, the German agriculturists were expected to become farmers like the Americans: farming, that is to say, an economic type of agriculture which aims at the highest profit, is dependent upon the business cycle, and calculates with the tools of stock-exchange profitableness. As is well-known, farming has broken down in the United States today."[111] However, there are complaints that "during the last few years, agriculture did not quite fully participate in the increase in income which took place in Germany," and Professor Carl Brinkmann reports that the "price-scissors" have appeared again.[112] Owing to better prices, farming certainly had become more profitable during the first years of the new regime. However, it has become apparent that the struggle of the Nazis with the law of diminishing returns has made

---

[109] *Der moderne Kapitalismus* (2 vols., Leipsic, 1902), I, 344.

[110] "Der Leistungsgedanke in der Erzeugungsschlacht," *Deutsche landwirtschaftliche Presse*, LXIII (1936), 349, 365, 375; reply by Max Schönberg, *ibid.*, p. 491.

[111] R. W. Darré, "Blut und Boden, ein Grundgedanke des Nationalsozialismus," *Zeitschrift der Akademie für Deutsches Recht*, II (April, 1935), 193.

[112] Rosemann, "Eine Abschlussbilanz der Landwirtschaft, 1937/38," *Deutsche landwirtschaftliche Presse*, December 3, 1938, p. 636; Brinkmann, *Jahrbücher für Nationalökonomie und Statistik*, CIL (1939), 120.

farming the less profitable the higher the output is. The small farmer is benefited very little by higher prices. Consequently, the average size of holdings sold at auction has decreased from 30.6 hectares in 1931 to 6.3 hectares in 1938.[113] As to the results of Germany's attempt to attain agricultural self-sufficiency, it must suffice at this time to quote the conclusion of a well-informed observer that "the whole agricultural production has not been substantially increased and imports have not been substantially reduced."[114]

[113] *Statistisches Jahrbuch für das Deutsche Reich*, 1938, p. 429; *Wirtschaft und Statistik*, 1939, p. 493.

[114] B. H. Higgins, "Germany's Bid for Agricultural Self-Sufficiency," *Journal of Farm Economics*, XXI (1939), 456.

SELECTED BIBLIOGRAPHY

I. FOUNDATIONS OF LAND TENURE POLICY

Abrams, C. *Revolution in Land.* New York, Harper & Bros., 1939.

Baker, O. E., Borsodi, Ralph, and Wilson, M. L. *Agriculture and Modern Life.* New York, Harper & Bros., 1939.

Black, J. D. "The Problem of Determining an Economic Policy for American Agriculture," *Conference on Economic Policy for American Agriculture at the University of Chicago.* Ed., E. A. Duddy. Chicago, University of Chicago Press, 1932.

Brandt, K. "Public Control of Land Use in Europe," *Journal of Farm Economics,* XXI (1939), 57 ff.

Cohen, R. L. *Economics of Agriculture.* Cambridge Economic Series. London, Nisbet, 1940.

Davis, J. S. "Observations on Agricultural Policy," *Journal of Farm Economics,* XIX (1937), 861 ff.

Dietze, C. von. "Land Tenure and the Social Control of the Use of Land," *Proceedings,* Fifth International Conference of Agricultural Economists, 1938. London, Oxford University Press, 1939.

Ely, R. T., and Wehrwein, G. S. *Land Economics.* New York, Macmillan Co., 1940.

Gray, L. C. "Land Policies and National Progress," *Proceedings,* Association of Land-Grant Colleges and Universities, Fiftieth Annual Convention, 1936.

Hibbard, B. H. *A History of the Public Land Policies.* New York, Macmillan Co., 1924.

Kelso, M. M. "A Critique of Land Tenure Research," *Journal of Land & Public Utility Economics,* X (1934), 391 ff.

Kraemer, E. "Tenure of New Agricultural Holdings in Several European Countries," *Social Research Report,* No. 2. Washington, Farm Security Administration and Bureau of Agricultural Economics, 1937.

Taylor, H. C. "Land Tenure and the Social Control of the Use of Land," *Proceedings,* Fifth International Conference of Agricultural Economists, 1938. Special reprint. London, Oxford University Press, 1939.

———. *Outlines of Agricultural Economics.* Rev. ed. New York, Macmillan Co., 1931.

Wehrwein, G. S. "Public Control of Land Use in the United States," *Journal of Farm Economics,* XXI (1939), 74 ff.

II. THE LEGAL BACKGROUND OF LAND TENURE IN THE UNITED STATES

Book, A. B. "A Note on the Legal Status of Share-Tenants and Share-Croppers in the South," *Law and Contemporary Problems,* IV (1937), 538 ff.

Bordwell, Percy. "Land Transfer," *Encyclopaedia of the Social Sciences*, IX, 127-31. New York, Macmillan Co., 1933.

Cotton, A. H. "Regulations of Farm Landlord-Tenant Relationships," *Law and Contemporary Problems*, IV (1937), 508 ff.

Fairchild, W. "Economic Aspects of Land Titles," *Cornell Law Quarterly*, XXII (1937), 229 ff.

Geldaert, W. M. "Some Aspects of the Law of Property in England," *Property, Its Duties and Rights*. Ed., Bishop of Oxford. New ed. London, Macmillan & Co., 1922.

Harris, M., Cotton, A. H., and Schickele, R. *Some Legal Aspects of Landlord-Tenant Relationships*, Bulletin No. 371. Ames, Iowa Agricultural Experiment Station, 1938.

Kruse, F. V. *The Right of Property*. Translated from Danish by P. T. Federspiel. London, Oxford University Press, 1939.

McKeon, R. "The Development of the Concept of Property in Political Philosophy," *Ethics*, XLVIII (1938), 297 ff.

Morris, R. B. *Studies in the History of American Law*. New York, Columbia University Press, 1930.

Noyes, C. R. *The Institution of Property*. New York, Longmans, Green & Co., 1936.

Pollock, Sir Frederick, and Maitland, F. W. *History of English Law*, 2nd ed. Cambridge, Cambridge University Press, 1903.

Sato, Shosuke. *History of the Land Question in the United States*. Baltimore, Johns Hopkins Press, 1886.

Tiedemann, C. G. *American Law of Real Property*. Rev. by McCune Gill. 4th ed. St. Louis, Thomas Law Book Co., 1924.

Tiffany, Herbert T. *The Law of Real Property*. 3rd ed., by Basil Jones. 6 vols. Chicago, Callaghan & Co., 1939.

Vance, W. R. "Alienation of Property," *Encyclopaedia of the Social Sciences*, I, 639-41. New York, Macmillan Co., 1931.

III. FACTS AND FACTORS IN EUROPEAN AND AMERICAN LAND TENURE

THE INHERITANCE OF FARM LAND

Gray, L. C. "The System of Inheritance," *Yearbook of Agriculture*, 1938, pp. 115 ff.

Morris, R. B. "Primogeniture and Entailed Estates in America," *Columbia Law Review*, XXVII (1927), 24 ff.

Reppy, A., and Tompkins, L. J. *Historical and Statutory Background of the Law of Wills*. Chicago, Callaghan & Co., 1928.

Spaulding, J. L. "Inheritance as a Function of the Agricultural Ladder." 1938. Typewritten manuscript in the files of Dr. G. S. Wehrwein, University of Wisconsin.

Wehrwein, G. S. "The Problem of Inheritance in Land Tenure," *Journal of Farm Economics*, IX (1927), 163 ff.

Wedgewood, J. *The Economics of Inheritance*. First published in 1929. Reprinted by Penguin Books. London, 1939.

THE TENURE OF FOREST LAND

Fairchild, F. R., *et al. Forest Taxation in the United States.* Miscellaneous Publication No. 218. Washington, United States Department of Agriculture, 1935.

Forest Land Resources, Requirements, Problems, and Policy. Report on Land Planning, Pt. VII. Washington, National Resources Board, 1935.

Ise, J. "The Theory of Value as Applied to Natural Resources," *American Economic Review,* XV (1925), 284 ff.

Marquis, R. W. *Economics of Private Forestry.* New York, McGraw-Hill Co., 1939.

National Plan for American Forestry, A. 73rd Cong., 1st Sess., S. Doc. 12 (1933).

Pigou, A. C. *Economics of Welfare.* 4th ed. London, Macmillan & Co., 1932.

Sparhawk, W. N. "Property Rights and Forest Land Management in Europe," *Yearbook of Agriculture,* 1938, pp. 133 ff.

Troup, R. S. *Forestry and State Control.* Oxford, Clarendon Press, 1938.

TAXATION AND LAND TENURE

Coombs, W., *Taxation of Farm Property,* Technical Bulletin No. 172. United States Department of Agriculture, 1930.

Garland, J. M. *Economic Aspects of Australian Land Taxation.* London, Oxford University Press, 1934.

Hibbard, B. H. "Taxation in Relation to Land Utilization," *Conference on Economic Policy for American Agriculture at the University of Chicago.* Ed., E. A. Duddy. Chicago, University of Chicago Press, 1932.

Hinckley, R. J., and Haggerty, J. J. "Taxation in Aid of Farm Security," *Law and Contemporary Problems,* IV, (1937), 548 ff.

Sanders, J. T. "An Effective Homestead Exemption Will Reduce Farm Tenancy," *Current Farm Economics* (Oklahoma Agricultural Experiment Station). February, 1936, pp. 16 ff.

LAND TENURE AND COLLECTIVE ACTION

Costanzo, G. "Agricultural Cooperation in Italy," *International Review of Agriculture, Bulletin of Agricultural Economics and Sociology,* XXII (1931) 1 ff.

Cotta, F. *Agricultural Cooperation in Fascist Italy.* London, King, 1935.

Eddy, G. S. *Door of Opportunity; Or, An American Adventure in Cooperation with Sharecroppers.* New York, Page, Kirby, 1937.

Hobson, A. "Collective Leasing and Farming of Land in Italy," *Journal of Land and Public Utility Economics,* II (1926), 66 ff.

Kester, H. *Revolt Among the Sharecroppers.* New York, Covici, Friede, 1936.

Pienesco, M. V. "Agricultural Cooperation in Rumania," *International Review of Agriculture, Monthly Bulletin of Agricultural Economics and Sociology,* XXV (1934), 492 ff., 541 ff.

Schmidt, C. T. *The Plough and the Sword*. New York, Columbia University Press, 1938.

LAND TENURE AND FARM CREDIT

Explanation of the Provisions and Benefits of the Farmers' Relief Act, 1932-1935, An. Farmers' Relief Board, New South Wales. Sidney, Kent, 1935.

E. R. Hooker. *Readjustments of Agricultural Tenure in Ireland*. Chapel Hill, University of North Carolina Press, 1938.

———. *Recent Policies Designed to Promote Farm Ownership in Denmark*. Land-Use Planning Publication No. 15. Washington, Resettlement Administration, 1937.

Jensen, E. *Danish Agriculture*. Copenhagen, Schultz, 1937.

Johnson, E. C. "Farm Credit Policy as a Factor in Soil Conservation," *Journal of Land and Public Utility Economics*, XV (1939), 377 ff.

Morehouse, E. W. "Land Valuation," *Encyclopaedia of the Social Sciences*, IX, 137-39. New York, Macmillan Co., 1933.

Murray, W. G. *Farm Appraisal. Classification and Valuation of Farm Land and Buildings*. Ames, Iowa State College Press, 1940.

———. "Governmental Farm Credit and Tenancy," *Law and Contemporary Problems*, IV (1937), 489 ff.

Rush, D. R. "The Use of Agricultural Credit in a Land-Use Program," *Land Policy Review*, Vol. I (1938), No. 1, pp. 12 ff.

Reports on Operations, 1934 to 1938. Farmers' Relief Board, New South Wales, 1935 ff.

Young, E. C. "Farm Credit and Government," *Journal of Farm Economics*, XX (1938), 563 ff.

IV. FARM TENANCY POLICY

FARM TENANCY IN EUROPE AND IN THE UNITED STATES

Black, J. D., and Allen, R. H. "The Growth of Farm Tenancy in the United States," *Quarterly Journal of Economics*, LI (1937), 393 ff.

Farm Tenancy. Report of the President's Committee. Prepared under the Auspices of the National Resources Committee. Washington, 1937.

Farm Tenancy in the United States. Washington, Chamber of Commerce of the United States, 1937.

Farm Tenancy in the United States, 1918-1936. Agricultural Economics Bibliography No 70. Washington, United States Department of Agriculture, Bureau of Agricultural Economics, 1937.

Gray, L. C., et al. "Farm Ownership and Tenancy," *Yearbook of Agriculture*, pp. 507 ff. Washington, 1923.

Hunter, N. *Peasantry and Crisis in France*. London, Gollancz, 1938.

Kraemer, E. "European Agricultural Land Tenure Laws," *Yearbook of Agriculture*, pp. 129 ff. Washington, 1938.

Land Tenure Systems in Europe, The. League of Nations. European Conference on Rural Life, 1939. Contributions by the International Institute of Agriculture, Document No. 2. C. 19 M. 11. 1939. Conf. E. V. R. 7.

Schickele, R., and Himmel, J. P. *Problems of Land Tenure in Relation to Land Use Adjustments.* Resettlement Administration, Land-Use Planning Publication No. 9. Washington, 1936.
Schickele, R., and Norman, Charles A. *Tenancy Problems and Their Relation to Agricultural Conservation.* Iowa Agricultural Experiment Station, Bulletin No. 354. Ames, 1937.
Taylor, H. C. "What Should be Done about Farm Tenancy?" *Journal of Farm Economics,* XX (1938), 145 ff.
Vate, J. van der. "Farm Tenancy Legislation in the Netherlands," Bureau of Agricultural Economics, *Land Policy Circular,* January 1938, pp. 16 ff.
Warriner, D. *Economics of Peasant Farming.* New York, Oxford University Press, 1939.
Wehrwein, G. S. "Place of Tenancy in a System of Farm Land Tenure," *Journal of Land and Public Utility Economics,* I (1925), 71 ff.

THE FORMATION OF RENTS AND THE LEASE MARKET

Bye, C. R. *Developments and Issues in the Theory of Rent.* New York, Columbia University Press, 1940.
Garver, F. B., and Hansen, A. H. *Principles of Economics.* Rev. ed. Boston, Ginn & Co., 1937.
Ise, J. "Monopoly Elements in Rent," *American Economic Review,* XXX (1940), 33 ff.
Regan, M. M. *The Farm Real Estate Situation, 1936-37, 1937-38, and 1938-39.* United States Department of Agriculture, Circular No. 548. Washington, 1939.

THE ECONOMIC FOUNDATION OF FARM TENANCY POLICY

Pigou, A. C. *Economics of Welfare.* 4th ed. London, Macmillan & Co., 1932.
Schultz, T. W. "Capital Rationing, Uncertainty, and Farm Tenancy Reform," *Journal of Political Economy,* XLVIII (1940), 309 ff.

AMERICAN FARM TENANCY POLICIES

A. B. S. "Some Aspects of Farm Tenancy," *Georgetown Law Journal,* XXV (1937), 387 ff.
Baker, J. A. "A New Lease for a New South," *Land Policy Review,* I (1938), No. 2, 7 ff.
Brandt, K. "Farm Tenancy in the United States," *Social Research,* IV (1937), 133 ff.
———. "Potentialities of Agricultural Reform in the South," *Social Research,* III (1936), 434 ff.
Brief Report of the Preliminary Survey and the First Series of Farm Landlord-Tenant Hearings, A. Stillwater, Oklahoma A. and M. College, Extension Division, 1938.
Harris, M. "Changes in Landlord-Tenant Contracts," *Yearbook of Agriculture,* 1938, pp. 259 ff.
———. *Compensation as a Means of Improving the Farm Tenancy Situation.* Land-Use Planning Publication No. 14. Washington, Resettlement Administration, 1937.

———. "Farm Tenancy Legislation in the States," *Land Policy Circular*, July, 1937, pp. 10 ff. Washington, Resettlement Administration, 1937; *Yearbook of Agriculture*, 1938, pp. 259 ff.

———. "A Suggested Adjustment in the Farm Tenancy System," *Journal of Farm Economics*, XIX (1937), 892 ff.

Hoover, C. B. "Agrarian Reorganization in the South," *Journal of Farm Economics*, XX (1938), 474 ff.

House of Representatives, Committee on Agriculture: Amending the Bankhead-Jones Farm Tenant Act. *Hearing* on S. 1836 (H. R. 6768), 76th Cong., 3rd Sess., Serial H (1940).

House of Representatives, Committee on Agriculture: Farm Tenancy. *Hearing* on H. R. 8, 75th Cong., 1st Sess., Serial A (1937).

Maddox, J. G. "The Bankhead-Jones Farm Tenant Act," *Law and Contemporary Problems*, IV (1937), 434 ff.

Reports of the Administrator of the Farm Security Administration, 1938, 1939.

Report and Recommendations of the Farm Tenancy Committee. Des Moines, Iowa State Planning Board, 1938.

Schuler, E. A. *Social Status and Farm Tenure—Attitudes and Social Conditions of Corn Belt and Cotton Belt Farmers.* Social Research Report No. 4 (1938). United States Department of Agriculture, Farm Security Administration and Bureau of Agricultural Economics.

V. ENGLISH LAND TENURE POLICY

Addison, Lord. *A Policy for British Agriculture.* London, Gollancz, 1939.

Ashby, A. W. "Agricultural Conditions and Policies, 1910-1938," *Agriculture in the Twentieth Century*, Essays Presented to Sir Daniel Hall, ed. by A. W. Ashby, *et al.* New York, Oxford University Press, 1939.

Astor, Viscount, and Rowntree, B. Seebohm. *British Agriculture, The Principles of Future Policy.* London: Longmans, Green & Co., 1938. Reprinted in part by Penguin Books. London, 1939.

Brandt, K. "The English System of Regulating Landlord-Tenant Relations," *Journal of the American Society of Farm Managers and Rural Appraisers*, II (1938), pp. 3 ff.

Ernle, Lord. *English Farming, Past and Present.* 5th ed. by Sir Daniel Hall. London, Longmans, Green & Co., 1936.

Foà, E. C. *Outline of the Law of Landlord and Tenant.* 5th ed. London, Field Press, 1934.

Harris, M. *Agricultural Landlord-Tenant Relations in England and Wales.* Resettlement Administration, Land-Use Planning Publication No. 4a (1936).

Jackson, T. C. *Agricultural Holdings.* 8th ed. by W. H. Aggs. London, Sweet & Maxwell, 1934.

Orwin, C. S., and Peel, R. W. *The Tenure of Agricultural Land.* 2nd ed. Cambridge, Cambridge University Press, 1926.

Venn, J. A. *Foundations of Agricultural Economics.* 2nd ed. Cambridge, Cambridge University Press, 1933.

Woodfall, W. *Law of Landlord and Tenant.* 21st ed. by A. J. Spencer. London, Carswell, 1923.

VI. LAND TENURE UNDER THE SWASTIKA

GENERAL CHARACTERISTICS OF THE NEW AGRICULTURAL POLICY

Aereboe, Friedrich. *Agrarpolitik.* Berlin, 1928.

Beckmann, F., et al. *Deutsche Agrarpolitik im Rahmen der inneren und äusseren Wirtschaftspolitik.* 3 vols. Berlin, 1932 ff.

Bente, H. *Landwirtschaft und Bauerntum.* Berlin, 1937.

Böker, H., and Bülow, F. W. von. *The Rural Exodus in Germany,* Studies and Reports of the International Labour Office, Ser. K, No. 12. Geneva, 1933.

Brandt, K. "The German Back-to-the-Land Movement," *Journal of Land and Public Utility Economics,* XI (1935), 123 ff.

———. "Recent Agricultural Policies in Germany, Great Britain, and the United States," *Social Research,* III (1936), 167 ff.

Brentano, L. *Agrarpolitik.* 2nd ed. Stuttgart and Leipsic, 1925.

Häbich, T. *Deutsche Latifundien.* 2nd ed. Königsberg, 1930.

Hainisch, M. "Grossbetrieb und Kleinbetrieb in der Landwirtschaft unter dem Einflusse der Landflucht," *Jahrbücher für Nationalökonomie und Statistik,* CL (1939), 544 ff.

Heberle, R. "The Causes of Rural Urban Migration, A Survey of German Theories," *American Journal of Sociology,* XLIII (1938), 932 ff.

Holt, J. B. *German Agricultural Policy, 1918-1934.* Chapel Hill, University of North Carolina Press, 1936.

Jasny, M. P. "Some Aspects of German Agricultural Settlement," *Political Science Quarterly,* LII (1937), 208 ff.

Kraemer, E. "Supplementary Farm Homesteads in Recent German Land Settlement," *Journal of Land and Public Utility Economics,* XII (1936), 177 ff.

Loomis, C. P. *The Modern Settlement Movement in Germany.* Bureau of Agricultural Economics, Division of Farm Population and Rural Life. Washington, 1935.

Merkel, H., and Wöhrmann, O. *Deutsches Bauernrecht.* 2nd ed. Leipsic, 1939.

Rohr, H. E. von, ed. *Grossgrundbesitz im Umbruch der Zeit.* Berlin, 1935.

Seraphim, H. J. *Deutsche Bauern- und Landwirtschaftspolitik.* Leipsic, 1939.

———. "Die Neuschaffung von Bauerntum und die Erzeugungsschlacht der deutschen Landwirtschaft," *Zeitschrift für die gesamte Staatswissenschaft,* XCVIII (1938), 625 ff.

Sering, M., ed. "Die deutsche Landwirtschaft unter volks- und weltwirtschaftlichen Gesichtspunkten," *Berichte über Landwirtschaft,* N. S., Spec. No. 50. Berlin, 1932.

Sering, M., et al. *Deutsche Agrarpolitik auf geschichtlicher und landeskundlicher Grundlage.* Leipsic, 1934.

Steiner, E. *Agrarwirtschaft und Agrarpolitik.* Jena, 1939.

Turnor, C. *Land Settlement in Germany.* London, King, 1935.

FARM TENANCY POLICY

Brandt, K. "Untersuchungen über Entwicklung, Wesen und Formen der landwirtschaftlichen Pacht," *Landwirtschaftliche Jahrbücher,* LXVI (1927), 535 ff.

———. "Die Lehre von der landwirtschaftlichen Pacht," *Handbuch der Landwirtschaft,* I, 525 ff. Berlin, 1930.

Krause, H. "Pachtland und Betriebsgrössen," *Berichte über Landwirtschaft,* N. S., XXI, 733 ff.; XXII, 252 ff. (1937).

Landpachtgesetz. Entwurf des Reichsjustizministerium, Reichsministerium für Ernährung und Landwirtschaft, Reichsarbeitsministerium. Berlin, 1930.

Sauer. "Agrarpolitik und Landpachtproblem," *Recht des Reichsnährstandes,* V (1937), 213 ff.

———. "Erbhof und Pacht," *Recht des Reichsnährstandes,* IV (1936), 286 ff.

———. "Pachtpolitik in der Praxis," *Recht des Reichsnährstandes,* V (1937), 616 ff.

Spiegel, H. W. *Der Pachtvertrag der Kleingartenvereine,* Tübingen, 1933.

THE INHERITANCE OF LAND

Beutner, W. "Grundzüge eines allgemeinen Anerbenrechts in rechtsvergleichender Darstellung," *Gruchots Beiträge zur Erläuterung des Deutschen Rechts,* 1928, pp. 210 ff.

Blomeyer, K. "Neuerungen im Erbhofrecht," *Jahrbücher für Nationalökonomie und Statistik,* CXIVL (1937), 450 ff.

Brandt, K. "Junkers to the Fore Again," *Foreign Affairs,* XIV (1935), 120 ff.

Brentano, L. *Erbrechtspolitik; Alte und neue Feudalität; Gesammelte Aufsätze,* Vol. 1, Stuttgart, 1899.

Dölle, H. *Lehrbuch des Reichserbhofrechts.* Munich, 1935.

Galbraith, K. "Hereditary Land in the Third Reich," *Quarterly Journal of Economics,* LIII (1939), 465 ff.

Holt, J. B., and Jasny, M. P. "Changes in German Rural Life," *Rural Sociology,* II (1937), 266 ff.

Hopp, Karl. "Erbhofrecht in Zahlen," *Deutsche Justiz,* 1936, pp. 1563 ff.

———. *Erbhofrechtsverordnung und Erbhofverfahrensordnung.* Berlin and Leipsic, 1937.

Kaden, H. "The Peasant Inheritance Law in Germany," *Iowa Law Review,* XX (1935), 350 ff.

Saure, W. *Reichserbhofgesetz.* 4th ed. Berlin, 1938.

Sering, M., ed. *Die Vererbung des ländlichen Grundbesitzes im Königreich Preussen.* 14 vols. Berlin, 1897 ff.

Sering, M., and Dietze, C. von. "Die Vererbung des ländlichen Grundbesitzes in der Nachkriegszeit," *Verein für Sozialpolitik, Schriften,* Vol. 178. Munich and Leipsic, 1930.

Spiegel, H. W. "The Altenteil: German Farmers' Old-Age Security," *Rural Sociology*, IV (1939), pp. 203 ff.
Wagemann, Gustav, and Hopp, Karl, *Reichserbhofgesetz*, 3rd. ed. Berlin, 1935.

THE NEW FEUDALISM

Bertrand, R. *Le corporativisme agricole et l'organisation des marchés en Allemagne*. Paris, 1937.
Blomeyer, K. *Hat der Bauer Eigentum am Erbhof?* Jena, 1935.
Darré, R. W. *Das Bauerntum als Lebensquell der nordischen Rasse*. 4th ed. Munich, 1934.
————. *Neuadel aus Blut und Boden*. Munich, 1934.
Häberlin, L. *Das Verhältnis von Staat und Wirtschaft*. 2 vols. Berlin, 1938.
Herschel, W. *Das Erbhofeigentum*. Mannheim, 1936.
Huber, E. R. "Die Rechtsstellung des Volksgenossen, erläutert am Beispiel der Eigentumsordnung," *Zeitschrift für die gesamte Staatswissenschaft*, XCVI (1936), 438 ff.
Mehrens, B. *Die Marktordnung des Reichsnährstandes*. Berlin, 1938.

INDEX

www.ingramcontent.com/pod-product-compliance
Lightning Source LLC
Chambersburg PA
CBHW030651270326
41929CB00007B/315